GREEK COMEDY
AND IDEOLOGY

GREEK COMEDY
AND IDEOLOGY

David Konstan

New York   Oxford
OXFORD UNIVERSITY PRESS
1995

Oxford University Press

Oxford   New York
Athens   Auckland   Bangkok   Bombay
Calcutta   Cape Town   Dar es Salaam   Delhi
Florence   Hong Kong   Istanbul   Karachi
Kuala Lumpur   Madras   Madrid   Melbourne
Mexico City   Nairobi   Paris   Singapore
Taipei   Tokyo   Toronto

and associated companies in
Berlin   Ibadan

Copyright © 1995 by David Konstan

Published by Oxford University Press, Inc.,
200 Madison Avenue, New York, New York 10016

Oxford is a registered trademark of Oxford University Press

Library of Congress Cataloging-in-Publication Data
Konstan, David.
Greek comedy and ideology / David Konstan.
p.   cm.
Includes bibliographical references and index.
ISBN 0-19-509294-5
1. Greek drama (Comedy)—History and criticism. 2. Political
plays, Greek—History and criticism. 3. Politics and literature—
Greece. 4. Literature and society—Greece. 5. Social problems in
literature. I. Title.
PA3166.K66   1995
882'.05230901—dc20   94-6730

1 3 5 7 9 8 6 4 2

Printed in the United States of America
on acid-free paper

For Alan and Susan Ruskin

Preface and Acknowledgments

This book is conceived as a companion to my *Roman Comedy*. Once again, I interpret the texts as vehicles of social or ideological tensions in the classical city-state, which show up in the plays as complex or overdetermined elements in plot and characterization. However, the time span covered in this book is more generous, the kinds of comedy are more various, and evidence is drawn not only from Greek originals but also from Roman and modern adaptations. All translations from ancient and modern languages are my own, unless otherwise indicated.

Each of the eleven chapters has appeared elsewhere in one form or another; all have been brought up to date and revised, in some cases so extensively as to amount to entirely new essays. I wish to thank the following journals and publishers and their editors for permission to reprint relevant parts of the following materials:

"The Politics of Aristophanes' *Wasps*," which appeared in *Transactions of the American Philological Association* 115 (1985) 27–46, and is here adapted in Chapter 1.

"Aristophanes' *Birds* and the City in the Air," which appeared in *Arethusa* 23 (1990) 183–207, and is here adapted in Chapter 2.

"Women and the Body Politic: The Representation of Women in Aristophanes' *Lysistrata*," which appeared in S. Halliwell, J. Henderson, A. H. Sommerstein, and B. Zimmerman, eds., *Tragedy, Comedy and the Polis*, published by Levante Editori in Bari (1993) 431–44, and is here adapted in Chapter 3.

"Politique, poétique, et rituel dans les *Grenouilles* d'Aristofane," which apeared in *Mētis* 1 (1987) 291–308, and is here adapted in Chapter 4.

"The Ideology of Aristophanes' *Wealth*," written jointly with Matthew Dillon, which appeared in the *American Journal of Philology* 102 (1981) 371–94, and is here adapted in Chapter 5.

"A Dramatic History of Misanthropes," which appeared in *Comparative Drama* 17 (1983) 97–123, and is here adapted in Chapter 6.

"Between Courtesan and Wife: A Study of Menander's *Perikeiromene*," which appeared in *Phoenix*, journal of the Classical Association of Canada, 41 (1987) 21–39, and is here adapted in Chapter 7.

"The Young Concubine in Menandrean Comedy," which appeared in Ruth Scodel, ed., *Theater and Society in the Classical World*, published by the University of Michigan Press in Ann Arbor (1993) 139–60, and is here adapted in Chapter 8.

"Love in Terence's *Eunuch*: The Origins of Erotic Subjectivity," which appeared in the *American Journal of Philology* 107 (1986) 369–93, and is here adapted in Chapter 9.

"Premarital Sex, Illegitimacy, and Male Anxiety in Menander and Athens," which appeared in Alan Boegehold and Adele Scafuro, eds., *Athenian Identity and Civic Ideology*, published by the Johns Hopkins University Press in Baltimore (1994) 217–35, and is here adapted in Chapter 10.

"The Dramatic Fortunes of a Miser: Ideology and Form in Plautus and Molière," which appeared in Andrew Milner and Chris Worth, eds., *Discourse and Difference: Post-Structuralism, Feminism and the Moment of History*, published by the Centre for Comparative Literature and Cultural Studies (formerly the Centre for General and Comparative Literature) of Monash University in Melbourne (1990) 177–89, and is here adapted in Chapter 11.

I am especially grateful to Matthew Dillon of Loyola Marymount University for permission to include our jointly written paper on Aristophanes' *Wealth*.

It is a pleasure to acknowledge here my intellectual debts. Colleagues at Wesleyan University, where I taught from 1967 to 1987, Brown University, where I now teach, and the University of Sydney, where I spent a year's leave in 1990–91, were helpful at successive stages. I wish especially to mention Henry Abelove, Marylin Arthur, Elizabeth Bobrick, Stephen Dyson, the late Rena Grant, Barbara Harlow, Jonathan Haynes, Carol Kelley, Frances Muecke, Pura Nieto Hernández, Georgia Nugent, Kenneth Reckford, Michael Roberts, Ellen Rooney, Adele

Scafuro, Richard Slotkin, Andrew Szegedy-Maszak, Elizabeth Traube, Ruthann Whitten, and Bronwyn Williams.

I am very pleased to acknowledge grants by the National Endowment for the Humanities and by the American Council of Learned Societies, as well as a sabbatical leave from Brown University, which permitted me the freedom from other academic duties needed to complete the final version of the book.

It is a particular delight to acknowledge my dear friend Khachig Tölölyan, who urged me to undertake this book and gave me constant encouragement. I am grateful also to my children, Eve (called Tupi) and Geoff, and to Robyn Sprigg, for their love and friendship. To my father, Harry, my deepest thanks and love. Alan and Susan Ruskin, to whom I dedicate this book, know what they have meant to me.

Providence, Rhode Island   D.K.
August 1994

Contents

Introduction, 3

I. Aristophanic Comedy: Politics and Utopia

1. *Wasps*, 15

2. *Birds*, 29

• 3. *Lysistrata*, 45

4. *Frogs*, 61

5. *Wealth*, 75

II. Menandrean Comedy: Sex and Status

6. *Grouch*, 93

7. *Shorn Girl*, 107

8. *Self-Tormentor*, 120

9. *Eunuch*, 131

10. *Arbitrants*, 141

11. *The Miser*, 153

Conclusion, 165

Notes, 169

References, 211

Index, 235

GREEK COMEDY
AND IDEOLOGY

Introduction

Among the many dozens of Greek comic dramatists whose names are recorded in ancient sources, only two are known to us directly through plays preserved in whole or in substantial fragments: Aristophanes and Menander.[1] Both were Athenians. Aristophanes' productive career dates to the last quarter of the fifth century B.C. and the first decade of the fourth. During most of his active life, Athens was engaged in the conflict with Sparta and her allies known as the Peloponnesian War, which culminated in Athens' defeat and surrender. Menander produced his comedies in the late fourth and early third centuries, when the conquests of Alexander the Great had transformed life in the Greek city-states. He experienced the ten-year reign of the philosophically minded Demetrius of Phalerum, who ruled the city with the support of a foreign garrison from 317 to 307 B.C., and the subsequent restoration of the democratic constitution by Demetrius, the son of Antigonus.

Ancient critics, sensitive to the existence of two distinct forms, labeled the plays produced in the fifth century B.C. Old Comedy, while the dramas produced in the time of Menander were identified as New Comedy.[2] Old Comedy, as it is represented by the eleven extant plays of Aristophanes, was given to burlesque and topical humor. The plots are fanciful: on the eve of a truce in the great war, Trygaeus, the protagonist of *Peace*, conceives and executes the plan of flying to heaven on a giant dung beetle in order to free the goddess Peace, who is being kept in chains, and bring her back to earth; in *Birds*, a character in search of a more harmonious country than Athens sets himself up as ruler over a city of birds. Even where realism is not violated so extravagantly, the

3

comic heroes fasten upon and carry out wildly implausible schemes, like establishing a private treaty with the enemy (*Acharnians*), or bringing the Peloponnesian War to an end by means of a sex strike engineered by women on both sides (*Lysistrata*). Bold actions; earthy humor; immediate social or political relevance; personal attacks on contemporary figures that break the dramatic illusion; choruses in the guise of animals such as wasps, birds, and frogs, or dressed as clouds—all mark Old Comedy as an exuberant and satirical genre, rich in fantasy and spunk.[3]

New Comedy, by contrast, tends to naturalism. A famous remark by an ancient critic runs: "O Menander and life, which of you has imitated the other?" Menander's plays preserve the integrity of the dramatic scene and avoid mention of living figures. According to testimonies by classical writers, confirmed by the surviving evidence, all of Menander's comedies dealt with the theme of erotic passion. He favors the representation of young, middle-class lovers who must contend with strict parents and a lack of resources in order to achieve the object of their desire. His heroes are more hapless than bold, and they depend to a great extent on luck, which manifests itself through the brilliantly contrived coincidences that are characteristic of the genre.[4] While the characters and general story lines of the form are conventional, Menander adapts the plots to a subtle and sympathetic examination of contemporary social issues, such as the dependent condition of citizen wives or foreign courtesans, the social tension between rich and poor families, and conflicts between generations.[5] These same concerns are also evident, as I shall argue, in the plays by the Roman dramatist Terence that are based on Menandrean originals, two of which are examined in this book.

Aristophanes' comedies more overtly address contemporary social issues. Three plays are devoted to the ongoing war, others to problems of wealth and poverty, Athenian litigiousness, the dangers represented by new and corrosive philosophical doctrines or by popular leaders whom he regarded as demagogues, the function of public poetry (specifically tragedy), and the role of women in the state, to name but a few of the topics congenial to him. He could comment openly on social questions in his own voice, or thinly diguised behind the persona of the chorus, by means of the formal interlude called the *parabasis*, in which dramatic illusion is wholly abandoned and the poet speaks directly to his audience.[6]

The interpretations of Aristophanic and Menandrean comedy in the chapters that follow are ideological readings. They look to the ways in which the plays respond to cultural issues, shaping the narratives by which Athenians defined and understood themselves.[7] My approach is indebted to a tradition of critical theory that addresses a literary text as a site in which social tensions or contradictions are enacted. This does not mean that the comedies are an unmediated reflection of social conflicts. Rather, literature reconstitutes the cultural givens, refracting the prevailing images of the culture into new forms; in the words of John Frow, a text is "a labor of transformation carried out on a raw material of ideological values."[8] Where society is riven by tensions and inequalities of class, gender, and status, its ideology will be complex and unstable, and literary texts will betray signs of the strain involved in forging such refractory materials into a unified composition. There remain fissures, gaps, or slips that are indices of the diverse values with which the text operates. As Fredric Jameson puts it: "The deviation of the individual text from some deeper narrative structure directs our attention to those determinate changes in the historical situation which block a full manifestation or replication on the discursive level."[9] The tensions that inhabit a text are manifested symptomatically also in the construction of characters, or dramatis personae, as well as in the detours of the plot.[10] As Mieke Bal observes: "Characters embody contradictions; only if we endure lapses can we take them as existing in a stable and unchanging, if fictive, ontology."[11]

In the chapters that follow, I attend to the seams and sutures in the construction of ancient comedy, the places where the fusion of incompatible elements becomes visible. My purpose is not to find fault with Aristophanes or Menander for a lapse in aesthetic unity. Unity is not an ideal quality of a text, but a product of its ideological labor, and it is the task of the critic to lay bare the contradictory elements that the narrative welds together into an apparent whole. To quote Pierre Macherey:

> What begs to be explained in the work is not that false simplicity which derives from the apparent unity of its meaning, but the presence of a relation, or an opposition, between elements of the exposition or levels of the composition, those disparities which point to a conflict of meaning. . . . The book is not the extension of a meaning; it is generated from the incompatibility of several meanings, the strongest bond by which it is attached to reality, in a tense and ever-renewed confrontation.[12]

It is necessary to defend a social interpretation of ancient comedy, since some critics have insisted that the aim of both Aristophanes and Menander was entertainment, pure and simple, and that the political content of the plays is either accidental or else wholly chimerical, a result of the critic's prior assumptions and orientation.[13] Malcolm Heath, one of the most forceful proponents of this view, writes: "If we think of an Aristophanic comedy as unified . . . , it cannot be as the consistent exposition of some single theme or intention. But that is precisely the dominant approach to unity in recent criticism of Old Comedy, as of other Greek poetic genres."[14] Heath claims, with a provocative contrariness, that "the unifying element in Aristophanic comedy is—perhaps surprisingly—plot," though a well-constructed plot "is in turn functionally subordinate to the play's comic effects."[15] I wish to argue exactly the reverse: that Aristophanes' plays, like Menander's, are engaged with social themes, and that lapses in unity at the level of plot and characterization make manifest the effort of the text to synthesize diverse elements in the ideological repertoire. This ideological labor, and not a generic imperative to produce laughter at any cost, is the source of the overdetermined structure of the comedies.

While the plays are political in the sense of intervening in the processes of ideological production, they are not necessarily programmatic, conveying a specific message or bit of advice to the audience. This is the truth behind Simon Goldhill's observation that the "search to discover the place from which the figures of comedy speak will not uncover an author's voice speaking out from beyond the boundaries of comic interplay."[16] There is no unambiguous "Aristophanes" within the texts. There is, however, a complex of ideologically valorized elements that are not wholly reconcilable with each other, but which in combination yield determinate ideological effects: not a political line, necessarily, but an angle of vision, from which some social possibilities are occluded and others are rendered especially visible.[17]

I do not doubt that the comic playwrights intended to amuse their audiences, and I am confident that they succeeded. But they produced humor by playing off accepted attitudes and recognized social roles, reconstructing or rearranging them in order to bring out absurdities and expose unwarranted pretensions. In making fun of conventions and characters, they revealed what is arbitrary in them. In the process, they constituted the audience, or a part of it, as a community defined by a shared perception of what is funny. Goldhill remarks that "a joke about certain topics will not be funny in certain circles."[18] Comic playwrights test what is possible in their comedies, the limits of the semantic space they have in common with the audience. At the same time, they stretch the limits in certain ways and not others, and there is always the possibility that some in the audience will find that they no longer participate in the circle of shared meanings that constitute the comic space. By exclusions of this sort, humor works its political effects.

The worlds the comic poets portrayed in their dramas, then, are not coherent. They do not erase the contradictions in the society around them, but transform them imaginatively by combining conventional conceptions in new ways that are simultaneously funny, revealing, and politically loaded.[19] Their critical corrosiveness is not innocent, but operates through processes of selection and reconstruction that constitute the ideological orientation of the text.

The chapters of this book are divided into two sections. In Part I, I examine five of the eleven surviving plays by Aristophanes, written over the full range of his literary career, from the early *Wasps* of the 420s B.C. to *Wealth*, produced in the 380s B.C., and the latest of his extant works. *Wasps* dramatizes the efforts of a young Athenian to wean his father from his addiction to service in the popular jury courts and to convert him to the aristocratic pleasures of the symposium or drinking party. The overdetermined characterization of trial-happy old Philocleon as simultaneously a hero of the indigent jurors and a prosperous householder with connections, through his son, to the elite political coteries of Athens is the basis for a critique of the democratic jury system as a forum for self-indulgent posturing. *Birds* portrays a utopian regime that is complexly imagined as both passive and restlessly aggressive, united in a primitive communalism yet driven by libidinous impulses to domination and riven by hierarchical tensions. In the midst of Athens' bid in 414 B.C. for dominion over the entire Mediterranean, *Birds* projects a fantasy of limitless power that simultaneously reasserts the conservative ideal of a bygone age of social harmony. In *Lysistrata*, Aristophanes exploits the status of women as social outsiders to construct an alternative model of Greek solidarity based on identification and cooperation; the unity of the warring Greek cities is grounded in the image of the female body as the substratum of Hellenic identity. But the women's desire is simultaneously contained by their commitment to their individual households, and the play concludes by ratifying the competitive claims of the rival cities for their separate stakes in the feminized topography of Greece. Here again, the overdetermination of the women's motives in the drama functions as the vehicle for a contradictory ideological content, which leaves its mark also on the logic of the action.

Frogs evokes the age of Aeschylus as an ideal time in which civic membership coincided with the seemingly natural criterion of birth, while simultaneously conjuring up an inclusive vision of Greek and indeed human equality, in part grounded in the openness of the Eleusinian rites to all Hellenes, that threatens to shatter the parochialism of the classical polis. Dionysus is the most mutable of gods, and his several aspects as mock hero, initiate, and patron of the theater correspond to a sequence of contradictory moments in the ideological repertoire of Athens. Finally, *Wealth* fuses two different conceptions of a better world—one grounded in a redistribution of riches in favor of the just few, and the other looking to a golden age of limitless bounty in which scarcity is banished and everyone may prosper. The interpenetration of these two themes permits Aristophanes to transmute the problem of social inequity into a collective fantasy of plenty.

In each of the Aristophanic plays I've mentioned, there is a profoundly egalitarian or utopian impulse, which is capable of imagining an ideal of universal citizenship, the equality of women, the emancipation of slaves, or the abolition of property and class divisions. The age of Marathon, when the Athenians and Spartans united to repel the Persian invaders, is the touchstone of this golden age, which is symbolically embodied in the aged chorus of *Wasps* and the poetry of Aeschylus in *Frogs*. In *Wealth*, this bygone moment of natural solidarity is represented by the pre-Jovian regime of the god Plutus, while in *Birds* and in *Lysistrata*, the aspiration to communal identification is carried by the precivic population of birds, whose way of life is marked by the absence of money and property, and by the networks of sympathy that are imagined to obtain among women, who stand apart from the political and economic contentiousness that informs masculine values. This utopian fantasy is at once liberating and conservative, inasmuch as it grounds the aspiration to human equality in a nostalgic hankering for a simpler time that cannot pose a viable alternative to the hierarchies embedded in city-state life. Peter Rose writes in an optimistic vein: "The richness of a work of art seems a direct function of the tension between its commitment to a class-bound version of reality and its aesthetic capacity to open wider horizons, to set its own ideology in an inherently richer and freer aesthetic and cognitive context."[20] The stress under which the comedies of Aristophanes combine an idealistic universalism with an attachment to traditional hierarchies and divisions is manifested in the overdetermination or contradictoriness of plot and character.

In Part II, I examine five Menandrean plays, as well as Molière's *The Miser*. Of the five Menandrean plays, three are from the pen of Menander himself: *Grouch*, discovered just over thirty years ago and still the only complete example of Greek New Comedy to come down to us, and the fragmentary *Shorn Girl* and *Arbitrants*, which, thanks to recent papyrus finds, may now be reconstructed with a fair measure of confidence. Two other chapters discuss Latin adaptations or translations of Menandrean comedies by the Roman playwright Terence, writing in the 160s B.C. While the absence of Terence's Greek models makes it impossible to be certain how faithfully he rendered Menander, there is a general consensus among classical scholars that his versions are relatively close to their sources.[21] Where it is certain or likely that Terence altered a scene or passage in the original, I shall call attention to the significance of such changes. In general, as I shall argue, Terence underscores or embellishes the ideological issues of his model, and thus helps reveal their operation in the comedy. But the reader must understand that the decision to treat Terentian comedy as a reflex of Menandrean is not uncontroversial. Its justification depends in part on the results of the present investigation.

In *Grouch*, Menander exploits the complex representation of the curmudgeonly old Cnemo as a rabid misanthrope and as a hard-bitten, struggling farmer in order to conjure away class conflict by superimposing the tensions between rich and poor on the misanthrope's antagonism toward everyone alike. Cnemo is a scapegoat, and his defeat and humiliation reinforce the solidarity of the community, exemplified in a double wedding uniting a wealthy family and an impoverished one. In all the Menandrean plays, marriage is the sign of civic status and the solidarity of the citizen body. In turn, those who either will not enter into the nexus of connubial exchange, like the misanthrope who rejects all social ties, or who cannot do so because of a fault of status, as in the case of foundlings or resident aliens, inhabit the perimeter of the social space. Unmarriageable women assume, by the conventions of New Comedy, the role of courtesan or concubine in lieu of that of wife; ineligible men (when they are not slaves) appear as foreigners, often in the guise of mercenary soldiers. An example is Menander's *Shorn Girl*, in which a relationship of concubinage between a professional soldier and a foundling is resolved into a regular marital union upon the discovery of the girl's citizen lineage. The tension in the narrative derives from the girl's integrity in spite of her deficient social standing: her dignity and autonomy are a reproach to the arbitrary exclusiveness of the civic community, as well as to the passive and dependent condition of citizen women. Through its complex plot structure, *Shorn Girl* betrays the contradiction between an intuition of utopian inclusiveness based on qualities of character and the rigid status barriers characteristic of city-state ideology.

Terence's *Self-Tormentor*, based on an original of the same name by Menander, again develops the opposition between a code based on personal virtues and the exclusive connubial practices of the classical polis. The tension is particularly evident in the overdetermined representation of the young lover's girlfriend, who is cast simultaneously as a potential wife (in contrast to a professional courtesan) and as a novice courtesan (in contrast to a legitimate citizen woman). In Terence's *Eunuch*, once more derived from a Menandrean model with the same title, the focus is on the contradictory position of the courtesan as engaged in a purely commercial transaction, on the one hand, and as an autonomous subject who ostensibly freely reciprocates the authentic passion of her lover, on the other hand. The inward reflex of sincerity mediates the double role of the courtesan, permitting her to sell her favors to paying customers while maintaining the image of a heartfelt attachment to the hero of the comedy. Both the characterization of the lady and the movement of the plot betray the instabilities that are consequent upon this complex ideological maneuver within the play. Finally, in *Arbitrants*, Menander dramatizes the violation of a citizen woman that, upon discovery, induces her husband to leave her. The dissonance between the moral innocence of the wife and her husband's response to her misfortune is remarked upon explicitly in the play, but the force of the argument has been obscured by a misreading of the nature of the offense or stigma that prompts the man's reaction. A correct appreciation of the source of male anxiety in the play leads once again to the issue of citizen status and the way in which it informs the ideology of the classical city-state.

The comedy of Menander, like that of Aristophanes, betrays a tension between a universalizing or utopian impulse and the constraints of social practices, which surfaces symptomatically as lapses in the logic of the action or as the overdetermination of personal motives. Menandrean comedy, however, largely abandons the Aristophanic focus on communal solidarity in the face of wars and class conflict and concentrates instead on the contradiction between the recognition of individual excellence and the barriers to a full social life that are consequent upon a deficiency of status. The function of passionate love in New Comedy may be seen as a way of establishing a bond across status lines and thus of problematizing the exclusivity of social relations within the city-state.

The last chapter in Part II is on Molière's *The Miser* and investigates how the ideological presuppositions and structures that inform classical New Comedy undergo a fundamental transformation when they are adapted to a new social context. *The Miser (L'Avare)* is inspired by Plautus' *Aulularia (The Play of the Pot)*, which in turn is based on an original by Menander, or at all events by a comic poet very close to Menander in style and plot construction, as is evidenced by the resemblances between the Latin comedy and Menander's *Grouch*. While preserving elements of the formal structure of New Comedy, Molière finesses the challenge posed by the miser in the classical play to the nexus of connubial and economic exchange by which the agrarian city-state is constituted. Molière's miser, far from withdrawing, like

Menander's misanthrope, into lonely isolation, is wholly invested in financial transactions and threatens the cohesiveness of the proto-capitalist French nation, not by retiring from the community but by exploiting to the limit the new forms of commerce. This tension between the ancient paradigm and the modern disrupts the strategies of plot and characterization in Molière's comedy.

There is no single manner in which social and ideological contradictions become manifest in the texture of a literary work. The symptomatic presence of inconcinnities in the plot or the overdetermination of motivations is a sign of stress in the processing of ideological tensions, but these issues do not appear in simple or predictable forms. Each of the studies that follow is a probe into the relationship between a text riven by disruptions or dislocations and a set of contradictory social values characteristic of specific political formations. Taken together, they aspire to provide a view of ancient Greek comedy as an intervention in the ideological life of the classical city-state.

I

ARISTOPHANIC COMEDY: POLITICS AND UTOPIA

1

Wasps

As stories, the comedies of Aristophanes appear to bear a general resemblance to one another. The action centers on a protagonist, who achieves, against more or less organized social opposition, a reordering of the world that realizes a fantasy at once personal and collective.[1] In this respect, the earliest of the surviving plays by Aristophanes (*Acharnians*, 425 B.C.), in which Dicaeopolis makes a private peace with the Spartans and then negotiates with his fellow Athenians like the lord of a republic reduced to the dimensions of a single household, is like Aristophanes' latest play (*Wealth*, 388 B.C.), where Chremylus captures the god of wealth and inaugurates a reign of plenty. There are differences, too: Dicaeopolis is the vehicle, as Aristophanes presents him, for a widespread aspiration for the joys of peace, but his success is purely personal: he agrees to let a few of his fellow citizens in on his prosperity—for a price. Chremylus has a larger vision that embraces the whole society. As for their goals, Chremylus' is obviously utopian, while Dicaeopolis' represents a more realistic aspiration, even if his scheme to achieve it is fanciful.[2] But each puts a practical wiliness in the service of a fantastic vision of security and plenty. In this, *Acharnians* and *Wealth* are like a number of other Aristophanic comedies, such as *Peace* (421 B.C.), where Trygaeus liberates the goddess of peace and brings her to earth, *Birds* (414), *Lysistrata* (411), and *Assemblywomen* (392).

It does violence to Aristophanes to make all his comedies conform precisely to this scheme,[3] but Philocleon, the jury-mad protagonist of *Wasps* (422 B.C.), has the energy, the canniness, and the wishful fantasy of the comic hero, and his triumph over the efforts of his son to domes-

ticate him, culminating in a lively jig with ostensible members of the
audience, is something like the festive denouement in the other plays
I have mentioned.[4] Yet there are features specific to the design of *Wasps*
that complicate and even override resemblances with the predominant
Aristophanic pattern. From one point of view, in fact, the pattern seems
effectively to have been reversed in this comedy. As a juror, Philocleon
enjoys at the beginning of the play the absolute power, or at least the
illusion of absolute power, for which Pisthetaerus in *Birds*, for example,
must struggle. In the courts, Philocleon realizes a cosmic fantasy to such
a degree that he can compare himself with Zeus (619–27). What is more,
he realizes it in a collective way, in common with his fellow jurors,
while, at the conclusion of the play, his drunken, libertine violence
represents no general hope of well-being, but only the personal, juve-
nile lust of Philocleon himself.

The inversion of the utopian Aristophanic format becomes visible
when we look not simply to the bare categories of restraint and release,
for example, but also to the social meaning of the action at each stage
of the play. The special form of *Wasps* is a function of the critical stance
that Aristophanes adopts here toward the courts as a fundamental institution of Athenian life, a stance that undermines or resists a utopian
paradigm.[5] The form of *Wasps* is controlled by its politics.

It has frequently been observed that *Wasps* falls into two parts.[6] The
first problem in the play is weaning Philocleon from his addiction to
the courts; this done, he is introduced to an alternative and more genteel society, for which he proves too obstreperous. The initial action is
built in a straightforward way on the formula of containment: all else
having failed, Bdelycleon has locked his father in the house and placed
slaves to guard him, while Philocleon makes various attempts to escape.[7] Philocleon must be restrained, because his passion for the courts
is represented as something quite different from the motivation of any
other comic protagonist in Aristophanes. Philocleon is introduced to
the audience as suffering from a strange disease (71); toward the end of
the play (though in another context) he is called downright mad (1486).[8]
The extraordinary nature of Philocleon's condition is reinforced by the
suggestion at the beginning of the play that some kind of dangerous beast
is locked inside the house (4). His peculiar urge is described as a form
of *erōs*, the Greek term for an obstinate and unruly passion (89, 753),
and the compound *philēliastēs* (court-lover) is coined to name it (88). It
is clear what Aristophanes is depicting here: an obsession.

Among the surviving plays of Aristophanes, then, *Wasps* presents
us with a unique instance of a type to which the Renaissance label of a
humor is applicable—that is, a character "dominated by a ruling pas-

sion or obsession."[9] The figure is particularly at home in satirical comedy like *Wasps* and two other Aristophanic plays written about the same time as *Wasps*—*Knights* (424 B.C.) and *Clouds* (423 B.C.).[10] It is the narrow single-mindedness of his passion that marks the humor. A desire for peace and plenty, or for the restoration of civic and poetic decorum, as in *Frogs*, however intense, will not produce the humorous character unless it is represented as a pure obsession, detached, in the last analysis, from the acknowledged public value of its goal.

Philocleon's role as a humor, an obsessional character, in turn conditions the characterization of the son who confines him to his house. In Aristophanic comedy, there is commonly a generalized resistance to the hero's ambition for peace and prosperity, but it is usually diffused over several characters, some of whom yield to persuasion, while others are laughed off after a brief appearance: generals, informers, sycophants, and the like. In the utopian comedies, there is no single opponent matched with the protagonist, and even the more satirical *Knights* and *Clouds* lack the well-defined pair of antagonists that we have in the persons of Philocleon and Bdelycleon in *Wasps*. The names themselves, Cleon-Lover and Cleon-Hater, couple the two in struggle.

Bdelycleon is in some ways a conventional comic antagonist and has on his side common sense and conservative values, though it is odd that this function is assigned to a young man obliged to control the erratic behavior of an old.[11] Aristophanes facilitates the reversal through intimations of the old man's senility. The switch of roles, by which a sober son restrains an impulsive father, is further naturalized by the legal circumstance that Philocleon has surrendered control of his household to his son (cf. 612–13), who is thus the master of the household slaves (67, 142), while Philocleon is now their old or former master (442). Toward the end of the play, when he is drunk and feeling young, Philocleon talks to the slave girl he has kidnapped "rather as a lovesick youth with a stern father talks in much later comedies."[12]

> If you'll be nice to me now, as soon as my son's dead I'll redeem you from your owner, piglet, and have you as a concubine. As it is, I don't have control over my own money; I'm young, you see, and hedged in pretty strictly. It's my son who keeps an eye on me, and he's a hard man and a real skinflint into the bargain. That's why he's so afraid I'll go to the bad; I'm the only father he's got.

Philocleon takes his dependent legal status as license to behave childishly.[13]

As a juror, however, Philocleon retains an important measure of social authority, and, from one point of view, his son's efforts to dissociate him from the courts may be construed as an attempt to make Philocleon's retirement complete and consistent. However generous Bdelycleon's intention to support his father may be, it wholly abolishes the old man's independence, and Philocleon is clear that he does not want that.[14] Dramatically, there is an implicit logic at work, according to which Philocleon, having given up power over his own household and surrendered to the dominion of his son, becomes like an adolescent, willful and subject to an arbitrary passion, and this characterization corroborates the sense that Philocleon is unfit to perform the responsible duties of a juror. The Athenian democratic ideology conceived of the city-state as an association of heads of household (those who are, in Greek terms, *kurioi* over their *oikos*), and, accordingly, old men who have relinquished authority in domestic affairs are no longer suited to preside over affairs of state. Correspondingly, much of what seems silly or corrupt in the pleasures that Philocleon derives at court involves a childish desire for flattery (548–630) that transparently betrays the pathetic self-importance of the weak and helpless. Bdelycleon will expose his father's pretensions as a servile dependency upon Cleon and other demagogues, but it is important to recognize that his plan for Philocleon in fact offers him only a change of masters.[15]

Of course, Bdelycleon does not think to suggest that younger men, or legally responsible householders, should take over the role of dicasts.[16] As a number of critics have pointed out, Bdelycleon does not expose the faults or inadequacies of the court system in order to recommend remedies.[17] Who will replace the old jurors once Bdelycleon persuades them to retire is no concern of his. Within the play, which to some extent reflects the social reality, the courts are treated as an old man's forum. As such, they are also represented as an institution of the relatively powerless, a powerlessness that is symbolized by a waning vigor of body and mind, but which corresponds as well to an outmoded way of life characteristic, so Aristophanes suggests, of a generation whose time has passed.

The older generation as a whole is characterized by the testiness that defines the jurors' temperament. While only Philocleon is represented as suffering from a full-blown obsession or addiction to the courts, he shares with the aged jurymen who make up the chorus of *Wasps* an old-fashioned cast of mind, indicated by a preference for the early tragic poet Phrynichus and for traditional art forms in general. All alike are disposed to reminisce about campaigns in the Persian war—Aristophanes' benchmark for the good old days—and other bygone campaigns.[18] The churlish combativeness of Philocleon and the chorus, their proud anger which is so intimidating to those who must plead their case before them, their plain delight in prankish thefts and candidly selfish behavior with no seeming awareness of the threat it might pose to civic solidarity, are also signs of a passé style of behavior.

Certainly the most noticeable feature in the temperament of the jurors is their sharp temper. The term *orgē*, which like the English word "temper" was in Aristophanes' time more or less obsolete in the sense of temperament and normally connoted anger, is applied to them a dozen times or so, along with various synonymous expressions.[19] The fault that Aristophanes above all castigates in the jurors is their uncompromising severity: they enjoy the sufferings of defendants and care nothing for the justice of their cause. Nevertheless, this waspish disposition to anger is not simply a moral flaw, or a symptom of senile crotchetiness. There is also an admirable aspect to *orgē*, a high-spirited capacity for indignation that has something of a hero's pride about it and compared with which an accommodating good nature is a feeble and contemptible thing. Thus Aristophanes boasts (1030) of having an anger like that of Heracles, which has enabled him from the beginning of his career to stand up to opponents like Cleon rather than take refuge in petty jibes.[20] This is the kind of anger and sharpness with which the old jurors, chewing their lips and stinging away, fought the Persians from their land (1082–90), and they carry this same sharp and irritable spirit into the courtroom (1104–5). The complement of this proud rage is fearlessness, as the old men say (1091). Slaves and demagogues are afraid in *Wasps* (427, 715); Philocleon's crowning argument in defense of the juror's life is that everyone, even his own son, fears him, but he himself would die if he feared his son (628–30).[21]

If we recognize that the jurors' anger is a sign of an old-fashioned, rugged spontaneity and individualism, we may understand better the prominent role that theft plays in *Wasps*. References to stealing occur nearly twenty times in the course of the play.[22] Sir Kenneth Dover includes theft in a kind of formal indictment of the character of Philocleon, and confesses that he is "astonished at the hidden strength of antinomian sentiment" which his own sympathy and affection for the old reprobate imply.[23] Dover tentatively suggests that Philocleon's sick desire for jury service puts him in quite another category from the bravado of other comic heroes such as Dicaeopolis or Trygaeus in *Acharnians* and *Peace*.[24]

Philocleon indeed reminisces wistfully about the days when he could make off with some small skewers, while now he is watched like the ferret that has stolen the meat (356–64). But the recollection is inspired by the chorus, who think back fondly upon their youth when they stole a mixing bowl (236–38). Philocleon claims that his bravest exploit was the theft of some vine poles (1200–1), and he caps off these former achievements by carrying off the flute girl from the drinking party to which his son had invited him (1345, 1369). Such escapades are clearly regarded, at least by the older generation, as proper to young men: in the scene with the flute girl, for instance, Philocleon thinks of himself as again youthful, as we have seen. Bdelycleon, by comparison, seems prematurely straitlaced.

This indulgent attitude toward petty expropriations, which are taken as signs of a mettlesome temper, does not prevent either Philocleon or the chorus from feeling outrage at the kind of theft that results in large-scale social inequities, once they become aware of it. Thus, after Philo-cleon is persuaded by his son that Cleon has systematically defrauded the jurors, he wants a chance to condemn the man (758–59). The chorus is similarly resentful at the thought that young and unscrupulous men have cheated them out of the fruits of the empire acquired by their labors (1098–1101), and they are quite prepared to attack Laches for illegal accumulation of wealth (240–44). And yet Philocleon is, by his own admission, receptive to an appeal for sympathy on the part of an em-bezzler of state funds when he is reminded that he himself has not al-ways been above shaving a bit off his unit's provisions when he was in charge of mess funds (553–57).

Here, perhaps, is the nub of the issue: not that Philocleon or the old jurors are scoundrels, but that their frank acceptance of the impulse to take what one can get is no longer an adequate ethic in a society where a developed state machinery and the financial resources of an empire are a basis of real class power for those who can control them.[25] Within the ideology projected by the play, the old men represent a way of life that receives a certain nostalgic respect but is fundamentally unsuited to the position of political power that their role as jurors confers on them, under social conditions that they cannot clearly comprehend or con-trol.[26] Having grown up at a time when there was no thought for rheto-ric or sycophancy (1094–97), they are now easy prey for demagogues.

We may also read Philocleon's statement that as a young man he could, when on campaign, run away with impunity (357–59), not as a mark of cowardice, as Dover charges, but rather as an indication that a disposition to go where one pleased was not incompatible with the in-terests of the group in former times, when no one was posted to main-tain discipline. I am not for a moment suggesting that so sublime a harmony between private desires and communal needs actually ob-tained at the time of the Persian invasion, only that the image of such a harmony was available and effective in setting off, by way of contrast, perceived tensions in Aristophanes' own world. Within the world of the play, at any rate, there is no hint that Philocleon's military deportment is anything like that of the infamous Cleonymus, who is accused of abandoning his shield in battle (15–27, 822–23).[27]

There is a way, then, in which Philocleon and the jurors stand not for antinomianism or some abstract state of nature but for an anterior social order. Philocleon, however infantile he may seem, represents an ethic and a tradition that are both respected and diminished by the action of the play.

There is an analogy between the representation of Philocleon in *Wasps* and that of Strepsiades in *Clouds*.[28] Strepsiades is an old rascal, seeking to tap the sophistical expertise of Socrates to evade paying his debts, but his roguishness is not in itself a danger to Athenian social life; it is the kind of selfish cunning that the Greeks admired in Odysseus, Themistocles, and a variety of other cultural heroes. In less complicated times, the cocky individualism of a Philocleon or a Strepsiades did no harm. It was the rough and ready ethic of the peasant farmer, and in its way it served the state well. In the new circumstances of imperial power, however, modern methods of analysis and techniques of rhetoric have augmented the power of those who can master them, while at the same time they undermine those values that were traditional in Athenian society. While Strepsiades is happy to defraud a neighbor, he responds with horror to the idea of a son beating his parents—and this not only because the stick is in his own son's hand. Strepsiades may be seduced by philosophy's subversiveness, but it is only the upstart members of the younger generation who are capable of altogether rejecting conventional constraints.

If the jurors in *Wasps* are aged and old-fashioned, they also, with the kind of overdetermination that is characteristic of literature, represent the social class of poor free citizens.[29] The dialogue between the chorus and their young sons who lead them on stage makes their station evident: they worry about wasting lamp oil (251–53), consider dried figs an extravagance, consume their meager juror's pay on barley and firewood, and are at a loss how to provide dinner should the court not sit that day (293–316; cf. 1112–13). Mention of weather leads, as though by reflex, to thoughts of crops (264–65), which suggests that they are farmers. But in the main they think of themselves simply as the poor (463; cf. 703), and Bdelycleon can even compare them to olive pickers— that is to say, day laborers or hired hands, the most despised form of labor—for their dependency on wages (712). Consistent with their poverty, they see the rich as their natural antagonists, instantly suspecting Bdelycleon of collusion with the class of wealthy citizens when they learn why he is confining his father (342–43).[30] In a similar vein,

Philocleon sees among the great merits of jury duty the chance to insult the rich, and his change of gear at the end of the play, when he has given up serving in the courts, marks him as having now joined the wealthy set.[31] The chorus's repeated charge that Bdelycleon is aspiring to tyranny in attacking the jurors is an expression of their sense of social identity cast in the contemporary formula of class conflict.[32] Bdelycleon effectively ridicules the accusation by observing that every vegetable dealer screams tyranny if one shops next door (488–507), but the point, though witty, reveals only that the chorus is mistaken about Bdelycleon's personal motives, which, he says, are to provide for his father's comfort (503–6). Aristophanes thereby genially finesses the fact that the jurors, as poor people, see the courts as a bulwark of democracy. This rousing of the chorus's political apprehensions, only to dissolve them through a comic turn of argument, artfully evades the social issue.

Bdelycleon's filial interest, by which the chorus's suspicions are undercut, points to a fundamental inconsistency in the characterization of the jurors, the kind of fissure in the text that is the mark of its ideological burden. For all Philocleon's exemplary status as spokesman for the jurors' way of life and fiercest soul among them (277), he alone does not depend on the courts for his living; for him, jury service is merely a personal passion. His fanatical devotion to the juror's life may be represented as an obsession precisely because another and, by universal consent, more comfortable life is open to him (cf. 1453–73). Philocleon's bond with the chorus is primarily sentimental, based on their common age and shared experiences of an earlier and idealized moment in Athenian history.[33] Practically, however, he is the retired head of a relatively opulent household and has access, through his son's connections, at least, to circles of considerable influence in the state. The juror's life is at odds with Philocleon's social class.

Philocleon's conversion from the rigors of the courts to the easy life that his son promises carries the chorus with it, even though for them there is no possibility of a comparable change in circumstances. They regard the formal debate between Philocleon and Bdelycleon as a discussion of ultimate social issues, upon the outcome of which their own fate will depend (535; cf. 518, 540–47). The debate itself is cleverly cast as an argument about power: Bdelycleon sets the terms, and Philocleon rises to the challenge (515–19). Philocleon makes his case essentially on the deference shown to jurors by men of all classes, but above all by the rich and powerful (553–58, 575, 592–602); as an afterthought he adds the domestic independence that he derives from his juror's pay (605–18). Philocleon's argument rests on his identification with the common people (*tou plēthous*, 593; *tōi dēmōi*, 594). Bdelycleon's answer is that the jurors' authority, which they regard as royal (546, 549; cf. 587) and even godlike (571, 619), is illusory, because the pay that they receive represents only a small fraction of the state's revenues (656–718).

To the extent that Philocleon's passion for the courts is a reflex of pure egotism, Bdelycleon's argument strikes home, leaving aside the silly economics of his calculations.[34] As an address to class interests, moreover, Bdelycleon's rhetoric is effective in two ways: it undermines the confidence of the jurors in the men they have taken to be their leaders, and it suggests by its display of mathematical computations—however bogus the reasoning may really be—that the strong and spontaneous emotions of the old men cannot protect them against the wiles of modern politicians. Throughout Philocleon's presentation, Bdelycleon has been taking notes with ostentatious deliberateness (529, 538, 559, 576), and his emphasis on careful calculation (656; cf. 745) exhibits the sort of mind needed to reckon with the demagogues.[35] Thus, persuaded of the futility of their judicial powers, the chorus wholeheartedly endorse Bdelycleon's offer to support his father, and they go so far as to wish they had a relative who could offer such advice (731–32), not pausing to reflect that retirement from jury service will not solve the problem of their poverty. Later, when they observe the conveniences of Philocleon's private court at home, they conclude that Bdelycleon is the best friend the common people have had in his generation (869–73, 887–90). Indeed, after the debate the class status of the chorus is quietly elided in favor of their identification as genuine Athenians of the old stripe (1060–1121).

Logically, the chorus might have responded to Bdelycleon's argument by demanding an increase in the juror's daily fee; at all events, they might have contemplated using their legal role to control large-scale peculation.[36] It was surely not beyond Aristophanes to have staged the idea of all Athenians living in luxury on state income in one of his utopian comedies (compare, for example, *Assemblywomen* or *Wealth*), and Xenophon was to propose something of the sort in all seriousness in the middle of the following century.[37] Given Aristophanes' generally critical attitude toward the courts, however, it is safe to say that he would not have looked to them as an instrument of utopian reform.[38] In *Wasps*, the overdetermined status of the chorus—the conflation of class and generational characteristics—enables a semantic slide by which a problem of class tension is illusorily resolved by the prospect of comfortable retirement, even though this possibility can be realized by only one of the jurors, namely Philocleon. *Wasps* thus raises the issue of class only to conjure it away by an image of individual withdrawal.

Under the post-Periclean Athenian democracy, however, such individual withdrawal itself had a political aspect. Donald Lateiner has observed that Aristophanes and Euripides "represent an important, if controversial, disinclination for politics that is clearly evident by the beginning of the Peloponnesian War." "Most rich men," Lateiner notes, "rarely known as active democrats, find it useful to assert this quiet lack of involvement." Lateiner quotes from a speech of Lysias (19.55): "For I have reached the age of thirty without ever having talked back to my father. No citizen has ever haled me into court. Although our house neighbors on the Agora, I have never even been seen near the law court or the Council's hall before this suit fell on me."[39] The reasons for this condescending modesty are again best given in Lateiner's own words:

> The democratization of Athens, the relaxation of traditional social and political constraints, the emergence of a new class of politicians—all movements dependent to some degree on the growth, success, and revenues of the Athenian empire—encouraged a retreat by the socially and economically advantaged class from the world of politics and political manoeuvring in the courts. . . . As the men of traditional status were deprived of the monopoloy of political power, they came to devalue political participation.[40]

The lower classes, on the contrary, perceived the courts as a bulwark of popular rights, and not only because the very poor or decrepit might supplement their livelihood by the juror's fee of three obols a day. The chorus in *Wasps* instinctively regard a critic of the jury system like Bdelycleon as an enemy of the people.[41] The chorus's approbation of Philocleon's withdrawal from the courts, which presents itself as the cure to his personal obsession, is on the social level an endorsement of a class alternative in political style.

Insofar as the chorus evokes a time of natural solidarity, when there was no need of courts, there is a specious identity of interests, or at least of point of view, between the old jurors and Bdelycleon in his advocacy of withdrawal from judicial activities. That is to say, the genteel class could cloak its withdrawal from public life and encounters at law in an idealized memory of a time before the law, representing their class attitude as a gesture of pristine social harmony. Democratic litigiousness could be seen as the opposite both of early communality and of aristocratic aloofness, all the more easily to the extent that the upper classes succeeded in casting themselves as the bearers of traditional ways. The difference lies, of course, in the combative significance of the aristocratic denigration of the courts and manifests itself in Bdelycleon's mastery of forensic rhetoric. Bdelycleon has no choice but to enter into a contest of persuasion in order to reveal the dangers inherent in persuasion itself; he must prove himself superior to Cleon and his sort at their own game. What distinguishes Bdelycleon from popular demagogues is the rationality that is assigned to his discourse by the terms of the play.[42]

When Bdelycleon perceives that his arguments in the formal debate, which is itself a kind of trial, have convinced his father but still have not freed him from his passion for jurying, he proposes to stage a trial at home, with a farcical mock-up of court paraphernalia. This introduces a brilliant bit of comic invention in which a dog is accused of stealing a piece of Sicilian cheese. The scene has multiple functions within the play. It is a satirical enactment of the "prejudice and irresponsibility" of Athenian jurors, as Aristophanes saw them;[43] with transparent allegory, it caricatures a dispute between Cleon and Laches, a general close to the conservative leader Nicias, largely to the advantage of the latter; it serves a second and decisive defeat to Philocleon when he is tricked into voting for acquittal by a switch in ballot urns—an unpardonable violation of his principles that breaks his will (999–1002, 1008; cf. 973–74). We may observe also that it achieves Bdelycleon's original object of confining his father at home.[44] The entire conceit of a trial at home is thematically significant, for it dissociates Philocleon from the collective aspect of the jury system that is fundamental to its nature as an institution of the democracy, and, in effect, atomizes and domesticates the jurors.[45] The reduction of public life and the civic solidarity embodied in the judicial institutions of the populace to the scope of the individual household realizes the kind of privatism affected by the class of which Bdelycleon is a symbol, a style available in an exemplary way to the well-to-do. Philocleon even alludes to an oracle according to which everyone will have his own little court within his gate (799–804), a comment which, addressed as it seems to the audience (Bdelycleon has dashed inside the house and the chorus is not engaged in the action at this point) and not especially witty in itself, perhaps refers to or parodies some prophecy in circulation just then.[46] For Philocleon, the idea of the commonwealth has been reduced to the individual, that is, himself, alone (917).

If it is correct to see a social meaning in Philocleon's addiction to jury service—Bdelycleon himself refers to it as a disease inveterate in the city (651)—and to read the household trial as a figure for the domestication of a popular democratic institution and the contraction of civic consciousness, at least among the upper classes, to the perimeter of the household walls, then the victory of Bdelycleon's social ideals is already implicit in the trial scene itself. We may accordingly construe

the trick of the voting urns by which Bdelycleon determines the ver-
dict as an emblem of his new power. He has his father at home, where
he wants him; as actual master of the house, he is in control there; the
court as such is powerless, and Bdelycleon is in a position to decide the
acquittal of Laches. Philocleon's breakdown, and the final cure of his
jury mania, are simply an acknowledgement of this new state of affairs.
What is more, the conversion of class allegiance implied in Philocleon's
and the chorus's withdrawal from the public and collective role of jurors
signals the transition to the final scenes of the play.

After he has been cured of his mania for jury duty, Philocleon joins,
at his son's invitation, a drinking party or symposium at which prominent public figures are gathered, and disrupts it by his rowdy behavior.
John Vaio has shown how references to costume, manners, riddles and
wine, music and dance generate a contrast over the play between the
humble lives of jurors and the symposia to which "a larger part of the
social life of the nobles was devoted."[47] Thomas Banks remarks that
Philocleon is alienated both from the courts and from the symposium,
and stands as a symbol of nature against all claims of convention.[48] But
the distancing of Philocleon from the "communal and social essence"
of the law courts is not a mere function of Philocleon's irrepressible
character, his role as "natural man," in Jeffrey Henderson's phrase.[49]
Rather, it is predicated on the real social distinction between Philocleon
and the jurors of the chorus, and is engineered by Bdelycleon in such a
way as to command the assent of the chorus itself. Philocleon is pried
loose from the courts, and if Aristophanes then turns to satirizing the
entertainments of the nouveaux riches, this is in large measure a means
of exposing the social inferiority of Cleon and his friends, who are named
among the symposiasts (1219–21).[50] Wealth and influence alone do not
confer the status of gentleman.[51]

The caricature of the drinking party does score some hits against
aristocratic abuses, such as an ostentatious affectation of foreign styles,
including that of the Spartans (1136–66), and an inclination to treat
lower-class citizens in a violent or contemptuous manner. The charge
of assault is leveled four times at the inebriated Philocleon (1303, 1319,
1418, 1441). In part, this spoof on upper-class arrogance answers to the
earlier critique of the democratic courts, but it is decidedly weaker insofar as it is a former juror himself who is the most egregious offender:
it falls to Bdelycleon to offer compensation to an outraged victim
(1419–20) who professes a respectable distaste for lawsuits (1426).

G.E.M. de Ste. Croix has argued that Aristophanes was politically
a conservative in the mold of Cimon and that "he used many of his plays,
even while they of course remained primarily comedies, as vehicles for

the expression of serious political views."[52] With respect to the Athenian jury-courts, he suggests that Aristophanes saw "the whole system as a form of popular tyranny, and [was] out to discredit it by ridicule" (362). I agree. I hope, however, to have advanced the discussion from the citation of scenes and comments that are derogatory toward the courts (excellently summarized by Ste. Croix) to an analysis of how Aristophanes' ideological stance is manifested in the structure of the narrative. In particular, I have attempted to show how the conflation of thematically loaded characteristics such as age, generation, class, and personal vagaries in Philocleon and other characters in Wasps works to mask the popular character of the court system and valorize the upper-class ideals of withdrawal and privatism. When Dover, for example, writes that the mode of Wasps is "moralizing, not politics," and that "it belongs . . . within the tradition of didacticism directed not towards structural change but upon human attitudes and patterns of behaviour," he convicts Philocleon of a childish egotism but ignores the complex ideological construction of his persona.[53] It is the business of the literary critic to dissolve the apparent unity and coherence of character and narrative form and bring to light the complex and contradictory elements out of which they are produced.

But the appearance of harmony or unity in a text also has a social basis. The collapse of the class distinction between Philocleon and his fellow jurors reflects the ideological solidarity among citizens of all classes in Athens as against slaves or resident aliens, who did not have the right to own property in land. Citizens rich or poor shared a common aspiration to autarky, and were therefore susceptible to the dream of perfect autonomy represented by Philocleon's private court.[54] There are several swipes at foreigners in Wasps (cf. 82–84, 718, 1197, 1221), but the most telling lines are addressed by the chorus to a slave who has just emerged from the house in which the symposium is going on, having been beaten by the rampaging Philocleon: "What is it, boy? For it is right to call even an old man boy if he takes a beating" (1297–98). The equation between class and age group here is casually explicit: the slave's want of freedom leaves him forever in the dependent condition of the child.[55] Over against this kind of infantilization, citizens young and old are united as adults, with rights and responsibilities in the state. Philocleon's aggression is fairly indiscriminate, and he knocks his own son down when he tries to take away his flute girl (1379–86), but violence against a fellow citizen was an actionable offense.[56] The text insists on persuasion rather than force as the means of inducing the chorus and the normally unbudgeable Philocleon to desert the courts.[57]

And yet, words prove effective only after the show of force by which

Philocleon is prevented from leaving his home to attend the court ses-
sions. By this recourse to violence, in the restraints placed upon
Philocleon when argument would not avail, and by its profound ambivalence toward argument itself as a kind of charm and subversion,
Aristophanes' *Wasps*—read politically—betrays the stubborn fact of
class conflict within the citizen body of the Athenians.

2

Birds

In the opening scene of *Birds*, which Aristophanes exhibited at the dramatic festival of the city Dionysia in the year 414 B.C., two Athenian citizens, weary of constant lawsuits back home, take off in search of a better, or at all events less litigious, city in which to take up residence.[1] They seek out first an odd creature, the former king of Thrace named Tereus, who, legend had it, had been transformed for his sins into a hoopoe.[2] The idea is that this hoopoe, knowing what both humans and the soaring birds have seen, is best equipped to point them in the right direction (119). The hoopoe turns out to have established himself as a figure of authority among the birds. Thus Pisthetaerus, the cannier of the two Athenian wanderers, after hearing, and rejecting, a couple of possible sites for relocation, suddenly hits on a different plan: to found a city among the birds themselves. That will be the new, litigation-free community they seek.

What is more, such a city will be in a position to achieve limitless power, and even challenge the gods themselves for supremacy over the universe. The reason is geopolitical: the birds occupy the air, which is the region between the earth, where humans dwell, and the heavenly abode of the gods. If the birds will fortify this zone by surrounding it with a wall, and declare it off limits to all trade and trespass unless official permission is granted, then the birds can strictly control the passage from earth to heaven of sacrificial aromas—that is, the substance on which the gods depend for their nourishment. In a word, the birds can starve the gods into submission. As for humans, the birds can offer extraordinary benefits—for example, an end to plagues of locusts,

29

but also much finer things, like wings and longevity. Contrariwise, they can inflict dire punishment upon the recalcitrant, such as pecking out the eyes of cattle and their own style of aerial bombardment. Thus, mortals are bound to submit to the new avian regime, and gladly.

And so it happens. Men not only yield to the birds, they ape their ways and flock to the new city in order to borrow wings and enjoy its special blessings. The gods, for their part, put up some resistance, but hunger gets the better of them, and the final scene shows Pisthetaerus, now king of the omnipotent city of the birds, marrying the goddess Sovereignty, and thereby confirming in a sacred celebration the new order of things.

Such, in outline, is the plot of *Birds*. Two problems are apparent even in this brief summary. First, the original impulse behind the venture of the two Athenians, namely, to find a calmer, less contentious place, seems to have been all but forgotten in the new scheme, which is to erect an all-powerful state among the birds and seize control over the universe from the gods, all under the leadership of Pisthetaerus.[3] Second, the birds not only achieve sovereignty over gods and men alike, they also become a kind of model city which mortals seek to join or imitate. Not only benefits but also wings are conferred on human beings, beginning with Pisthetaerus and his companion, Euelpides, at the moment when they first persuade the birds to adopt their ambitious plan. Is the city of the birds a different place, an ideal community blessed with all good things? Or is it a caricature of human cities, and more particularly of Athens, so that Pisthetaerus and Euelpides, in their pursuit of a peaceful land, have succeeded only in reproducing the very kind of society they had abandoned, full of struggle and restless desire? On the one hand, the solidarity of the birds is contrasted with the competitive strife that characterizes Athens; on the other hand, a vision of peace and plenty coincides with a reign of limitless imperial desire. These paradoxical intersections are a reflex of tensions in Athenian ideology at the time of the Peloponnesian War, and testify to the contradictory elements of which it is composed—elements that Aristophanes reworks into a novel narrative structure.

In the minds of Athenians in the years 415–414 B.C. was one event in particular: the launching of the great naval expedition against Sicily, with the aim of conquering the Greek cities on the island. These cities favored the Spartan side in the conflict with Athens, recently suspended in a wary truce between the two powers. The larger object of the campaign was to cut the Peloponnesian peninsula off from its overseas allies. If Athens could gain complete control over the western, as well as the eastern, Mediterranean, it might then isolate the Lacedaemonians and compel their surrender. One need not rehearse the extraordinary excitement that attended the launching. Thucydides has given us a brilliant record of the hopes and ambitions that rode with the armada, the greatest military undertaking, he says, in Greek history (6.31). Some voices, to be sure, were raised against it, notably that of the distinguished general Nicias, who was nevertheless placed in charge of the expedition. Alcibiades was avid for it, but charges of impiety levelled against him by opponents—with what truth it is impossible to say— induced him to abandon both the fleet and his native city and join the Spartan cause. The upshot, as we know but the Athenians in the audience at the production of *Birds* did not, was the utter defeat of the armada off Syracuse.

This cursory sketch of the circumstances in which the performance of *Birds* took place will readily indicate why it has been tempting to draw a parallel between Athens' ambition to conquer the seaways, and Pisthetaerus' plan by which the birds will take over the sky and place an embargo on sacrificial odors until the gods give in. As Jeffrey Henderson writes, "the resemblance of the plot to the sensational events of the preceding year . . . is close enough that no spectator could fail to see it."[4] Various attempts at an allegorical reading have foundered, however, as systematic identifications between figures in the drama and contemporary political personalities have yielded inconsistent results and contradictory messages.

The practice was launched early in the nineteenth century by J. W. Suevern.[5] I quote from a summary of Suevern's view in an old school edition: "*The Birds* is a kind of allegory to dissuade the Athenians from the Sicilian expedition by exposing its folly. The birds are the Athenians; Cloud-cuckoo-land their visionary empire; the planners of it are certain politicians and orators; Pisthetaerus is Alcibiades with a dash of Gorgias . . . ; the gods are the Lacedaemonians, to be surrounded in the Peloponnese and starved out."[6]

This theory was influential in its time,[7] but by the end of the century, W. C. Green, whom I have been quoting, could dismiss it without much argument. Green comments simply that "the Bird-city founded in the play with complete success, a city to which is given all that Aristophanes . . . thought good, and from which is excluded all that he thought bad . . . this city cannot be held up by the poet as a warning, and as a folly to be avoided." For good measure, Green cites the opinion of H.A.T. Köchly, who, while remaining committed to the allegorical method, took a view just the reverse of Suevern's. According to Köchly, the city of the birds is not a warning but an ideal: "It is to be a democracy, but yet to have a head: a Periclean democracy. And the head recommended or hinted at . . . is Alcibiades." Given such fundamental disagreement, Green despaired not only of an allegorical reading of the play, but of a political reading on any terms. The play was written by the poet, he declared, "to relieve and amuse his audience." Here and there may lurk allusions to the contemporary world, but the characters in the comedy are universal, and "they suit all time."[8]

The issues canvased by Green over a hundred years ago are still very much alive. In a brilliant essay, William Arrowsmith revived the theory that the city of the birds is a warning to the Athenians: it is "Aristophanes' image of what all human *physis* (nature) would be if it truly dared to assert itself against the *nomos* (law, custom) of society and religion."[9] It represents what Arrowsmith calls the "fantasy politics" that bore Athens to its heroic defeat, a politics grounded not in moderation or self-control, but in *erōs*, the fatal passion for empire. Arrowsmith reminds us that Alcibiades, according to Plutarch, carried an image of the god Eros on his golden shield as he set sail for Sicily,[10] and that the chorus of birds, in their new vision of cosmic mastery, claim Eros as the ancestor of their race (698–99, 703–4). Passionate desire thus characterizes both the city of the birds and the policy of a specific party in Athens, and such desire, for Arrowsmith and doubtless for some Athenians as well, is marked negatively as excess. At least one critic, moreover, has reasserted the contrary idea that the city of the birds represents the ideal rule of the Athenian *dēmos* (people): "The Olympian gods are, in the play, the enemies of human beings; they are, moreover, symbols for the enemies of the democracy."[11] Finally, a number of scholars today flatly reject a political reading. Cedric Whitman, for example, asserts: "The theme of the *Birds* is absurdity itself. . . . It is about meaninglessness" and "is strangely free of political concerns."[12]

Interpretations of *Birds* thus continue to gravitate between positive and negative allegories of the new city founded by Pisthetaerus and his companion, or else to abandon a political reading altogether and dismiss the entire adventure as sheer comic extravaganza. Recently, Gregory Dobrov has sounded a wise caution against the alternatives "of treating *Birds* as either an autonomous text or as a simple mirror of contemporary politics."[13] If *Birds* is a political drama, it is nevertheless not an immediate reflection or imitation of conditions in the Athenian city-state in the year 414 B.C. In this sense, there is no actual historical referent, a world "out there" represented in the text.[14] The object of criticism is rather to analyze the elements that enter into the complex and contradictory image of the city of the birds and to display the operations by which they are organized in the narrative and made to cohabit in a single imaginary space.[15] We must recognize at the same time that these elements are themselves given by the culture and are thus signs of social values, subject in their own right to complex determinations.[16]

In discussing the nature of science fiction, Umberto Eco remarks: "What distinguishes the fantastic narrative from the realistic . . . is the fact that its possible world is *structurally* different from the real one."[17] Eco proceeds to enumerate "several paths that fantastic literature can take," assigning to the various species names such as allotopia, uchronia, metachronia, and metatopia, as well as the familiar utopia. Eco's classification invites attention to the ways in which a utopian community stands in relation to a society's conventional representation of itself. Fantastic literature, he says, asks "What would happen if the real world was not similar to itself, if its structure, that is, were different?" Eco chooses the roots of *topos* (place) and *chronos* (time), as the basis for his neologisms. For the analysis of Aristophanes' *Birds*, however, it is more useful to attend to relations between Aristophanes' fantasy utopia and prevailing social norms. In this spirit, I offer a technical vocabulary based on the term *nomos* (plural *nomoi*), the meaning of which in classical Greek covers the range of ideas we express by the words "law," "custom," and "rule." It can also refer to a certain type of poem, and, with a different placement of the accent, to a pasture or feeding ground (including that of birds).[18] A Dutch scholar has recently argued for the centrality of this term in all its senses to Aristophanes' *Birds*, in which the song of the birds, "as sweet and holy as the surrounding nature," is contrasted with human "law and morality."[19] I shall exploit the idea of *nomos* in order to discriminate several ways in which a utopian society may be distinguished structurally from an order represented as traditional.

The Greeks perceived human communities to be characterized by specific sets of rules or customs. Herodotus, for example, introduces each major ethnic group in his *Histories* with a description of its *nomoi*.[20] The *nomoi* define a social space, a place that is marked out as distinctive by virtue of its organization under laws that differentiate it from other regions.[21] The problem, accordingly, is to understand the ways in which an imaginary space, a No-place or Utopia in the name coined by Thomas More, is defined against the customs of known places. I have identified four broad kinds of relation between a utopia and a given place characterized by *nomoi*, to each of which I have assigned a name. These types are offered as an aid to the analysis of the city of the birds and the complexity of its ideological determinations.

Anomia. A utopian society may be defined by absolute negation, that is, as having no rules or *nomoi* at all. Such a form may be posited as an ideal type, even if in practice one may doubt that such a community can be described or imagined. Any form of social differentiation among roles or prescribed behaviors presupposes some code or codes of conduct, and the complete absence of *nomoi* would mean the collapse of all social distinctions. But we may call a community that tends toward such an absolute lawlessness anomian, marked, that is, by the absence of rules, *anomia* (anomy).[22]

Antinomia. Another imaginary society we may identify as antinomian. Such a society is marked not by the absence of *nomoi*, but by their reversal or inversion, *antinomia* (antinomy). This is the world turned upside down, as the Renaissance emblem pictured it, the world of the antipodes, where everything is done backwards. What is illegal at home is lawful there, and vice versa.[23]

Eunomia. We may distinguish a third kind of utopia with the label *eunomia* (eunomy). This is a society in which the laws and conventions are imagined as just or excellent, rather than as a mirror image of one's own. Thomas More himself toyed with the name *eutopia* (the good place), for his ideal polity (in the last verse of the second of the poems from *Utopia*).[24] Such a conception is evidently an extrapolation from some accepted version of good or just *nomoi*, the model for which will be values or laws immanent within one's own culture and projected as ideal.

Megalonomia. Finally, a fantastic place may be characterized by hypertrophy with respect to the laws, a tendency to exceed all limits. The distinction here is quantitative rather than qualitative. The order of things is not better, it is simply grander, a magnified world without boundaries in which the rules give scope for ambition and desire. It is a type particularly hospitable to satire. As a neologism for this sort of exaggeration or inflation of the norms, perhaps *megalonomia* (megalonomy) will do.

None of these four kinds of social otherness is likely to be represented in pure form, if indeed they logically can be. Nevertheless, one can call to mind examples in which one or another type seems to predominate in the characterization of an ideal or distant place. Plato presents his republic as just. Herodotus' Egyptians have customs the reverse of Greek practices. The cyclopes are represented in Homer as lacking *nomoi*. The competitive state of nature imagined by such sophists as Callicles and Thrasymachus (according to Plato) valorizes aggression and the pursuit of power, which are taken to be proper norms for human societies.[25] What is remarkable about the fabulous territory of *Nephelokokkugia*, or Cloudcuckooland, to adopt the most familiar English version of the name, is the way in which all four of the utopian forms I have identified enter into the image of it. I shall illustrate them in the order in which they have been mentioned.

In their primitive or natural condition, before the birds have experienced the benefits—if they are benefits—of their encounter with humans, the region that they inhabit has an anomian quality. To begin with, the birds carry no purses (157), and so are free from corruption, as Euelpides says, and also from the invidiousness of distinctions based on money or power (apart from the retinue of the hoopoe, who was formerly human, there is also no slavery among them).[26] Such simplicity, while it may be charming, strikes the Athenian visitors as a sign of witlessness, and Pisthetaerus, when he conceives his great plan for the birds, advises the hoopoe that they must, first and foremost, cease flying about everywhere with their jaws gaping. The gaping mouth is a standard Aristophanic image for dumb wonder.[27] But the subtler point in Pisthetaerus' advice lies, I suspect, in the adverb "everywhere" (*pantachēi*, 165). This kind of flightiness is, says Pisthetaerus, a dishonorable business: the Greek word he uses is *atimon*, literally, without *timē*, which indeed means honor, but, more concretely, applies to privileges of rank or office, and to the financial compensation for those and other services. To be *atimos* (without *timē*) is the legal status of a citizen who has been deprived of his civic rights, of the distinctions pertaining to membership in the polity of Athens.[28] A person who is unstable (*astathmētos*)—that is, without a fixed abode (*stathmos*); one who is undefined or unfixed (*atekmartos*), the kind who has no marker or boundary (no *tekmar*)—such a one is, according to Pisthetaerus, called a bird back home in Athens. The hoopoe acknowledges the justice in this, and inquires what the birds can do about it. Pisthetaerus' answer is: build a city.

In this exchange, we may observe how the opposition between nature and culture, between the unconstrained freedom of the birds and the civilized order of human communities, is reduced to an elementary opposition: boundaries versus unboundedness, rest versus motion, a here and a there ("there, among us," says Pisthetaerus, 167) versus an everywhere. The domain of the birds is without *termini*, without the marks of difference. The birds do not "remain in the same place" (170). The terms of this contrast seem in part derived from a culturally valorized opposition between settled cities and nomadic groups.[29] But Aristophanes gives to the polarity an abstract turn. For the birds, in their perpetual changefulness, nothing is self-identical. The two adventurous Athenians, in their journey to the realm of the birds, have indeed arrived at a nowhere.

At the very beginning of the play, Pisthetaerus and Euelpides cannot decipher the cries of the crow and raven they have been carrying to guide them to the habitation of the birds. One seems to be urging them forward, the other back (1–2). They are in fact at the right spot, except that they are below the residence of the hoopoe. Thus, compass-point directions do not apply.[30] Nor do they know any longer in which direction Athens lies (10–11). Playfully, Aristophanes evokes a mysterious indeterminacy, a kind of metaphysical lostness, about the realm of the birds. Spatial vagueness functions as a sign of a primitive lack of differentiation, like Homer's Aethiopians, dear to the gods, who live near the rising and the setting of the sun.[31]

The hoopoe cannot conceive how the birds can build a city, but Pisthetaerus is quick to instruct him. "Look down," he says, and the hoopoe does. "Now look up"; again the hoopoe obliges. With these commands, I should like to suggest, the lesson on how to build a city is already begun. Pisthetaerus has drawn a line; he has defined the difference between higher and lower—a boundary which, as Pisthetaerus will immediately observe, is of considerable importance if the birds can realize the advantage of their position. "What do you see?" Pisthetaerus asks the hoopoe. "The clouds and the sky," Tereus answers. "Now isn't this in fact the birds' firmament?" "Firmament? How's that?" says the bird. To follow Pisthetaerus' explanation, we shall have to spend a moment with the Greek text.

The word that I have translated as firmament is *polos*, from which is derived the English word *pole*, in the sense of the axis of the heavens. Loosely, it means "sky" in Greek. Pisthetaerus remarks that a *polos* is essentially a kind of place (*topos*, 180); implicitly, this equation demarcates the region as a bounded space. It is no longer quite an everywhere. Pisthetaerus explains that it is called *polos* because it *poleitai*, that is, because it moves around and about, and everything passes through it. But if the birds will settle it and fence it around, then instead of a *polos*, pole, it will be called a *polis*, a city-state. Pisthetaerus adds that the birds will then be able to rule over mankind and conquer the gods. The reason for this is, as has been said, that the air, which the birds inhabit, is "in the middle" (*en mesōi*, 187), between earth and heaven. That the location is strategic is evident. But the point is that for the birds there now is such a thing as a middle, a locus marked by position. What hitherto was by its nature mobile and permeable is now perceived as a fixed place and potential barrier. Thus the birds, by commanding this intermediate zone, can exact a transit fare from the gods, without which they will refuse permission for the savor of sacrificial animals to pass to heaven. It is not just a question of the wall, but of a different way of conceiving space as territorial, a field marked by limits of property. The hoopoe is immediately sold on the idea and prepares to summon the other birds to a council, remarking, for the benefit of his Athenian guests, that he has already taken the trouble to instruct the barbarous creatures in Greek (199–200).

While the precivilized condition of the birds may be described as a utopia of the anomian variety, without law or differentiation, the city of Cloudcuckooland that comes into being has a different constitution, based as it is on boundaries that are marked off and on an established discipline or order among the birds. The city of the birds is not the regime that Pisthetaerus and Euelpides find; it is a city they invent. But it is not posssible to discriminate too exactly between the older dispensation and the new. For the birds preserve, even in their walled city, a kind of natural solidarity among themselves that needs no laws or rules to enforce it. Cloudcuckooland sends packing those emissaries from the real city who come bearing anything that smacks of political structure or contention. The inspector and the decree salesman, like the informer, are unceremoniously banished.[32] So, too, is the geometer Meton, who offers to measure off the sky into individual plots of land (995–96). The birds do not proceed so far in the process of internal differentiation as to attain to private property and the city-state conception of citizenship that is underwritten by property. Thus, in answer to Meton's question whether there is civil strife (*stasis*) in the new city, Pisthetaerus answers that all are of one mind among the birds, and that they crush swaggerers (1014–16).

The city of the birds is already a complex affair, containing elements of both precivil and civic life. The idea of a naturally harmonious society has roots in several cultural traditions among the Greeks. It is implicit in visions of a golden age preceding the reign of Zeus, free of want and of injustice.[33] Aesopian fables are set in a remote time when animals could still converse with men. Distant tribes, like the Argippaeans, who neighbor upon the Scythians (Herodotus 4.23), might be invested with a blessed peacefulness. One may perceive, in this reconstitution of a city without the inner stresses to which conflicting interests and class tensions give rise, a kind of primitivist nostalgia, a desire for civilization without its discontents, that is conveniently projected by a colonizing population onto what they perceive as simpler beings, whether beasts or native peoples, who dwell at the margins of the world known to history.[34] Thus Ariel Dorfman, who examines the series of children's stories based on the character Babar the elephant, observes how European civilization has required the fantasy of "some island, some shore of the universe which is still uncontaminated, where all the positive aspects of 'progress' can be reconstituted without the at-

tendant flaws and dilemmas."[35] The territory of the barbarous birds
assumes this function in Aristophanes' play.

This same contradiction between social structure and an undifferentiated presocial condition pertains also to the prehistory of the birds.
Pisthetaerus, as has been said, wins the hoopoe to his grandiose scheme
with the promise of limitless power, but with the native birds—those
who, unlike Tereus, never had been human—he takes a slightly different approach. Pisthetaerus first arouses in them a desire for universal
sovereignty by representing it as something they had formerly possessed,
but have since lost. With them, that is, he must first implant a sense of
lack, a nostalgia for an originary plenitude which, until he tells them
otherwise, they have never missed. Inscription within human society
takes the form of an initiation into desire, which is predicated on the
memory—here self-consciously constructed as a myth—of former sufficiency. Thus, the birds are made to project their own plenitude onto a
prehistoric past, which thereby constitutes them as fallen creatures,
now entered into the realm of desire. In former times, Pisthetaerus tells
them, the birds were kings. Upon learning this, the birds inquire, "Of
what?" (or perhaps, "Of whom?," *tinos*, 467). It is a good question, given
that this was before the reign of Kronos and the Titans, before gods,
mortals, and the earth itself had come into existence (469–70). Pisthetaerus asserts that the birds, as the earliest beings in creation, are naturally entitled to rule (477), and also that, in earliest times, it was they,
rather than the gods, who held sway over mankind (481–82). Conceiv-
ably one is to understand here a process with discrete stages, but it is
likely that the hierarchical principle of kingship is simply projected back
onto an original, undifferentiated state of the cosmos to which it does
not logically apply. The image of a pre-Olympian state of nature is thus
fused with a vision of power and domination. Precisely this fusion characterizes the new city of the birds that will take shape under the inspiration of Pisthetaerus.[36]

In seeking escape from the pervasive litigation that is characteristic of Athens, as Pisthetaerus and Euelpides represent it, the two Athenians encounter a place that is lacking the differentiations on which
law itself depends, or rather, which law installs. Order imagines as its
opposite a lack of structure, a dissolution of distinctions, which it
projects onto an other, opposed either by species, as here, or by some
other difference, such as gender in *Assemblywomen*, where women
inaugurate a regime in which the rules of property and kinship are abolished.[37] But difference is present in the encounter between civilized
humans and presocial birds, and from this encounter proceeds both

structure and desire. I shall examine the logic and the consequences of this new arrangement shortly.

There is more than one way in which to imagine the opposite of structure. One may collapse the distinctions it sustains, or, alternatively, reverse the signs of the elements that it orders. Thus, it is no great distance, in comic visions of utopia, from anomy to antinomianism, from the absence of law, that is, with the corresponding ideal of a natural harmony, to an inversion of the law, in which the authority of the old law, not utterly canceled by its negation, remains evident in the selfish delight with which it is violated. Pisthetaerus and Euelpides begin their journey out of a desire to escape the lawsuits of Athens, but they do not on that account stand simply for a commitment to just behavior. They unashamedly reveal to the hoopoe that they, like him, are looking to evade their debts (115–16). The hoopoe, who had been human, retains enough of his former nature to keep a slave, for which the native birds have no use (70–76). Later, when the plan to fortify Cloudcuckooland has been adopted, the chorus of birds invites the audience in the theater directly (in the formal address known as the parabasis) to join them in the pleasant life, "for all the things that are ruled out as shameful according to the law (nomos) where you are are the very things that are virtuous among us birds" (755–56). They go on to explain that while beating one's father is deemed disgraceful according to Athenian custom (nomos, 757)—the example is commonplace for outrageous behavior—it is entirely respectable conduct in their own realm.[38] Slaves, foreigners, and sympathizers of the disenfranchized (atimois, 766) are all welcome in the new polity. In this topsy-turvy world, shame and honor, authority and obedience are not so much abolished as turned inside out. There is a certain slide into the anomian vision. Slaves do not reverse places with masters, as in the saturnalian festival, nor do foreigners with native citizens; rather, distinctions in status seem to be suspended in the new realm. But the idea of slaves welcomed as citizens is articulated as a transgression rather than as a social leveling, and so is assimilated to the trope of the verkehrte Welt (the world upside-down).

Later in the play, a father-beater takes up the invitation of the chorus and comes to establish residence among the birds, passionate, as he says, for their nomoi (1345).[39] Pisthetaerus acknowledges that it is indeed considered manly among the birds for a nestling to strike its father, but he adds that there is also an ancient custom, inscribed among the tablets of the storks,[40] that when the parent has reared his young so that they may fly from the nest, they are then in turn responsible for his support. Such an obligation was traditional at Athens,[41] and the father-beater naturally complains that his voyage was of no great use if he must also feed his father in Cloudcuckooland. Pisthetaerus then gives him the old-fashioned advice he himself received as a youth, that he had best not strike a parent, but, if he is pugnacious by disposition, let him go off and fight the Thracians, where he can, at the same time, sustain himself on a soldier's pay.

Clearly, there is a shift here from the antinomian image of utopia, in which the violation of conventional rules is endorsed in a spirit of unrestrained freedom, to the vision of a well-ordered polity. Contrariness gives way to a heightened sense of decency, inspired by reasonable persuasion that is marvelously effective in Cloudcuckooland. This is the city in its eunomian aspect, with a ready obedience to custom and the deference due to station and degree. This excellent constitution of the birds is ancestral. It is a product both of good legislation and of a spirit of respect for the law which is associated with the mores of former times. The virtues of the antique constitution were a universal touchstone of good legislation in Athens.[42] It is natural, moreover, that there should be a certain blurring of the lines between the ideal of the well-ordered society associated with the ancestral constitution and the tradition of a precivic golden age before the law. In both versions, the past serves as a screen on which the image of an order free from strife is projected, in contrast to the divisions within the contemporary polity. In this way, too, the solidarity characteristic of the anomian world is made a feature of the rule of law. Aggressive energy is directed outward beyond the perimeter of the city (a perimeter that does not exist in the absence of *nomoi*), toward savage enemies in Thrace. And because the carnivalian spirit of the inversion of custom lies so close to the anomian liberation from the constraints of law, it too may be made to coexist with the image of an ideal constitution, without too keen a note of paradox. The ancient order is not repressive. Thus, there is an air of unconstrained goodness among the birds that is capable of reconciling virtue and desire and of uniting, in the antique legislation of the storks, social order and the state of nature.

But the city of the birds has also a restless, expansionist drive that is at odds with the image of a settled, well-governed polity. It has been seen that Pisthetaerus succeeds in rousing desire among the birds. Having submitted to his leadership (548, 637–38), they are infected by new longings. Where they were once contented, gawking creatures, they are now seized by a violent urge to regain their lordship over the universe by any and every means, for without it, they say, life is not worth living (548–49). The hoopoe declares that there is no longer time for dozing or delay; the birds must act now with all possible speed (639– 41).[43] This passionate will to power, which culminates in mastery over gods and mortals, transforms the quiet community of the birds into an efficiently aggressive polity unconstrained by the inhibitions of conventional wisdom.[44] Moderation is out of court. This is the megalonomian dispensation, which gives rein to ambition without limit.

The vision of limitless power is grounded in the former plenitude of the birds, when they both ruled the universe and were alone in it. The idea of complete sufficiency is associated with traditions of the golden age, when the earth, under an earlier dynasty of gods, spontaneously yielded up its bounty. There is a suggestion of this earthly paradise in the benefits that the birds are prepared to confer upon mankind in exchange for recognition of their sovereignty. The birds will eliminate agricultural pests such as locusts and burrowing flies, will announce fair weather for sailing so that merchants will prosper, will reveal the sites of buried treasure and extend the lives of men by granting them longevity from their own store of years. Thus mortals will happily revere them as they do god, life, earth, Cronus, and Poseidon (586–87), the reference to Cronus evoking the fecundity of the pre-Jovian world.[45] The image is a mixed one, inasmuch as commerce, navigation, and mineral wealth are commonly associated with decline, but the overall sense of ease and plenty belongs to the dream of a pastoral age. The birds, then, represent these blessings in their identity as creatures prior to the law of Zeus; at the same time, however, their fallen state, as it is established for them in the myth of origins insinuated by Pisthetaerus, relocates this fullness as the object of the birds' desire. The birds thus simultaneously stand for a primeval wholeness and want it. This double character is written into the organization of the birds as a polity. They form a city in order to reclaim their heritage. The very act of marking off its perimeter defines the territory they have to conquer and projects the ideal of a mythic past as the object of a will to power.[46]

One may see here how the city of the birds can be the subject of inconsistent or contradictory political allegories. As a world of natural bounty, free of contention, it stands for the sufficiency of the golden age. But this plenitude at the same time inspires an ambition for universal conquest or domination, and is thus a figure for Athenian expansionism. The two aspects are simultaneous moments in the constitution of the city of the birds, and they reciprocally condition each other. It is in the eyes of Pisthetaerus and Euelpides that the birds are both the representatives of natural solidarity and witless, gaping creatures, needing to be organized to realize their potential power. The anomian and the megalonomian utopias arise in the same instant.

The source of the remarkable vigor of the city of the birds resides in the birds' solidarity, which, as has been said, appears as a residue of their precivic homogeneity, free of strife and litigation. Their extraordinary energy is harnessed in the marvelous construction of the wall around the city, which the birds, working in unison, complete so quickly that Pisthetaerus himself is astonished (1164–67). No longer, he observes, will anyone wish to hire wage-laborers (1152). Internal dissension is represented as the objective limit on the power of the city-state, while the cohesiveness or cooperation characteristic of the anomian community, which is miraculously preserved in the process of incorporation into the new city, renders the city invincible. The birds' use of their power, in turn, is true to the nostalgic image of their archaic unity inasmuch as it inaugurates the return of a golden age.

But the city of the birds is not wholly without division. Pisthetaerus is the leader—he is called archon (1123)—and his role is necessary. In their unorganized condition, the birds are passionate but ineffectual. Angry as they are at the intrusion of humans into their domain, they are easily held at bay by Pisthetaerus and Euelpides who are armed with skewers for swords and pots for shields (357–61).[47] Early in the play, Euelpides had denied the hoopoe's charge that he aspired to rule as an aristocrat (*aristokrateisthai*, 125). But as the city takes shape, there emerges an elementary hierarchy with Pisthetaerus as king and the birds subject to him. In the end, Pisthetaerus is described as an autocrat (*turannos*, 1708), and the power of Cloudcuckooland is his.[48] We learn also that some of the birds have risen up against the popular party, and Pisthetaerus is seen roasting their flesh for dinner (1583–85, cf. 1688).

It may well be that an allegorical reference to contemporary politics has entered the text here as a subtle hint of dissension in the promised land.[49] The tyranny of Pisthetaerus mirrors the role of Athens as the tyrant city, suppressing domestic opposition to its dream of empire.[50] Amid the commotion of the wedding songs for Pisthetaerus and the goddess Sovereignty,[51] it may pass all but unnoticed that the human being is deified, while the birds are reduced to a chorus of admirers (see esp. 1743). At the moment of the birds' triumph, there seems to be a hint of innocence betrayed.

But the principle of leadership in the city of the birds is also grounded in the union of civic order and natural community that drives the entire vision of Cloudcuckooland. The coexistence of two kinds of community—the one collective, the other political and socially differentiated—is figured in the division between the human leader and the crowd of birds.[52] Pisthetaerus is motivated by the desire for power and, to this

extent, perhaps, represents the kind of ambitious individualism associated with a sophistic conception of human nature, which takes advantage of the weakness or credulousness of simpler creatures. But
this role may also be a synecdoche for the imperial power of the city
of the birds as a whole, the polis as tyrant with a tyrant's grandiose
aspirations and untrammeled license. If Pisthetaerus vaunts and struts,
it is because he represents here the megalonomian moment of Cloudcuckooland itself, just as, elsewhere, he is characterized in accord with
other aspects of the birds' utopia. Thus the rogue who sought a place
to evade debts and enjoy lubricious pleasures can, in another context,
advise a youth on respect for parents. The inconsistency of characterization is a product of the complex ideological construction of the
birds' domain.

The four types of utopia that have been identified as variations on
the customary order or *nomoi* intersect with one another and prohibit
an allegorical reading that would associate figures in the drama with
specific social referents. In this respect, *Birds* differs from *Wasps*, where
the jurors and the courts to which they are devoted signify a recogniz-
able social class and the institutional expression of its power. There too,
as we have seen, Philocleon and the chorus of jurors are complex and
multiply determined. In *Birds*, however, the crisscrossing configurations
of Cloudcuckooland scramble the allusive pattern more completely.

But this is not to say that the play is unpolitical. Rather, it is an
example of what Catherine Belsey calls an "interrogative text," which
"invites an answer or answers to the questions it poses." Belsey argues
that "to smooth over the contradictions" in such texts by attributing
to them "a non-contradictory ideology . . . is to refuse to enter into the
debates about revolution, authority and tyranny initiated in the texts."[53]

The city of the birds is, indeed, a city, but it is a city of natural
creatures, who have no need of wealth, slaves, or property.[54] It is thus
simultaneously a token of the golden age, in which people lived in harmony and the earth spontaneously yielded its bounty, and a well-
ordered civic community from which the tensions and litigiousness of
Athens (such as resulted, perhaps, in the accusations against Alcibiades)
are banished. Restraints are abolished in a spirit of carnivalian liberty;
hence the city may resemble the topsy-turvy world of the antipodes,
where the rules are all backward. But the inscription of a restrospective
ideal of complete sufficiency into the differentiated and competitive
structure of a civic polity offers the promise of fulfillment to an unlim-
ited desire for mastery. The *megalonomia* of the city of the birds is presented as the cross product of lawlessness—*anomia*—and the rule of

law. The city of the birds is contradictory because Aristophanes fashioned out of conventional materials a place both social and presocial, harmonious and divided, benign and aggressive. Cloudcuckooland is not, however, an arbitrary fantasy. It is a complex image of Athens' own contradictions—its communal solidarity and its political and social divisions, along with the conservatism that looked to the image of an ancestral constitution and an imperial will to power.

3

Lysistrata

In Shakespeare's *Comedy of Errors*, one of the twins called Antipholus, who has arrived at Ephesus from Syracuse, is mistaken for his brother by his brother's wife, and admitted into his house. The wife's maid, Luce or Nell, is in love with the servant, Dromio. Now, Dromio too has a twin of the same name, who happens to be in the service of the Syracusan Antipholus. Luce, then, makes the same mistake as her mistress and pursues the wrong Dromio. When this Dromio is reunited with his master, he jokes vulgarly about Luce's girth:

ANTIPHOLUS S.: Then she bears some breadth?

DROMIO S.: No longer from head to foot than from hip to hip. She is spherical, like a globe; I could find out countries in her.

ANT. S.: In what part of her body stands Ireland?

DRO. S.: Marry, sir, in her buttocks. I found it out by the bogs.

ANT. S.: Where Scotland?

DRO. S.: I found it by the barrenness; hard in the palm of her hand.

ANT. S.: Where France?

DRO. S.: In her forehead, armed and reverted, making war against her heir.

ANT. S.: Where England?

DRO. S.: I looked for the chalky cliffs, but I could find no whiteness in them; but I guess it stood in her chin, by the salt rheum that ran between France and it.

45

There are more questions in this vein concerning Spain, the West Indies, and finally the Netherlands, to which Dromio replies, "O, sir! I did not look so low."[1]

This coarse anatomy bears a resemblance to the division of the allegorical figure Diallagē, or Reconciliation, at the end of Aristophanes' *Lysistrata*, on whose body the Athenian and Spartan men stake out the various parts of Greece:

> SPARTAN AMBASSADOR: We must demand this promontory here return to us.
>
> LYSISTRATA: Which one?
>
> SPARTAN AMBASSADOR: This one in back: we count on having, we can almost feel it.
>
> ATHENIAN AMBASSADOR: By the God of Earthquakes, that you'll never get!
>
> LYSISTRATA: You'll give it up, sir.
>
> ATHENIAN AMBASSADOR: What do *we* get, then?
>
> LYSISTRATA: You'll ask for something that's of equal value.
>
> ATHENIAN AMBASSADOR: Let's see now, I know, give us first of all the furry triangle here, the gulf that runs behind it, also the two connecting legs.[2]

The dialogue continues with a few more tasteless bits along these lines.

In both scenes, the body of a woman is imagined by men as a map or globe, divided into discrete geographical regions. It is thus rendered divisible, as though composed of independent parts that may be the object of territorial ambitions or opposed as rival states. This complex image of the female body, simultaneously unitary and yet exposed to a kind of political dissection, may be taken as an emblem of the way in which women as a political body are represented in *Lysistrata*.[3]

In *Comedy of Errors*, political and commercial rivalries divide the comic world that is mapped onto the body of a woman, just as they do in *Lysistrata*. At the same time, there is the suggestion of a fraternal connection between the cities of Ephesus and Syracuse, which harbor identical twins as citizens. Again, the case of *Lysistrata* is analogous. In her reproach to the warring Athenians and Spartans, Lysistrata says: "Don't you share a cup at common altars, for common gods, like brothers at the Olympic games, Thermópylae and Delphi? (1129–31)."[4] The cities that are locked in struggle have a common identity imaged in the relationship between brothers or kinsmen (*xungeneis*). Beneath their mutual antagonism Lysistrata can appeal to a familial unity or oneness among the Greeks. But women are the agency by which this collective bond is realized.

In *Lysistrata*, the women of Greece constitute themselves as an organized opposition across barriers of age, class (456–58), and nationality, in order to put an end to the war between the Athenian and Spartan alliances. Their most salient quality is solidarity, and in this they are dramatically differentiated from the men's commitment to pursuing the conflict. One may be forgiven for seeing here a parallel with the role of the working class in Marxian communism. In each case, a disempowered section of the population is represented as overcoming national rivalries and making league with their confrères (or consoeurs) abroad in order to put an end to wars among states.

. — The women's primary motive for ending the hostilities between the Athenian and Spartan alliances is sex—they long for their husbands, who are endlessly away on distant military campaigns (99–112)—and the device Lysistrata hits upon to compel the men to reach an accord is a sex strike, the stratagem for which the comedy is best remembered. — To account for the women's desperation, Aristophanes exploits the stereotype of women as libidinous, and adds for good measure the conventional attributes of bibulousness and thievery, that is, a general concern with private pleasures as opposed to public decorum.[5] As the women assemble at Lysistrata's summons, the Athenian Calonice inquires about the purpose of the meeting in the early hours of the morning: "Is it something big?" "Yes." "And thick?" "Thick too, by Zeus." "So how come we're not all here?" "That's not the kind of thing it is" (23–25). Lysistrata is impatient, but Calonice's lubriciousness is not irrelevant: sexual deprivation is, after all, what the strike is about. Lysistrata introduces a suggestion of domestic concerns when she inquires: "Don't you miss the fathers of your children who are away on campaign?" (99–100), but her next remark shifts the focus back to sex: "There's not even a scintilla of a lover left" (107), she complains, and the importation of dildoes has also dried up since the rebellion of Miletus. Later, Lysistrata will have her hands full keeping the women from going back on their oath of abstinence.

The women's urgent appetite for sex is not entirely compatible, however, with the motive of humbling the men by withholding sexual intercourse. The men are for the most part away at the front—that is why they are unavailable to their wives—and are apparently enduring their barracks life with no thought of suing for peace. If their distress at their privation is less severe than that of the women, how will a sex strike alter their resolve to continue the war?[6] Since they have not hitherto been troubled by the lack of sex, there is no reason why the strike should have more effect on them than on the women themselves. There is an inconsistency in motivation, whereby the women appear to be depriving the men of what they themselves especially desire.

The problem of motive is in part addressed by the concern for children and home intimated in Lysistrata's initial probe of the women's sentiments about the war (99). Despite the conventional image of female randiness, the women are not fighting simply for sexual satisfaction. They are also disturbed by the disruption to the home caused by the war and the absence of their husbands. Aristophanes is at pains in *Lysistrata* to portray women as preservers of the household. Lysistrata later explains to an Athenian commissioner who has come to negotiate with the women: "Just when it is right to have fun and enjoy the fruits of youth, we have to sleep alone on account of campaigns. Okay, I'll leave us out of it; but I suffer for the young girls who are growing old in their bedrooms." The commissioner asks: "Don't men also grow old?" "But it's not the same thing, by Zeus," Lysistrata replies (591–94). War is worse for unmarried women because the bloom of youth quickly fades, while men can find a young girl to wed even when their hair is gray (595–97). It is marriage, and not just sex, that is at stake. This same note of shattered homelife is struck when the excited Cinesias appeals to his wife Myrrhina with their infant in his arms (877). The women's sexual motive coexists with their commitment to marriage and the home.

In an important article, John Vaio has inquired why Aristophanes tolerated the inconsistent motivation of the women in the opening scene in the play, "when he could easily have omitted any reference to the separation of husband and wife." Vaio replies: "By sacrificing dramatic logic Aristophanes establishes a major theme at the start of the play: the disruptive effect of war on family life. It is partly to cure this ill that the women's action is directed, and the success of this action at the end of the play enables husband and wife to return home together in an atmosphere of peace and reconciliation."[7]

One may, however, reverse the question: Why does Aristophanes insist on the women's sexual motive for halting the war, rather than on their concern for domestic life, if the latter is indeed his primary theme? Lysistrata plainly hints that uninhibited sexual desire may find satisfaction in extramarital affairs, and Aristophanes is obliged to foreclose that option with the explanation that the war has made lovers as well as husbands scarce (107, 212)—rather a lame reason for the women's utter desperation. Besides, slaves, who were exempt from the fighting, might have served as lovers, as Aristophanes suggests in *Women at Festival* (491–92), which was produced in the same year as *Lysistrata*.

In representing women simultaneously as licentious and as concerned for home and family, Aristophanes has fused two distinct and mutually contradictory images. The women's sexual passion is at odds with their custodial relation to the home.

Of course, the women's randiness makes for some good fun at the women's expense, and this may be justification enough for the motif, even at the cost of logic and consistency of characterization. But female sexuality is also an element in the image of women constituted as a unified body as opposed to the antagonistic division of the men. The transgressive quality of feminine desire is coded as corrosive of the boundaries fixed by civic structures, rendering women the locus of primal solidarity and the vehicle of an appeal to the collective identification of all Greeks. Correspondingly, the idea of autonomous female desire threatens the integrity of the household. Women's eroticism must be contained. Aristophanes makes the women's sexual deprivation the basis for a plan intended to reaffirm the values of the household and to defend its exclusivity against the dangers that arise in the masculine, public space of politics and war. He both insinuates and seeks to control the danger of women's desire.

The very possibility of organizing a sex strike presupposes a collective and concerted action on the part of the women of Greece—an action that transcends the dispersion of women into discrete households, where the space for women is defined. In their effort to defend the home, the women are obliged to abandon it, at least temporarily, and join together as a corporate body. The anomaly of women inaugurating a political conference is underscored by the difficulty they experience in escaping from their houses, to the chagrin of an impatient Lysistrata. Once assembled, the women act out a parody of masculine debate and ceremony, the only model available for political behavior. Despite its farcical character, the collective action of the women imports a new element into the drama, which goes beyond the antinomy between adulterous eroticism and fidelity to the home. For libertine sexuality and marital fidelity are both defined in relation to the home as the presumed locus of a woman's life, segregated from the public sphere of male activity. The household is still recognized as a woman's proper place, even if its boundaries are respected in the breach, so long as each transgression is conceived of as an individual affair. But women meeting in assembly in order to influence state policy exceed this simple opposition, and challenge the ideological basis of the opposition between men's and women's spheres. By representing them as engaging in a political action against the war, Aristophanes conjures up the image of women as a countersociety, a kind of mirror world of the masculine civic space.

Here is the germ of the representation of women as an alternative public or *dēmos*, with their own state institutions, that will be developed further in *Women at Festival*, where a women's rite is imagined as a public assembly (*ekklēsia*).[8]

Perhaps the most striking feature of the plot of *Lysistrata* is the casual way in which two quite different stratagems by the women are woven together in order to compel the men of Greece to accept a peace treaty. On the one hand, there is the sex strike; on the other hand, there is the capture or occupation of the acropolis, the citadel of Athens where the treasury was located. The second scheme is introduced after the women, following the lead of the Spartan delegate Lampito, agree to Lysistrata's proposal that they abstain from sexual intercourse with their husbands. Lysistrata has met the objection that the women may be forced by recommending that they resist passively, if all else fails (162–63), for sex gives no pleasure under compulsion. Lampito then suddenly, and to all appearances inconsequentially, interjects that the Athenians will not reliably adhere to a peace treaty so long as their ships have rigging and their inexhaustible silver is stored safely in the temple of the goddess Athena (173–74). Lysistrata reveals that the oldest women of Athens have already been assigned to seize the citadel under the pretense of performing a sacrifice. With this settled, the women proceed to take the oath of abstinence.

In the play as a whole, the two strands of the plot defined by the alternative stratagems remain largely independent of each other. Thus, the chorus of old men, who attempt to break into the acropolis after Lysistrata and her friends have occupied it (245–46), are motivated not by sexual desire but by the determination to recover the citadel which, as they see it, has fallen into enemy hands; they compare the women's action with a Spartan takeover that occurred a century earlier (273–80). Neither is the commissioner, who is the next to arrive, in the grip of lust. Wilamowitz suggested that it needed the passage of time before the effects of the women's strike were felt.[9] The effects of the economic freeze, however, are immediately palpable: the commissioner enters for the express purpose of collecting funds to supply the navy with timber and oars (421–22). The action reverts to the sexual theme only when Lysistrata emerges from the citadel, more than halfway through the play, to complain about the women inside, who are running her ragged by their attempts to slip back home for sex (708–15). Once they are brought under control, Cinesias, the husband of Myrrhina (one of Lysistrata's allies), arrives and is teased into agreeing to a truce, although a last-minute equivocation costs him his satisfaction (951). When a Spartan herald turns up and is mistakenly suspected of harboring a weapon under his tunic (the classical analogue to Mae West's line, "Is that a gun you're carrying or are you just glad to see me?"), the Athenian commissioner at last realizes the extent of the women's conspiracy, and consents to summon ambassadors with the authority to strike a peace pact (1007–12).

To be sure, the transfer of the scene of action to the citadel facilitates the sex strike, inasmuch as it is possible to lock the passionate husbands out and, even more important, keep the passionate wives inside. But the move to the acropolis also transforms the sex strike from an essentially individual affair, to be put into practice household by household, into a collective action of the women united as a kind of city themselves, defending their own walls and occupying their own separate civic space. The women's solidarity as a community within Athens mirrors their unity on the international scale. Both at home and abroad, women are seen as overcoming or abolishing divisions that are constitutive of the masculine order.

It is worth emphasizing this contrast between the private character of the sex strike, where each woman will cling to her own doorpost in order to prevent her husband from hauling her into bed, and the collective or communal aspect of the seizure of the acropolis, where the women act as a single body. John Vaio sees a thematic connection between the two movements in the play: in both, the playwright emphasizes the domestic life of women. The occupation of the acropolis by the women effectively turns the city into a larger version of the home, with which the women have all along been primarily concerned. As Vaio puts it, "the women turn public into domestic economy, city-center into private household," and he adds: "Home and city merge in the language of the play."[10] The city, under occupation by the women, is indeed run as a household, but not as a private household. Rather, the distinction between public and private collapses here. The collective action of the women establishes their new domain as a communal space, the locus of the city's solidarity as a single body. The private households, for the time being, have been abandoned.

By taking control of the acropolis, the women openly organize themselves into a separate community, and any suggestion of individual resistance to husbands at home is tacitly dropped. All the women, young and old, are now gathered together and are in a position to withstand an assault collectively. By locating themselves at the ritual center of the Athenian state, moreover, the women cease simply to function as a kind of shadow society, with a parallel organization to that of the men, and insert themselves into the male domain in fact.

After the women have occupied the upper city, they do not merely hold the treasury hostage until their demands for a peace treaty are met, though this is, to all appearances, their original intention. Rather, Lysistrata announces, to the consternation of the commissioner sent to draw on the treasury, that she will act as manager of the public funds (493), and in that capacity will cease financing military operations on the grounds that the war is unnecessary. She is fully conscious of the reversal between private and public roles that such a usurpation represents. Formerly, as she says, women were kept silent within the house (509–16); now they have formally elected to save Greece by their collective will (525–26). To dramatize the inversion, they dress the commissioner in a veil and women's garments and declare that henceforth war is women's business.

The women's right to govern the state rests on two kinds of claim. First, they are loyal and responsible citizens, distinguished by their participation in the women's rituals and festivals, and have contributed to the city its most valuable form of wealth, that is, its men (639–51). Note the public character of this claim, especially in respect to civic festivals, which recalls Lysistrata's original instructions to the oldest women of Athens to occupy the citadel on the pretext of performing a sacrifice (179).[11] Such rites were the only occasion on which women acted collectively and in public, and they provide the women with a model for the governance of the commonwealth as an autonomous body, parallel to the corporate association of males. Thanks to their role in public cults, the women are preeminently suited to offer advice to the city.

Second, implicit in Lysistrata's elaborate analogy between statecraft and the working of wool (565–86) is the point that the skills required for domestic chores, and in general for managing a household, equip women perfectly for the administration of public affairs.[12] The premise is that women are in fact mistresses of the home and their tasks involve a substantial measure of competence and responsibility. The women, then, who had hitherto been mute and confined within the house, propose an alternative model of civic government based on principles of domestic economy.

There is, of course, a certain simplification involved in the women's depiction of Athenian politics, not to mention the men's motives for maintaining the war, but it is no worse than most political sloganeering. While it is cast in homespun language, the women's advice is preferred as a political solution to dissension in Athens and among the Greek states. True, the analogy between the city and the household on which the women make their case maintains the association between women and the domestic space, even as they push their claims for a civic role. But their program is addressed to public issues and suggests an alternative to masculine modes of administering the state.

However, the option of a new regime is not fully developed or exploited in *Lysistrata*. The question of the women's ability to govern, and the suitability of their methods, is dropped when the plot shifts back to the sex strike, unless perhaps it resurfaces in an attenuated form in the superior and almost maternal impartiality with which Lysistrata presides over the peace negotiations in the finale. Having captured the citadel, the women do nothing except guard the treasury until the men, reduced by erotic desire, arrange the truce.

In *Lysistrata*, the women do not aim to seize power permanently. Their plot is defined or limited by the single goal of effecting a reconciliation among the warring parties. After that, they will return to their individual homes, which are seen as the locus of traditional values. They are a one-purpose army, disbanded at the end of their campaign and recontained within the domestic sphere. On this conception of the women's goals, there is no scope for them to put their economic and political ideals into effect and rule the city as a commune. The larger plan for the adminstration of the city is at odds with the women's intention to resume their private household functions.

The tension between the limited aim of holding the treasury hostage until the men consent to arrange a truce and the wider ambition of running the city along the lines of domestic economy reproduces the double aspect of the sex strike plot, in which women's sexuality is caricatured as illicit and ungovernable, and simultaneously harnessed to the interests of the home. In both strands of the plot, the women threaten to break down the property-based structure of the city-state, predicated on the dispersion of women among discrete households under the authority of a presiding male. The moment they take action, the women conjure up the specter of a communal identity that, despite their professed commitment to the home, clashes with the norms of Athenian social life. It is as though the body of women, on which will be written, in the finale of the comedy, the division of the Greek world into separate territories, irrepressibly asserts its undifferentiated unity as the essence of social solidarity.[13]

It would have to await *Assemblywomen* (*Ecclesiazusae*), produced in the early years of the following century, before Aristophanes would take off from the analogy between the management of the home and the governance of the city to launch a complete inversion of the social order under a women's regime, where the walls between houses are torn down, all property is held in common, men and women are allowed indiscriminate sexual congress (in the interest of fairness, the ugliest have first choice), and the entire city is restructured along the lines of a single vast household.[14] This revolutionary dispensation is introduced

abruptly in the play. Praxagora, the heroine, originally proposes that the
women pack the Athenian assembly in disguise and elect themselves
into power on the grounds that their domestic experience renders them
uniquely fit to end the mismanagement of state resources and to institute a clean and competent regime. Only after authority has been voted
to the women (with considerable support from the males at the meeting) do they inaugurate, suddenly and unexpectedly, their social revolution, which does not follow directly from Praxagora's claims to superior talent in the administration of the state. Aristophanes evidently
regarded it as natural that women, once in power, should propose such
a scheme. They are closely associated with the household, the structure of which is imitated in their public arrangements. What is more,
as the social other, conceived in their collective identity as the anti-
thesis of the masculine order, women represent the potential negation
of the privatism in economic and sexual relations on which city-state
society is based.

The narrative design of *Lysistrata* resembles that of several other
utopian comedies of Aristophanes, from early works like *Acharnians*
and *Peace* to late plays such as *Frogs, Assemblywomen,* and *Wealth,* in
which a hero or heroine conceives an audacious scheme to renew or
refashion society and normally wins the support of a sometimes recalcitrant set of allies, including members of the chorus—or, in the case
of *Lysistrata,* the semi-chorus of old women. Analogies with *Birds,*
produced three years before *Lysistrata,* are especially conspicuous. The
birds, under the leadership of Pisthetaerus, form the polis of Cloudcuckooland and encircle it with walls, just as Lysistrata and the women
gain control of a walled space, here the acropolis, or, as it is called in
the play (and in Attic literature generally), the polis. The women, like
the birds, defend their territory against petitioners from the lower city,
such as the commissioner, the half-chorus of old men, and Cinesias,
who bears the same name (probably by coincidence) as one of the visitors to Cloudcuckooland (the root *kin* has a slang meaning appropriate
to the sexual excitement felt by Myrrhina's husband). Like Lysistrata,
the birds oblige their opponents, here the gods, to submit by virtue of
their control of an essential resource, the aroma of sacrifices wafting
toward heaven on which the gods depend for sustenance. Both plays
conclude with the epiphany of a mute female figure—Reconciliation
in *Lysistrata* and Sovereignty in *Birds*—in a scene of erotic triumph and
communion. Like women, the birds are outsiders and constitute a natural locus for an alternative order, based on elementary forms of social
solidarity.

The birds, however, inspired by the megalomania of Pisthetaerus, establish a new regime characterized, in accord with their primitive mode of life, by an absence of private property and other forms of social differentiation, and they go on to humble the Olympian gods and take their place as lords of the universe. This is a far cry from the mellow affirmation of peace, reconciliation, and domestic life in *Lysistrata*, despite the festive spirit of the conclusion. The erotic force celebrated in *Birds* is, in *Lysistrata*, harnessed to aspirations for quiet contentment, an end to conflict and competition, and a return to the pleasures of the home. Thus, Lysistrata does not exploit the full possibilities of the women's political organization and settles for the more limited objective of inducing the Athenian and Spartan men to come to terms, upon which the women will be reassimilated into the private spaces of their individual households.

The women in *Lysistrata* do not rehearse in a serious way the kinds of deals on which a truce with Sparta might depend, and it has been doubted whether an immediate resolution of the war was conceivable in the political climate of 411 B.C.[15] Early in the year, when *Lysistrata* was produced, the situation at Athens was still desperate.[16] The great armada that had been sent to subdue Sicily had been defeated. Thucydides gives a vivid description of the reception of the news at Athens in 413 B.C.:

> For a long while they disbelieved even the most respectable of the soldiers who had themselves escaped from the scene of action and clearly reported the matter, a destruction so complete not being thought credible. . . . Already distressed at all points and in all quarters, after what had now happened, they were seized by a fear and consternation quite without example. It was grievous enough for the state and for every man in his proper person to lose so many heavy infantry, cavalry, and able-bodied troops, and to see none left to replace them; but when they saw, also, that they had not sufficient ships in their docks, or money in the treasury, or crews for the ships, they began to despair of salvation.[17]

The Athenians did not remain passive. They took the extraordinary step of appointing a special board of ten commissioners (*probouloi*) to oversee the conduct of the war (the commissioner who makes an appearance in *Lysistrata* is one of these), and acted to prevent the defection of allied or subject states. Nevertheless, within three months of the production of *Lysistrata*—if, as seems likely, the play was put on in February—an antidemocratic faction succeeded in dissolving the Athenian assembly and installing itself in power, ruling as a council of 400 with a special force of armed Greeks as a local guard.[18]

The conflict concerning the war thus presented itself as a class issue. As Henderson puts it: "Aristophanes' irritation was directed in particular at the new leaders of the demos, men not belonging to the old leading families, who, in his view, duped the people for their private gain."[19] He is presupposing in *Lysistrata* a politicized contrast between the populace gullibly following its militant demagogues and respectable men of property and family who were broadly inclined to reach a settlement with Sparta. The internal controversy within Athens over the prosecution of the Peloponnesian War and the negotiations for peace is projected onto the division between the sexes. The realignment or transposition of this social conflict into a struggle between the genders enables an identification between the aristocratic peace party—broadly construed—on the one hand, and the nostalgic values of domestic order and communal solidarity, on the other.

Lysistrata lacks a proper parabasis (choral address) to the audience, since the chorus remains divided till near the end of the play (1014–75), and Lysistrata's argument with the Athenian commissioner, properly part of the formal debate (*agōn*) in the structure of the play, effectively takes over this function.[20] Her advice thus occupies the place reserved for the comic poet's own political counsel to his fellow citizens. Lysistrata recommends the incorporation of all allied populations into a single civic community (579–86; cf. Henderson 1987: 144), and defends a thoroughgoing panhellenism based on the kinship of all the Greeks (1128–34). It is a remarkable program that does not correspond to anything supported by the democratic or the oligarchic partisans in Athens. Here the utopian impulse of the comedy exceeds the confines of pragmatic politics. It is not accidental that this advice is tendered by an actor in the guise of a woman. Women are not conceived of as having the same stake as men in the narrow exclusivity of the city: they are outsiders to the hierarchy that discriminates between imperial Athens and its subject cities, colonies, and free allies, as well as to the division of Greece into rival leagues.[21]

To be sure, Aristophanes expresses analogous sentiments in other plays (cf. especially *Frogs* 701–2 for a more inclusive attitude toward the allies).[22] But Lysistrata is not merely an advocate of the policy of reconciliation; she has already achieved it in practice among the women of Greece, whether allies or enemies, at the beginning of the action. Dramatically, the strongest argument in favor of peace is the image of the women representatives of the several Greek states cooperating effortlessly with one another, mutually determined to put an end to the conflict among the men. The oath among the women of the several warring nationalities is an image of panhellenic identification and prefigures the swearing of the truce in the conclusion (1185). Given the preexisting alliance among the women, the commitment of the men to the war must seem perverse.

It is, of course, a comic absurdity that Lysistrata can arrange a meeting of women from all over Greece and across battle lines in the wee hours of the morning, so that they can slip undetected out of their houses. Old Comedy was tolerant of such fantastic devices, like Dicaeopolis' private truce with the Spartans in *Acharnians*. But the women's collaboration on an international level may be seen as an extension of their local organization within Athens itself, a kind of subterranean cohesion outside the public spaces where men regularly convened. In a word, the women rely on networking, that parallel system of relations that men represent as covert or mysterious.[23] The idea that women maintain their own forms of communication takes the edge off the implausible device of a panhellenic women's conference in wartime Athens. Moreover, the international solidarity among the women is different from Dicaeopolis' isolated pact with the enemy. It is women as a group who are capable of transcending factional and national differences and acting in concert against the war. Their spirit of solidarity is projected beyond Athens to the whole of Greece.

Near the beginning of the play, when the women first assemble at the summons of Lysistrata, Lysistrata greets the Spartan envoy Lampito:

LYSISTRATA: Lampito, darling, greetings from us all.
What a gorgeous specimen, you lovely thing!
What healthy skin, what firmness of physique!
You could take on a bull!

LAMPITO: Is not impossible.
I go to gym, I make my buttocks hard.

CALONICE: I've never seen a pair of boobs like that!

LAMPITO: You feel them: like blue-ribbon ox, you think!

LYSISTRATA: And this young lady here, where's she from?

LAMPITO: Distinguished comrade from collective farm of Thebes.

MYRRHINE: I knew she had to be from Thebes: she looks so natural and organic.

CALONICE: Yes, her organs have a cultivated look.

LYSISTRATA: And who is this one?

LAMPITO: Representative from Gulf [i.e., Corinth].

CALONICE: She's got some pretty gulfs herself. Here's one in front, and here's another one.[24]

The banter here seems to be of a piece with the men's appreciation of the parts of Reconciliation's body at the end of the play, though it is noticeably less aggressive. But nothing goes on among the men themselves that corresponds to this frank sexual interest among the women.

Of course, in ancient Greece men might find a boy attractive in the same way as a woman. In this tradition, an epigram by the fourth-century A.D. Roman poet Ausonius speaks of a youth who died in his sixteenth year as having "already ceased to seem either boy or girl."[25] But it was a disgrace for an adult male to be treated as the passive object of another man's desire; thus, erotic relations are normally incompatible with the bond between friends (*philoi*), who are presumed to be equals.[26] Aristophanes avoids any suggestion of sexual attraction between the deprived men in *Lysistrata*: his aim is to create a spirit of mutual respect, and he has no wish to insult either the Athenians or the Spartans by casting them as sexually passive or immature. In the case of the women, however, it seems to have been permissible to exhibit such sexual byplay among adult friends (*philai*) without offense, presumably because they were imagined as naturally occupying the passive position with respect to men. It was of course acceptable for a grown woman to be the object of erotic desire, and while an active sexual interest might be coded as masculine, the positive pole in the amatory relation did not automatically carry a stigma.[27] The solidarity of the women could thus find expression also in a sexualized form.[28]

The image of a female body as an emblem of Greek unity in *Lysistrata* may, then, have an analogue in the suggestion of women's sexual intimacy. To be sure, the scene just described is brief and perhaps open to different interpretations. But the connection between sexuality among women and their corporate identification has been suggested in modern feminist literature. Jane Gallop, for example, observes that, according to the theories of feminist psychologists such as Nancy Chodorow, "Any daughter, that is, any woman, has a self that is not completely individuated but rather is constitutively connected to another woman. Thus the formation of groups of women draws upon the permeability of female self-boundaries. The collectivity reactivates, reenacts the mother-daughter bond."[29] Tania Modleski takes the argument a step further: "As feminists have recently stressed, the mother/daughter relationship is one of the chief factors contributing to the bisexuality of women. . . . The female's attachment to the mother, Freud came to understand, often goes 'unresolved' throughout woman's life and coexists with her later heterosexual relationships."[30] Whether as a result of psychological processes of for other reasons, representations of women's sexuality in classical Greece may have lacked the asymmetrical structure of power that was characteristic of male erotic behavior and could thus provide the model for a noncompetitive and reciprocal type of bonding that could be called into service as a trope for peaceful relations among the city-states.[31]

There is a suggestion of a specifically female mode of relating, perhaps, in Lysistrata's instructions to the women toward the end of the play to draw the Athenians and Spartans together, "not with a rough or violent hand, and not the way our husbands used to do in their ignorance, but as women ought, very familiarly (oikeiōs)" (1116–18). Behind the coarse humor is the suggestion that women have a different sexual style from that of men, which is aggressive rather than gentle and integrative.

In the finale of the play, the aroused men are reconciled with each other by naming and appropriating the parts of a woman who is the object of their erotic desire.[32] Competition among men is thus mediated by passion for the female body (as opposed to the direct and reciprocal desire of the women), and is resolved by carving up the body into discrete fetishized sections. At the same time, the woman's body serves as an image of wholeness that figures the coalescing of the contending parties into a greater unity.

It is Lysistrata herself, acting as a kind of pander, who presents the figure of Reconciliation to the inspection of the Spartans and Athenians and exposes her to be divided up according to their desires. Lysistrata has the air of a statesman: she argues on equal terms with men like the commissioner and explains that even though she is a woman, she has intelligence because she has listened to the discussions of her father and other elder men (1124–27).[33] She is clear-headed, decisive, and self-controlled. Unlike the rest of the women, Lysistrata seems free from domestic constraints and has no difficulty organizing and participating in the plans for the sex strike and the seizure of the acropolis. She also stands above the sexual obsessions of the others. Her age and marital status are indeterminate.[34] It is now known that the priestess of Athena Polias, "Athena of the City," in the year 411 bore the name Lysimache, the meaning of which, "Dissolver of War," is roughly the same as the meaning of Lysistrata, "Dissolver of Armies."[35] Lysistrata clinches the identification when she declares that the women will be remembered among the Greeks as Lysimaches, once Eros and Aphrodite have worked their magic (551–54).

Jeffrey Henderson remarks, "there are no earlier examples of a female protagonist like Lysistrata," and he adds: "Greek tradition contains no parallel to the organized defiance of Lysistrata and her comrades."[36] But if Lysistrata is rebellious, she is simultaneously accommodating.

She supervises the dissection of Reconciliation, and the women have no hesitation about appealing to the traditional responsibility of the Athenians, enshrined in the ephebic oath, to preserve and extend their empire (652–55). Because their differences with the men, even as they promote universal reconciliation, are restricted to the immediate issue of the war with Sparta, the women do not effectively challenge the division of Greece into separate political entities.

Having assumed a public role in order to achieve unity among the Greeks, the women withdraw again into their separate households at the end of the play. Although the household had served the women as a model for the communal solidarity of the city under their regime, it is here the emblem of their dispersion into separate families, thus canceling their extraordinary civic presence. By representing the women as the bearers of domestic values in *Lysistrata*, Aristophanes could exploit a double symbolic dimension, casting them both as proponents of a utopian ideal of social integration and as isolated members of their husbands' homes. The overdetermined position of the women is the point at which the contradictory strands in the narrative intersect.

The figure by which Greek identity is condensed in the body of a woman threatens to collapse the public sphere of masculine difference and competition. The cohesion of women is thus represented as transgressive even as it is pressed into service as a symbol of collective union. At the end of the play, with the women comfortably dispersed under the authority of male heads of household, the rival Greek states stake out their territories on the body of a woman without a thought for the ideal of pan-Hellenic citizenship proposed by Lysistrata. The utopian gesture has been recontained.

4

Frogs

At the beginning of *Frogs*, Dionysus, moved by his reading of Euripides' *Andromeda*, decides to retrieve the recently dead poet from the underworld. After he reaches Hades, Dionysus learns that a contest is under way between Euripides and Aeschylus for the title of best poet. Dionysus, installed as judge, decides in favor of Aeschylus and brings him—not Euripides—back to Athens. Critics have proposed various explanations for this shift in plan.

According to an early view, Aristophanes began working on *Frogs* after Euripides' death in Macedon, but while Sophocles was still alive. Upon Sophocles' death in 405 B.C., Aristophanes revised his original intention, which was the recovery of Euripides, in order to take up the general question of poetic values now that the last of the three great tragedians was gone. The accident by which Dionysus arrives in Hades just as a contest is in progress allows for an easy transition from the first theme to the second. References early in the play to the death of Sophocles are, on this view, later insertions designed to bring the two halves into line.[1]

In an essay published in 1962, Eduard Fraenkel worked from the other end to explain the double plan of *Frogs*. Fraenkel, following Rogers and others, believed that Aristophanes had intended from the beginning to represent the competition between Aeschylus and Euripides, but had feared that so elevated a scene would not appeal to his unsophisticated audience. As a result, he tacked on the farcical business at the beginning of the play, with Dionysus dressed as Heracles and inspired by a silly passion for Euripides.[2]

More recently, some critics have abandoned the idea that the dual plan in *Frogs* is the result of an extrinsic motive, and have sought to explain the inner dramatic purpose behind the shift. Charles Segal and Cedric Whitman, for example, have both argued that Dionysus has a change of heart because, in the course of the play, he has been educated away from Euripides' clever effects to the high-minded seriousness of Aeschylus. The shift in plan thus expresses the theme of the play, which is Aeschylus' superiority as a poet and teacher.[3]

The contest between the poets is the most memorable part of the comedy, at least to modern readers, who may be inclined to take the earlier scenes as a mere prelude. This segment, however, has its own articulation, which suggests that, contrary to the general consensus, the structure of *Frogs* is tripartite rather than bipartite.[4] Its three major movements are the descent into Hades, during which Dionysus adopts the guise of Heracles; the action at Hades' door, where Dionysus meets the chorus of initiates in the sacred mysteries; and the poetry contest. These broad episodes are related by correspondences of theme, and their implicit logic defines the central ideological issues of the play.

Leo Strauss seems to have been the first modern scholar to ask why Dionysus chooses to assume the attire of Heracles in his attempt to rescue Euripides.[5] Strauss suggested camouflage as the reason, on the grounds that "the Heraklean appearance is the only one that cannot possibly arouse in Hades the suspicion that its wearer is after a poet."[6] Since there is not the least hint in the text that Dionysus was concerned to keep the object of his mission a secret, we can safely dismiss Strauss' answer. The question, however, remains an important one and invites a different kind of reply: Heracles is chosen because he was a mortal and had become a god.[7]

As vivid evidence that it is possible for human beings to overcome or survive death, Heracles in the first part of the play serves the same function that the chorus of initiates serves in the second section. Moreover, they represent the possibility of resurrection or survival in a state of eternal happiness. Finally, what is at stake in the contest between Aeschylus and Euripides at the end of the play is again a return to life for the victor, although in this case it is not imagined as a permanent survival. Thus, each of the three segments or moments in *Frogs* is informed by the idea of human resurrection.

If Heracles, the chorus of mystae or initiates, and the winner of the poetry contest all represent the possibility of surviving death, they overcome mortality in very different ways. Heracles' apotheosis is not directly mentioned in *Frogs*, but his victory over death is alluded to symbolically in his successful assault upon Hades, when he stole the guard dog Cerberus that was the immediate object of his mission (111). In the process, he offended the nether gods by his violent and unseemly behavior. Heracles' behavior in the underworld will have consequences for the reception of Dionysus when he appears dressed in the hero's lion skin and bearing a club. Here, however, I wish to emphasize that Heracles stormed the underworld by force, did violence to its order, and regained the upper regions by virtue of his extraordinary strength and courage. The means of Heracles' triumph over Hades is his individual heroism.

The mode in which the chorus of initiates overcomes death is diametrically opposed to that of Heracles. They earn their return to the light and to everlasting life by their piety and justice (454–59), rather than by heroic violence. Their means are not aggresssive, but peaceful, almost passive. Their reward is to play forever in an eternal garden.[8] It is a reward not so much for what the mystae have done in their lives as for what they have refrained from doing, as is indicated by their own long list of prohibited kinds of conduct (354–68). As opposed to the mighty, fearless, and brawling actions of Heracles, they are characterized by tranquillity and fellow-feeling. What is more, the survival of the chorus is collective. In contrast to Heracles' individual salvation, theirs is an undifferentiated, communal survival. They are represented essentially as a group, bound together by their common experience of the mysteries and a shared holiness. The individual violence of the hero is thus doubly opposed to the collective sanctity of the initiates.

The return to Athens of the victor in the contest between Aeschylus and Euripides represents, I believe, yet a third mode of resurrection. Here, survival is the reward of service to the city; both Aeschylus and Euripides agree that the poet's skill and counsel are directed toward improving citizens (1008–10). Such, too, is the basis of Aeschylus' own claim to deathlessness (868–69). Poets are teachers: though the use of the term *didaskō* for staging a dramatic production may originally have referred to the poet's role in instructing the chorus and actors (see, for example, the usage in 954–55), it is clear that for Aristophanes it also connotes the kind of moral education that playwrights ought to provide for the citizen audience, intended to make them noble and courageous.[9] In contrast, then, both to the heroic violence of Heracles and the moral sanctity of the initiates, the poet's path to immortality is based on civic responsibility and political service to his fellow citizens.

While the hero wins the prize of immortality in individual combat, and the mystae participate in a collective experience of initiation, the arena in which the poet displays his excellence is the contest (*agōn*). The contest, or competitive game, represents a controlled antagonism that shares both in the mode of struggle that characterizes heroic action and in the solidarity that characterizes the community in its cultic aspect. In this sense, we may see the contest between Aeschylus and Euripides, and, more broadly, the forms of competitive excellence that mark Greek political life in general, as a mediation between heroic individualism and mystic communalism. On the most abstract plane, we can perhaps say that the heroic mode represents virtue in the form of the single figure against the world, and that the cultic or initiatory mode represents it in the community of the many, while the political mode is essentially contestatory and thus dyadic: its number, so to speak, is neither the singular nor the plural, but the dual.[10]

Heroic excellence is predicated on violence; the virtues of the chorus are a function of inner disposition, a state of the soul; but the medium of poetic or political virtue is the word, which is the prime matter of the poet's art, "the dialogue, the lyrics, the sinews of tragedy," as Euripides puts it (862; cf. 881, 885, 904, etc.). Heracles' strength is in action: the virtue of the mystics, if not passive, is nevertheless more like a state of being; but the poet's virtue is dialogical, and is expressed in the form of influence upon others. In the root meaning of the word, the poet is responsible, he answers to another. Here again, the poet, and the civic principle he represents, may be said to mediate between the solitary achievement of the hero and the collective identity of the initiates. The poet stands for the individual in relation to the community, and for the reciprocal obligations by which the city is defined.[11]

There is one further relationship among the three tableaux in *Frogs* that deserves mention: each seems to bear a specific connection to Dionysus in one or another of his manifestations.[12] To begin with Heracles, both he and Dionysus were traditionally represented as conquering heroes who traveled through distant lands. Aristophanes points to their familial connection as sons of Zeus by having Dionysus address Heracles as "brother" (58); Heracles answers with the affectionate or condescending diminutive *adelphidion* (60; cf. also 164). Both, moreover, were legendary victims of Hera's jealousy, and both made descents into the underworld.[13] Thus, it may not be wholly in a spirit of parody that Dionysus is shown wearing the lion skin.

The initiates also have a special connection with Dionysus. Whether the Iacchus hailed by the chorus of mystae was at the end of the fifth century already identified with Bacchus is not certain, but Cedric Whitman is undoubtedly right that "Dionysus appears in the play not only as the god of the theater, but also as a deity affiliated, if only by initiation, with the Eleusinian mysteries."[14] It is worth noting in this connection that Heracles too was, in the words of C. Bérard, "an exemplary initiate."[15] Finally, Dionysus is associated with the contest between Euripides and Aeschylus in his capacity, already noted by Whitman, of presiding deity at the Athenian theater.

The sequence of emblematic tableaux, emphasizing individual heroism, mystic communion, and civic competition, casts Dionysus in different roles that elicit various aspects of his complex and shifting persona. The identities of the god come into focus successively, as the scene moves from the upper world down into the heart of Hades. Heracles' house is apparently located, in Frogs, at the point where the descent into the nether regions begins, on the boundary, that is, between the two worlds. After he crosses the lake into the underworld, Dionysus meets the mystic chorus at the portals of Hades. The last episode, the poetic contest, apparently takes place inside Hades itself.[16] The site of the contest seems to be imagined as a city in its own right, mirroring the society of Athens above. There is an aristocracy (783) that supports Aeschylus, while the populace at large (779), qualified as good-for-nothings, is sympathetic to Euripides. Moving outward, the mystae, whom we encounter at the gates, may be imagined as residing just outside the city. Finally, Heracles, whose abode is located where Hades' realm ends, is at the outermost limit of the civic space.

There is logic in this arrangement. Heracles' heroic deeds were performed chiefly in the outer world, beyond the confines of the city-state, where he encountered beasts and barbarians. At home, his violence could be dangerous and destructive. It is represented tragically in Euripides' Heracles, where the hero, having returned from his journey to the underworld, slays his own wife and children in a fit of madness. In the Hades of Frogs, insofar as it takes the form of a civic community, Heracles seems a wild interloper, and his behavior is cause for alarm. The Eleusinian cult, in turn, was celebrated within the territory of Attica but beyond the city walls. There, at Eleusis, Greeks of every nation and status were welcome, and the distinctions characteristic of Athenian social order were suspended.[17] Finally, the contest to determine which poet is best able to save Athens is situated within the underworld city, in the heart of the civic space.

The association between agonistic contests, like that of Aeschylus and Euripides, and the Athenian agora (public meeting place) seems to have been traditional. Bérard speaks of two complementary sites in Athenian life, the religious, centered on the acropolis, and "the agonistic wing, the competitions, centered in the agora, the theater of human discourse."[18] Nicole Loraux, in her study of Athenian civic imagery, indicates a further contrast between the space of the ceramicus outside the walls of the city, where public discourse tended to dwell on the autochthonous origins of the Athenians—imagining themselves as born from the earth, the undifferentiated children of their native land—and the agora, where the idea of autochthony was suppressed in favor of the theme of tribal units, according to which the Athenians regarded themselves as descended not from the earth and in common but severally from Cecrops, Erichthonius, and the other eponymous ancestors of the different tribes.[19] These two locations, then, outside and inside the city walls, seem to have been coordinate with the self-representation of the Athenians in their collective and their politically differentiated aspects, respectively, just as the mystae outside the gates are emblems of the oneness of the Athenian populace, while the competition inside gives expression to the spirit of civic rivalry.

The symbolic geography in *Frogs* thus corresponds to three moments or aspects of Athenian identity. Dionysus proceeds from the outermost limits of the underworld, where Heracles resides, to the doorway or anteroom of Hades, and finally appears at its civic center, so to speak. He thus traces a route from what we may think of as the proper arena for personal valor, at the perimeter of the realm, through the locus of initiatory solidarity, at last to emerge at the site of political or contestatory virtue, represented by the competition of the poets. At each of these scenes, moreover, Dionysus himself assumes an appropriate character, though always, to be sure, comically exaggerated. Thus, for all his mock fearfulness, Dionysus is not in fact daunted by Heracles' warnings about the difficulties that will face him on the road to Hades (117–18, 144–45), and not even when confronted with Hades' own terrors does he contemplate turning back. He undertakes the first part of his journey in the spirit, as well as the uniform, of Heracles—a heroic assault on the underworld.[20]

In the second stage of his journey, as he approaches Hades' threshold, Dionysus begins to lose the proud confidence to which he pretended earlier, when he dismissed Heracles himself as vain and envious (279–84). After an encounter with the bogey-figure Empusa, he is overcome with terror. When his slave Xanthias teasingly announces, "We are done for, my lord Heracles" (298), Dionysus implores him not to call him Heracles. Xanthias replies: "Dionysus, then," to which Dionysus answers, "This still less than the other" (298–300). W. B. Stanford explains Dionysus' reticence about the use of his name by reference to "a widespread belief that if a demon or ghost knows your name he has greater power over you" and cites peoples in parts of Africa in illustration of this superstition.[21] The difficulty with this view is that it does not account for Dionysus' consternation at the use of the name Heracles.

Alternatively, in the denial of his own name Dionysus anticipates the loss of identity that he will soon suffer before the gates of Hades.

On the level of the plot, Dionysus' exchange of costumes with his slave Xanthias, which he inaugurates with the plea, "you become I" (*su men genou'gō*, 495), is the consequence of his disguise as Heracles, who had made himself unwelcome during his visit to Hades, at least to some. To Persephone herself, however, Heracles had seemed attractive, and the appearance of her slave at the door motivates a second switch, and so forth. When Aeacus, in the role of infernal gatekeeper, emerges, Xanthias is once again dressed as Heracles, and to prove before this hostile figure that he has never been to Hades before, Xanthias suggests that Dionysus, as his slave, be forced to testify under torture. At Dionysus' request, torture is applied to both, on the grounds that a true god is insensitive to pain. There is a subtle shift here: the purpose of the trial by torture is no longer to prove which of the two is Heracles and which is not, but to demonstrate which is the god Dionysus, and which his slave. The test fails to distinguish man from god, and in the end Aeacus recommends that the pair enter Hades, where Pluto and Persephone, being themselves gods, will be able to recognize which is which (668–71).

The radical confusion of identities between Dionysus and Xanthias corresponds, I believe, to what Victor Turner, building on the work of Arnold Van Gennep, refers to as the liminal stage in the ritual process:

> Van Gennep has shown that all rites of passage or "transition" are marked by three phases: separation, margin (or *limen*, signifying "threshold" in Latin), and aggregation. The first phase (of separation) comprises symbolic behaviour signifying the detachment of the individual or group either from an earlier fixed point in the social structure, from a set of cultural conditions (a "state"), or from both. During the intervening "liminal" period, the characteristics of the ritual subject (the "passenger") are ambiguous. . . . In the third phase (reaggregation or reincorporation), the passage is consummated.[22]

Turner provides a list of contrasting features that distinguish the liminal state from the status system. These include such categories as equality versus inequality, anonymity versus system of nomenclature, absence of rank versus distinctions of rank, acceptance of pain versus avoidance of pain, and so forth.

I have selected from among Turner's features with a view to the situation in Aristophanes' *Frogs*, and it is clear that they apply well to the collapse of difference between Dionysus and Xanthias that follows their exchange of costumes. When Xanthias accuses Dionysus of being "the most cowardly of gods and men" (486), the confounding of status categories is already implied (cf. 1472, an angry outburst by Euripides). At the threshold (*limen*) of Hades, the distinctions between god and mortal, master and slave, are temporarily suspended. Dionysus' refusal of his own name, which I have mentioned, is part of the liminal pattern and is in contrast with the proud announcement of his name, complete with mock patronymic ("son of Flask," 22), at the beginning of the play, as well as with the recognition of the god and his elevation to the status of judge in the poetry contest in the last or "reaggregating" phase. (In the figure of Empusa, the spirit who frightens Dionysus, we may perhaps recognize another symbol of the liminal confusion of categories and loss of identity, for it is the nature of Empusa constantly to alter her form.[23])

The chorus of mystae also displays the attributes of liminality in their sacredness, their uniform clothing, and other indices of homogeneity as opposed to heterogeneity or status distinctions. As initiates, they incarnate the moment of marginality with respect to the ordinary or structured world. Their speech, which mixes the witty with the serious (389–90), is characterized by an ironic derisiveness (*skōptein* and related terms, 374, 392, 416; cf. 404). It may seem arbitrary to associate the farcical antics of Dionysus and Xanthias with the dignified humor of the chorus, but the two principles of inversion (the switching of roles) and leveling (the abolition of social distinctions) tend to go hand in hand in comedy, as Ian Donaldson has argued in his study of English comedy entitled *The World Upside-Down*.[24] Donaldson relates both principles to the festival (14–20), which as a publicly sanctioned, ritual suspension of the rules of ordinary life corresponds in certain ways to the liminal phase of initiatory rites.[25]

The three broad tableaux that constitute the structure of *Frogs*, in each of which is represented a particular mode of resurrection, are arranged in such a way as to suggest two kinds of motion or development. The first of these is linear, from the outer limits of culture, which is the place of the individual hero, who is marked by animal traits in the form of the lion-skin cloak, through the domain of the mystae and into the halls of Hades, which seem to be imagined at least in part on the model of a Greek agora. The second motion is not linear, but shaped like a V, representing a descent and return on the pattern of an initiation into the mysteries. Jane Harrison long ago suggested that Greek myths of death and resurrection unfolded in three stages and were formed on the analogy of rites of initiation.[26] We need not accept all of

Harrison's theoretical apparatus in order to agree with Walter Burkert that she had understood the essential structure of Greek ritual.[27]

Dionysus begins his journey in disguise, but no one is in doubt about his identity. At the threshold of Hades, which is the nadir of Dionysus' fortunes, he is unable to prove that he is not a mortal slave. In the final episode, within the city, his identity is restored. This pattern, in numerous variations, informs many stories in Greek literature, such as Odysseus' descent into the cyclops' cave, where he rebaptizes himself as No-one (only to reassert his name proudly upon his escape), Sophocles' *Philoctetes*, where at the center of the narrative the hero is deprived of his sacred bow as he lies unconscious within his cave, and Euripides' *Bacchae*, in which Dionysus, in disguise, is abused and imprisoned within the palace before he reveals himself in triumph as a god.[28] Eupolis' *Dēmoi* seems, in particular, to have been constructed on a similar plan to that of *Frogs*.[29] In each case, the hero recovers his name or emblem, passes through an entrance of some kind, and is restored to power.

There is a way in which each of the three modes of transcending death in *Frogs*, while complete and independent in itself, also may be seen as standing for one of the three stages in the initiatory process. Heracles' heroism is appropriate to the initial descent, which requires personal courage; the chorus represents the central or liminal moment; and the contest inside Hades' door may be taken as a metaphor for the return to the political life of the city. The mystae, on this reading, symbolize both a permanent state of blessedness, sandwiched between the apotheosis of Heracles and the resurrection of Aeschylus, and a transitional phase in the larger pattern of descent and return.

What I have identified as the liminal stage or episode in *Frogs*, at the gateway to Hades' house, is framed by the two great choral songs in the play. The first is the hymn addressed to Iacchus and Demeter, while the second is a slightly truncated parabasis (direct address to the audience), which opens with an invocation of the Muse (675). The theme of the parabasis is an appeal to the audience to restore full citizen rights to supporters of the oligarchical revolution of 411 B.C., who had been punished after the restoration of the democracy with partial *atimia* (disenfranchisement). This advice, if one may trust the prefatory hypothesis to *Frogs*, was received with such enthusiasm that the play was awarded the special privilege of a second performance.

Aristophanes argues that those who have been disenfranchised deserve the opportunity to put their previous error behind them. He adds that it is in the best interests of the city that no one be deprived of rights.

He then offers as an example of a more liberal disposition among the
Athenians the freeing of the slaves who had fought in the recent naval
battle at Arginusae, and suggests that if a single campaign earned slaves
such a reward, it is all the more appropriate that those whose fathers,
like themselves, have often fought for Athens, and who are related by
kinship to the Athenians, should be pardoned for a single misadven-
ture (699).

Near the beginning of the play, Xanthias alludes to the extraordinary decision to enfranchise the slaves who served at Arginusae only
months before the production of *Frogs*; he says that, if he himself had
fought at sea, he would now have been free to reproach Dionysus for
making him carry his gear like an ass (33–34). The enfranchisement is
mentioned again during the negotiations for the ferry-crossing with
Charon, who refuses to bear a slave in his boat unless he took part in
the sea battle (190–91).[30] In the parabasis, the chorus seems grudging in
its approval of the action: "I wouldn't want to say that this was not
rightly done—in fact, I praise it" (695–96). The recently manumitted
citizens were in the audience and had of course to be accepted, but there
is nevertheless a sense of discomfort with the decision.[31] One may
imagine why: an example of the exceptional violation of traditional
status barriers is invoked (that of the enfranchisement of slaves) to justify what is, in effect, an assertion of the natural integrity of the citizen
community—that is, those who were born citizens should not be ex-
communicated. There is a connection between the two propositions in
the idea of generosity, but in respect to status distinctions, the incorporation of slaves into the citizen body runs exactly counter to the view
that native citizens ought on no account to be expelled from full participation in the city. If merit on the part of slaves can earn them the
franchise, then an offense against the constitution should by the same
logic deserve the privation of citizen status.

The confusion between Dionysus and Xanthias at the gate of Hades
mirrors, within the action of the play, the confusion of status categories in Athens at the time of the production of *Frogs*, when there were,
as Aristophanes presents it, citizens who had been disenfranchized and
slaves elevated to the rank of citizen. In a sense, then, Athens itself was
in a liminal state, its ordinary rules and distinctions partially suspended
in the course of the crises brought on by the Peloponnesian War, now in
its last year before the final defeat of the Athenians.[32] At all events, this
is how the state of things might appear on a more or less conservative
view of the situation.[33]

After the comparison between the dispossessed supporters of the
oligarchy and the freed slaves, the chorus recommends that anyone who

has fought for Athens should be accepted as kin and fellow citizen, with equal rights, and that Athens ought to shed its arrogant exclusiveness, lest a future age condemn it for poor judgment (700–5). It may be doubted whether Aristophanes is here promoting the conferral of citizenship upon resident aliens, for example, or endorsing a still more universalistic humanism, as Rogers, the great editor of Aristophanes, supposed. In context, the phrase "all men" (*pantas anthrōpous*, 701) need not look further than to the partisans of the regime in 411 B.C., in whose cause the chorus is speaking, although it is expressed in a universalizing language. A little earlier, Aristophanes alludes to the Thracian descent of Cleophon, one of the democratic leaders (679–82), and the chorus will again, shortly afterward, freely abuse foreigners, redheads (e.g., Thracians), and newcomers in general (730–32), while exhorting the audience to avail itself of its well-born citizens (the *kaloi kagathoi*, 719, 727–29). The stigma of alien origin remains even as the granting of citizenship to former slaves is applauded.

It has been seen that, while Aeacus is unable to recognize the true god as opposed to the slave Xanthias, the gods within do so, and thereby restore Dionysus to his proper position. Immediately after the parabasis, Xanthias emerges from Hades' gates with a servant—perhaps Aeacus once more—who announces: "By Zeus the savior, your master is a noble gentleman" (738–39). The appeal to a transcendent authority in order to reestablish conventional distinctions of status represents in miniature the issue at stake in the contest between Aeschylus and Euripides, and anticipates Dionysus' choice of Aeschylus as the poet who will best serve the needs of Athens. The chorus' exhortation to respect the differences between citizens and strangers suggests that the present confusion in Athens is somehow transitional. It will be the task of the successful poet to rescue the city from this confusion.

On one level, the victory of Aeschylus is simply a metaphor for the reassertion of the authority of noble citizens in Athens, since, as mentioned above, the division between classes in the city is reproduced in the underworld, with decent folk rallying to Aeschylus while Euripides is favored by the mob (cf. 359, 760). Aeschylus' party stands for traditional values, such as respect for families of distinguished lineage, dutifulness toward parents, landed wealth and the like.[34] More interesting, however, is the opposition between two conceptions of the function of discourse, represented by the two poets. If Aeschylus wins the vote of Dionysus, it is because his idea of poetry, as Aristophanes presents it, can lead Athens out of its liminal state and restore a lost order.

While Aeschylus and Euripides agree that the function of poetry is to improve citizens, "Aeschylus believes," according to a penetrating analysis by George Walsh, "that the moral qualities of poetry reproduce themselves directly in the souls of the audience." Aeschylus' characters "breathe" spears and helmets (1016), and their "souls are dense with the presence of things."[35] Euripides, on the contrary, describes what is. In this sense his words are empty forms, serving as signs rather than as substance. Aeschylus is scandalized by Euripides' representation on the stage of women dominated by passion, because "the poet must conceal what is base, not bring it on stage and teach it" (1053–54). As Walsh observes, "Euripides seems more puzzled by this than offended"; his answer is that the stories that he relates are true (*onta logon*, 1052).[36]

In his own time, says Aeschylus, men did not talk back to their superiors when they manned the ships, but limited their speech to the demand for bread and the rowers' chant, *rhuppapai* (1073). Walsh notes that this refrain is "unintelligible as language," but it has the power to inspire men in action, and in this sense "the poet who produces something like this chant truly creates."[37] In the most general terms, we may say that Euripidean art, as Aristophanes represents it, is based on the faithful correspondence of the signifier to the signified, while for Aeschylus the signifier has the power to shape or produce the signified. In this sense, Aeschylus is more truly the "productive" (*gonimos*) poet whom Dionysus set out to recover at the beginning of the play (96).

If the scene at the gateway to Hades is a figure for the felt collapse of social distinctions in Athens toward the end of the Peloponnesian War, then a poetic practice that faithfully describes the world may be adequate to representing such a condition, but cannot alter it. The formula of Simonides applies: *logos tōn pragmatōn eikōn esti* (language is the image of deeds).[38] Euripides' delight in oxymoron, such as "soulless soul" (1334), "living but not living" (1082), or his notorious division between tongue and mind which Aristophanes' so enjoyed parodying, is well adapted to expressing the confusion of categories. He portrays a world in which kings like Telephus appear in a beggar's rags while gods like Dionysus go about disguised as mortals (compare Dionysus in the garb of Heracles), and where the traditional gods are displaced by quasi-philosophical abstractions like Aither and Tongue (892–94). It is an atomized or privatized world of domestic realities (*oikeia pragmata*, 959); as Walsh remarks, "even his gods are private (*idiōtai theoi*, 891)."[39] Euripides' art at best reflects the prevailing disorder.

Aeschylus' magical or creative conception of language is, on the contrary, capable of reimposing form on the disordered state of Athenian political life, as Aristophanes depicts it. The power of the word to enchant is required to deliver the city from its liminal anonymity. The victory of Aeschylean poetics, then, offers a route back to traditional structures and enables the "reaggregation" that marks the third stage of the ritual process according to the scheme of Van Gennep.

If one grants that Aeschylus stands, in Aristophanes' ad hoc poetics, for the creative force of the signifier, it is nevertheless necessary to remark that he is certainly not the spokesman for the free play of language and its productive energies. His own use of language is embedded in the traditional symbolic order that he desires to restore. It is an order rooted in Athens' past, which Aeschylus, as a figure long dead, best serves to represent. In other words, there is an implicit structure of signifieds that ensures that Aeschylus' poetic magic will generate what is perceived as a noble and natural way of life. The account of Aeschylus' creative practice must be supplemented by the politically loaded association between Aeschylus and the worthy few. There is nothing to guarantee that poets or speakers of a more radical sort, uncommitted to the conservative image of Athens' past, will not use language as Aeschylus does to inspire their followers with an entirely different vision of the state.[40]

In this respect, the figure of Aeshylus is doubly determined as an emblem of the functioning Athenian democracy and as a representative of a traditional aristocratic style of politics. This ambivalent characterization corresponds to Aristophanes' own hesitancy over the extension of Athenian citizenship. At one moment, Aristophanes represents himself as prepared to welcome loyal slaves into the citizen body, and even, in an exuberant gesture of inclusiveness, to extend Athenian civic rights to all of mankind. But he is equally comfortable in endorsing a natural title to civic status on behalf of the traditional nobility and in impugning popular leaders as servile foreigners. The overdetermination of the character of Aeschylus is analogous in function to the complex representation of the chorus in *Wasps* and of Lysistrata and her partisans; it permits Aristophanes to exalt Athens for its generous openness to outsiders, while simultaneously restricting the ideal citizen body to a privileged segment of society.

The victory of Aeschylus is thus necessary to the fundamental theme of *Frogs*. Whether "Aristophanes may have intended his more sympathetic hearers to be sorry for Euripides' largely undeserved defeat," as Stanford suggested, or whether he desired that his audience approve of Aeschylus "without abandoning Euripides' critical reserve," as Walsh concludes, may be left moot. It requires the poet of the good old days to reimpose distinctions that have been eradicated in times of crisis.[41]

The linear movement in plot of *Frogs* from the individual heroic mode of transcendence represented by Heracles to the mode of ritual solidarity characteristic of the Eleusinian initiates culminates, as has been said, in the agonistic and dialogical scene of the poetry contest. The contest itself, together with such critical argument and judgment as Dionysus exercises, for all his comic silliness, represents within the play the sphere of the political.[42] The competition between Aeschylus and Euripides, under the aegis of Dionysus, is an image of the Athenian dramatic festival. The skills required to appreciate it are intelligence and careful measurement, symbolized by the scales employed to weigh the poets' choice of words. While the contest will produce a victor, it is political discourse as a process or activity, the clash of views before a discerning audience in the city's center, rather than the enchanting power of Aeschylus alone, that is the goal of Dionysus' journey to the underworld.

The contest between Aeschylus and Euripides at the end of the play corresponds with the singing match between Dionysus and the chorus of frogs in the first tableau, as the god is transported across the infernal lake. There, verbal conflict was represented as a matter of force, with each side attempting to shout down or outlast the other. The croaking of the frogs is inarticulate noise, and Dionysus responds in kind. It is neither the creative discourse of Aeschylus nor the critical discourse of Euripides, but pure ranting, analogous perhaps to the language of the demagogues, as Aristophanes saw it, or to that of his rival Phrynichus, if Nancy Demand is right in seeing a punning reference to his name (*phrunē* = toad) in the use of frogs.[43] However that may be, the competition with the frogs represents the mode of Heracles transposed into the domain of sound.

In the scene at Hades' door, one may perhaps recognize another *agōn* in the competition between Dionysus and Xanthias to say nothing under the stress of blows, and thereby prove themselves superior to pain. Here the effort to preserve silence may be seen as language in the mode of secrecy, or what we may call the linguistic form proper to the mysteries.[44] Only in the ultimate episode of the comedy, namely, the poetry contest, does argument take center stage as the highest form of discourse. This is the form characteristic of the city-state as a political community.

If the final scene of *Frogs* represents argument in action, the free play of political discourse is nevertheless recontained by the decision to award the victory to Aeschylus as the standard-bearer for traditional values, who can inspire the Athenians with an idealized vision of their past. Here again, as in *Wasps*, the men of Marathon serve as a complex symbol of a natural harmony in society and of a benevolent hierarchical order in contrast to the extreme leveling of the radical democracy. Once more, as in *Birds*, Aristophanes conjures up an image of a depoliticized utopia—the good old days—as a figure for the primitive vigor and solidarity of the Athenian polity.

5

Wealth

On the level of action, Aristophanes' *Plutus* (*Wealth*), produced in 388 B.C., is not rich in conflict. From the beginning, it is clear that the good citizen Chremylus will gain the god of wealth as his ally, and such obstacles as he encounters in Wealth's own cowardice or the opposition of ill-wishers, including the goddess Poverty, are easily disposed of. The narrative line of Chremylus' progress, and that of his demesmen, is direct: he restores sight to the blind Plutus, holds a greedy sycophant at bay, dispenses good fortune liberally and with a benign wink at petty squabbling, and finally establishes the god in the city treasury—the temple of Athena on the acropolis—for the benefit of all Athens. However, this straightforward trajectory, broadly conforming to the formula of Aristophanes' other utopian comedies, conceals a fundamental thematic tension between two quite different conceptions of the nature of want and sufficiency that are phased in and out throughout the argument. The first, in the order of narrative presentation in the text, represents wealth and poverty as a function of unequal social distribution. The rich achieve their wealth at the expense of the honest poor, who are poor because they remain honest. The second conception is predicated on a notion of universal scarcity, as a result of which all alike are more or less indigent. The solutions to these two ways of representing poverty are correspondingly different: the first, or social, conception invites a program of redistribution; the second demands a general improvement in resources, whether through technological progress or a lucky increase in the earth's fertility, the idealized image of which is a return of the spontaneous bounty of the golden age.

The opening words of the play announce the role of money in establishing the social distinction between masters and slaves: the slave
may know better than his master, laments Chremylus' man Cario, but
he must share the consequences of his master's ill judgment; "for the
daimōn does not permit the rightful owner [*kurios*] of his body to control it, but the one who has purchased it" (6–7).[1] It is reasonable to identify the *daimōn* here as Plutus himself.[2] Cario's lament concerns his
master's attachment to an enigmatic blind man, after he has been advised by Apollo to bring home with him the first person he should encounter upon leaving the oracle. Chremylus explains his motive for
having consulted the oracle: although he is pious and just, he has fared
badly and remained poor; those who get rich are the public speakers,
informers, and troublemakers in general. Accordingly, since his own
life is shot, he was inquiring of Apollo whether his only son would be
better off changing his habits and becoming utterly unscrupulous and
immoral (28–37). The slave Cario ventures to interpret Apollo's instructions differently: Chremylus' son must assume the local character, he
explains, because even a blind man can see that sick conduct is most
advantageous at the present time (45–50). Chremylus rejects this ex-
egesis, but the point, by now, is clear: corruption is abroad in the land,
and the wicked prosper while the just go empty-handed. After Plutus
identifies himself as the god of wealth, the topic is further developed.
First, Plutus explains why he is blind: he had boasted as a youth that
he would visit only the just and the wise and decent, and Zeus, spiteful
toward such worthy folk, had deprived him of his ability to discriminate (87–92).[3] Plutus still desires to attend upon the just, but for a long
time he has not seen any; "Nor have I," replies Chremylus, "and I can
see" (99). But Plutus is suspicious of Chremylus: all people pretend to
virtue until they get rich (107–9). "Not everybody is bad," says Chremylus; "Absolutely everybody, by Zeus!" replies Wealth (110–11).[4] With
this, Chremylus proposes his plan to restore the sight of Plutus.

The import of the passage is clear: wealth begets corruption, and
corruption wealth. Society is divided into rich and poor, honest and evil.
The fault lies not with a failure of natural abundance, but with the
character of the times, in which dishonesty is rewarded, virtue despised.
The solution is to reverse the situation: augment the fortunes of good
citizens, few as they may be, at the expense of the prosperous thieves.
And indeed, when Plutus regains his vision, this is precisely the effect.[5]
A sycophant or public informer arrives on the scene complaining bit-
terly of his misfortune, since on account of Wealth he has lost all his
possessions (856–58). A just citizen, who had entered shortly before to
pay honor to the god for having reversed his fortunes, deduces at once

that the newcomer is a bad type. The sycophant continues: "Where is the fellow who said he would make us all rich at once, if he could see again? Because it is really the case that he has destroyed some of us utterly" (864–67). The sycophant is accused of immorality, but turns the charge back upon Cario and the rest: "There is no good in any of you, and no way but what you have my money" (870–71). The gain of Chremylus and his friends is achieved at the sycophant's expense; in his view, they have acted criminally (876), done violence against a fellow citizen (886; cf. 899), been up to no good ("not yours, at any rate," replies the just citizen, 889), and feasted off his property (890).

All this, the sycophant laments, has been achieved at the cost of harm to a worthy and patriotic citizen (900), and with this claim the argument takes a new turn, or rather develops a theme that was only implicit in the preceding dialogue. "Are you a farmer?" asks the just citizen. "Do you think I'm that crazy?" the sycophant replies. "A trader, then? Or do you practice some craft?" (903–5, abridged). Finally: "How then do you make a living, since you do nothing?" (906). The sycophant's defense is that he assists the laws, that is, the administration of justice, in the city, bringing charges against those who violate them (a responsibility which, in the absence of a system of public prosecution, did in fact fall to private citizens, though these were normally ones with a personal stake in a given case). Sycophants were often regarded more or less as informers, officious meddlers who stirred up trouble for its own sake and thrived on others' losses; in a passage already cited, they are lumped with orators—that is, demagogues in the assembly, or less disparagingly, politicians—and with good-for-nothings in general (30–31).[6] The contrast with farmers, merchants, and artisans in the present passage is the nub of the argument: on the one side are those engaged in useful labor, on the other, those who exploit the apparatus of the state for their own gain, making a profession of political activity—in the popular phrase, being a busybody (*polupragmonein*, 913)—without performing any productive service for society.[7] What had previously been represented as widespread corruption, a general rapacity and decline in morals so extensive that Plutus could affirm that absolutely everyone was evil (111), is here redefined as an opposition, not between good men and bad per se, but between two sorts of occupation, the one honest and useful, the other mischievous and unproductive. The economic problem remains one of unfair distribution, but it is cast this time not simply in ethical but in social terms. Reform, correspondingly, is not so much a matter of a broad improvement in morals as an attack on a specific class of parasites. Get rid of them, and there will be wealth enough to meet the needs of those who created it.

Both views were commonplace in Athens, and the transition from one to the other is easily effected by the equation of sycophants and their like with the depraved portion of the citizen body. The audience has long since been prepared for the move because the chorus, which Chremylus summons early in the play to share equally in the new wealth (223–26), consists of hardworking farmers like himself (224; cf. 33), fellow-demesmen (322), all of whom (286) will enjoy the bounty of the god. Aristophanes, however, facilitates the shift in a scene between Chremylus and his friend, Blepsidemus, who enters to check out the barbershop rumors of Chremylus' sudden prosperity; Blepsidemus cannot imagine that honest work can have been the source of it (340–41). Chremylus' cryptic remarks concerning the risks of his plan (to restore the sight of Plutus, of course, although Blepsidemus is still in the dark about it, 350–51) seem to confirm the drift of Blepsidemus' suspicions, and he proceeds to caution preachily against theft and the temptations of greed (352–63). Blepsidemus continues to lament the lapse in his friend's former standard of conduct (365), while Chremylus repeatedly indicates his intention to share his good fortune with Blepsidemus and everyone else who is good and righteous and well behaved (345, 386–88). The misunderstanding is at last resolved when Chremylus explains that he has Plutus with him. Blepsidemus, reassured that the wealth was not dishonestly acquired, immediately demands a portion of it (398–400). The effect of the scene is to undo Blepsidemus' automatic association of wealth with theft. It is not true that riches are necessarily a sign of corruption, and with this anxiety assuaged, the audience, like Blepsidemus, can forget the pervasive moral squeamishness about sudden gains, along with the connection between avarice and ethical decline. The common people in the play are good and will be rewarded. The real problem, as Chremylus goes on to say, is restoring Plutus' sight. One may comfortably infer, at this point in the play, that only the traditional types of malefactor, sycophants and their sort, will have cause to regret the god's vision.

The evil characters, then, have been identified and the sycophant stands for them all as a sort of scapegoat. But the sycophant himself was, to the Athenians, an ideologically complex figure, and the debate between him and the just citizen takes, at one point, a surprising turn. The just man asks: "Wouldn't you like this, to have some peace and quiet and live at leisure?" (921–22). The sycophant replies that a life without occupation is that of a sheep, and that not for Plutus himself and all the tea in China (or, as the Greek expression has it, all the silphium of Cyrene) would he change. To understand the train of thought here, one must recall that one of the conventional traits of the sycophant was an inner restlessness or urge to excessive activity that drove him to take on, in addition to his own, the affairs of others (931). This idea of meddlesomeness presupposes as the norm a notion of minding one's own business that was well suited to the Athenian regard for independence and the self-sufficiency of the individual household estate. Nor is it a wonder that such autonomy was a matter of pride, for it could be difficult to maintain, and the farmer's life—that of the chorus in our play—was commonly represented, as here, as one of toil.[8] An image of better times would naturally include an essential component of leisure. But the sycophant, who has, it would seem, some freedom from his own responsibilities, invests his time compulsively in the affairs of others. He is thus unfit by disposition to profit from the bounty of a golden age; were he rich as Midas, he would still labor at what he thinks of as public business. This is all, as has been said, conventional in the representation of the sycophant, but it is incongruous in the present context because the issue that has been emphasized so far is that of dishonesty and greed, not activity for its own sake. A sycophant who is prepared to renounce wealth in order to maintain his profession is no very satisfactory emblem of the unjust division between rich and poor, which was the original motive for Chremylus' appeal to Apollo.[9] The inconsistency arises at a juncture between the two major motifs in the play: parasitical rapacity and the unfair division of wealth on the one hand, and general poverty in this age of iron on the other. The seams are visible under analysis, but this is not a fault in artistry or the sign of irony and deliberate paradox; rather it is evidence of the work of the text as an engagement with social meanings rather than the passive reflection of stable and inert ideas.[10]

The complexity of *Wealth* does not lie in its narrative structure. Restoration of the god's vision is quickly established as the crucial task (115–16), and the scenes that follow clear the way for execution of the plan. Chremylus first overcomes the opposition of Plutus himself by arguing that he, as god of wealth, is mightier even than Zeus. Next Chremylus enlists the support of the chorus and his friend Blepsidemus, whose suspicions of dishonesty are put to rest. At the center of the play is the debate with Penia, Poverty, who represents the most serious threat to the scheme and must be driven off by force. A choral interlude marks the passage of night, and then Cario reports in a long messenger-type speech how Plutus was healed in the temple of Asclepius. The nature of the new regime is revealed in the familiar series of "exemplificatory" scenes, beginning with the epiphany of the god at the head of a procession. Roughly, the scenes come in pairs, each involving two new characters: the just citizen and the sycophant; an old woman and her young lover; and finally, Hermes and a priest of Zeus—politics, sex, and religion, which is to say, the essentials. This straightforward movement of the plot, however, is offset by a thematic crosscurrent that appears intermittently throughout the play and becomes increasingly significant once Plutus' vision is restored.

The approach of the newly healed god is heralded with great excitement. Cario describes how he is attended by vast crowds, for those who had previously been just greeted him with joy; those, on the other hand, who had acquired their wealth unjustly frowned and were sullen (750–56). Stations have been altered, there is restitution and retribution, but the emphasis of the passage is on the liberal bounty of the god, and Cario concludes his speech with a general invitation to dance and skip together (760–63), for no one shall do without. Plutus himself appears with a prayer in the high style, repenting of his former errors, when he consorted with miscreants and avoided those worthy of his company (774–77). Now, however, he will not even accept the traditional offering of nuts and figs which Chremylus' wife has brought out to greet him with; upon his first visit to the house, now that he can see, he feels it proper to take nothing out, only in (791–93).[11] He will receive the customary offerings inside.

The speech of Cario, who reports what has been happening in the house since Plutus entered, paints a picture of burgeoning splendor, a fertile profusion of grain and wine, silver and gold, oil and incense and fruits, that conjures up the abundance of the golden age. To be sure, there remains a reference to moral probity, for Cario notes wittily that "a pile of goods has burst into the house upon us, though we have not done anything wrong" (804–5). But the point is not so much that just behavior is rewarded as that wealth now sprouts so freely that injustice has nothing to do with acquiring it. Under the new dispensation, wealth does not accrue to one at the expense of another. The conventional association between wealth and crime or fraud is no longer pertinent, for there is now enough and more than enough for everybody. The superfluity of wealth has changed the rules of the game: no longer is it a matter of just distribution, for the prosperity of Chremylus and the rest has nothing to do with the fortunes of others. The limitless largesse of the god sets aside any question of social inequity. To be sure, the audience will shortly be reminded that the sycophant, as representative of the worse sort, has lost his stores. But this has nothing to do with compensating his former victims; it is simply a matter of just deserts. In the last analysis, too, it is not even a matter of his losses or gains, but of his personal preference for his profession, without regard to the possibility of idle riches. The sycophant's problem is not that he will fare worse under the golden age, but that he is by nature unfit to enjoy it.

For the Athenians, the idea of wealth was bound up with that of autarky: the receipt of wages could be stigmatized as tantamount to slavery, for it meant dependency on the will of another.[12] Thanks to Plutus, a young man who as served as the lover of an old woman no longer needs to sell his favors to her. (The old woman's complaint against the god is that a golden age is a golden age, and everybody's wants should be satisfied.[13])

In the final scenes of *Wealth*, the new dispensation is ratified by the submission of the Olympian deities to the god of wealth. Hermes enters violently with the message that Zeus is planning to blast them all to hell (1107–9). The reason is that from the time Plutus began to see, no one has been sacrificing the least thing to the gods. "Nor will anyone, by Zeus," replies Cario, "for you took pretty poor care of us back then" (1116–17). Apart from the association of Plutus' vision with his capacity to reward virtue, his healing at the hands of Asclepius has also a more general significance as the symbol of his new power in the world, before which that of the Olympians has receded. There follows some characteristic comic banter about food, after which Hermes requests to be accepted as a fellow citizen (1147). The opportunism of this switch in sides is duly noted, and then Cario wonders what use Hermes might now be to them: as guardian of the doorposts, he might keep watch, but Cario reminds him that they have no need of such devices.[14] "Of the marketplace, then," suggests Hermes, but Cario reminds him that they are all rich, and do not have to support a god of retailers. Hermes offers his role as trickster, but Cario replies that this they need least of all. "The guide, perhaps"; "But the god can see now." "Of the games, then. What do you say? It will be particularly useful to Plutus to set up contests in athletics and the arts." This, at last, serves, and earns from Cario a wry comment on how fine a thing it is to have many epithets (1164). The point of all this is clear: Hermes' skills and duplicity were appropriate in the reign of scarcity; now, in the kingdom of plenty, there is a place only for his marginal, festive aspect.

The last character to turn up is the priest of Zeus, who complains that he too is dying of starvation. The motif is broadly reminiscent of the plot of *Birds*, but the reason for withholding sacrifices here is that "everybody is rich" (1178). With this "everybody," the theme of injustice and the unfair distribution of wealth evanesces utterly. Aristophanes has not a thought to spare here for the evildoers who at the beginning of the play included everyone, according to Plutus (111), or not quite everyone, according to Chremylus (110)—evildoers who, by the logic of the distribution theme, should now be the legions of the poor. Under the sign of wealth, everything is right. The priest himself prepares to abandon Zeus and remain with Chremylus (1186–87), whose house now has something of the status of a city. In fact, however, there is nothing to worry about, since Zeus is also on board, having come voluntarily.[15] All that is left is to establish Plutus once again as the guardian of the treasury in the temple of Athena on the acropolis (1191–93), where he may extend his beneficence to the entire community. And even the old woman, it is hinted, will have her lad this evening (1201).

The idea at work throughout this section—that the reign of Zeus is one of hardship and poverty for mankind, in contrast to some Eden either lost or still to come of goodness and fertility—was part of Greek popular theology. The best-known versions involve the role of Prometheus, who in various, sometimes mysterious ways is implicated in Zeus' hostility toward the human race.[16] One or another tradition of this hostility is alluded to in Plutus' account of the cause of his blindness early in the play, where he explains that Zeus deprived him of his sight out of ill will toward man (87–92). The recovery of Plutus' sight is the emblem of a contest for power between Zeus and Plutus, as is evident in the dialogue in which Plutus is persuaded to risk Zeus' displeasure and abolish his tyranny (124). Plutus is unaware of his real strength. Once he realizes it, the epoch of Zeus will be at an end. The will to regain his vision, to see again as he did in the past (95), is simply a matter of courage (118, 122, 203). When Chremylus declares his intention to demonstrate that Plutus is far more powerful than Zeus, he swears by Heaven or Ouranos, exceptionally for this play (cf. also 403)—oaths are most often by Zeus; it seems likely that there is a deliberate evocation of the dynastic succession of deities, which began with Ouranos and will now reach a new stage (or recover the quality of a former one) with Plutus.[17]

There was, of course, an answer to this denigration of Zeus. Toil and want might also be regarded as the best environment for a hardy breed of men—the strong, self-disciplined, honest, active race that had created civilized life, held enemies at bay, and brought art and morality to their zenith. This is the sentiment that inspires Odysseus' praise of Ithaca as a rugged land, good for raising men and horses; or Hesiod's respect for the farmer's life, tough but righteous. The doctrine that Zeus' harsh reign was instituted for the moral and intellectual benefit of mankind was articulated most fully in Hellenistic and Roman times, notably in Virgil's *Georgics*, but there are intimations of this theodicy much earlier, e.g. in *Prometheus Bound*, and it is likely that it was developed as a topos by the sophists.[18] In our play, Poverty develops in

her own defense the idea that all good things derive from her, for sur-
feit is the death of effort. Some of Penia's reasoning is mere sophistry,
such as the argument that if everyone were wealthy, no one would
work—not even slave dealers, for theirs is a risky trade, and thus there
would be no slaves. As a result, everyone would be obliged to labor for
himself, and life would be worse than it is now (510–34).[19] The crux of
this paradox is the equation of wealth with money or gold (528); Penia
asks, "With money alone and not the things it can buy, what is it to be
rich?" (531). In essence, this is but a rhetorical version of the tale of
Midas' touch. But the idea that modest means—not raw indigence or
beggary, but modest means—prompt human beings to labor passes over
into the familiar diatribe on the virtues of the rigorous life, which produces men who are sere and wiry and bitter to their enemies (561), well
mannered (564), and concerned for the public welfare (567–68); the hard
way is the just way (578). Penia's dialectic is too sharp for Chremylus,
who, when he does not apply threats and invective, resorts to repeating
the proposition that much is better than little: "You won't persuade me,
not even if you do" (600) is the flourish with which he caps his case.[20]

Chremylus' difficulty, however, is that he has lost sight of his own
position. He had not argued for paradisical opulence; he had proposed
only that it is just for good men to fare well, and the reverse for bad
(490–91); at present, the opposite obtains (500–4). Penia does not respond
to this charge at all, but shifts the grounds of the debate. Chremylus
poses the question of fairness in the social distribution of wealth; Penia
responds with a sermon on the advantages of the spare life which assumes a more or less universal scarcity, in which specific inequalities
are mere perturbations in the system, and may be overlooked for the
sake of the argument. To be sure, Penia endorses a world that is at the
opposite pole from that inaugurated by Plutus in the finale of the play.
Plutus restores the original prosperity of an age preceding Zeus, while
Penia, insisting that Zeus also goes poor, dismisses the picture of Olympian splendor drawn by Chremylus and Blepsidemus as a Cronus-like
dimness (Kronikais lēmais, 581), playing on the common idea of Cronus
as an old man, but alluding also to their purblind faith in the golden
age over which Cronus, the father of Zeus, was believed to have pre-
sided. Precisely as opposites, however, Penia and Plutus present two
sides of the same issue: the relative benefits of generalized want or
plenty, which is a different concern from that originally articulated by
Chremylus.

So that his characters might not seem wholly to speak past each
other, Aristophanes here and there masks the distance between them
with an ambiguous or inconsistent phrase. Thus Chremylus asks what

harm it will do to Penia if he provides some good to all men (460–62);
the "all" is quite inconsistent with the thrust of his primary complaint.
More subtle is the way Penia formulates her hypothetical premise: "if
Plutus should see once more and distribute himself equally" (510). As
has been seen, Chremylus was not in the first instance concerned with
equality, despite the reference just cited to "all men." What is more,
Penia's own position is not incompatible with an equal apportionment
of wealth. Penia should not want to insist that the kind of poverty that
nourishes virtue is necessarily the unfair penury of the just members
of the population. Rather, the expression is simply a bridge, which reso-
nates with Chremylus' arguments about justice without being so specific as to jar noticeably with Penia's main thought. If poverty is abroad,
there must be some inequality, and the audience will have a sense of
continuity in the argument without paying much heed to the details of
the logic.[21]

There is an argument employed by Chremylus and Cario in their
effort to assure Plutus of his supreme power that has a certain resemblance to some of the things Penia says. Penia asserts that without
poverty there would be no skills, no striving, no work (cf. esp. 527–34);
Chremylus claims that all crafts and skills were discovered on account
of Plutus (160–61; the idea is developed in the verses following). Chremylus means that people exert themselves only for the sake of profit. His
view thus seems correlative to that of Penia: she contends that men
work because they have little, he because they want more. The context,
however, reveals that the points of view are entirely disparate. Apart
from some sophistical banter which we have already noted, Penia's case
rests on a moral vision of the simple, rugged life and its creative energy,
a life in implicit contrast to the softness and decadence of a rich, safe
society. The worship of luxury to which Plutus testifies is a sign of that
very decadence. It points not to the way people should be, but to the
way they are. In this sense, Plutus is already in power. Everyone is
motivated by the desire for money, and those who appear not to be are
merely sugarcoating their baser purposes (158–59). What is more, money
is the one thing of which there is never enough (187–89). Aristophanes'
folk wisdom here anticipates an insight of Aristotle, who observes in
the *Politics* (1256a–58a) that of all goods there is a natural limit, save
money, which is pure quantity. Plutus thus presides over a world in
which money has dissolved the relations of barter based on the production and exchange of use-values, in Marx's phrase, and the reigning
passion, accordingly, is greed. Kings, councils, armies, and whores: all
arise through the power of Wealth (170–79; cf. 149–57).

Clearly, such a world bears little resemblance to that over which

Plutus sheds his bounty at the end of the play, for it is based on a relative scarcity of riches and universal competition. Nor is there occasion for surprise that Plutus as he is depicted here is unlike his later self. At this stage of the action, the prevailing conception of wealth is still the social rather than the natural: boundless greed is the moral condition for the differentiation into rich and poor, in which wealth accrues typically to scoundrels, while the decent sort do without. In their panegyric to Wealth, Chremylus and Cario do not yet look to transforming this condition; they merely wish for their piece of the action. Some of the language in this passage points up the ambiguous ethical status of Chremylus, who wants, after all, to exchange places with the rich. He reassures the still hesitating Plutus of his plan by promising that they will have plenty of allies, "all those who, because they are just, haven't a groat." Plutus is not convinced: "Aiii! Those are wretched allies you've mentioned," to which Chremylus replies: "Not if they should grow rich again" (219–21). The term for wretched here—*poneros*—is loaded. It can have the morally neutral significance of "unfortunate" or "in distress," reflecting its derivation from *ponos* (toil), but throughout this play it is used in its pejorative sense of "bad" or "villainous."[22] Chremylus understands Plutus to mean only that his friends are poor, but there is perhaps a connotation also of knavishness. Whether or not it is the case here, however, there is no mistaking it in Chremylus' invitation to Plutus to enter his home: "This is the house which you must make full of money today, whether justly or unjustly" (231–33).[23] Chremylus wants what others have, and is happy to have it at their expense. There is nothing here of that spirit of community represented both by Penia, in her praise of poverty, and by Plutus in the final scenes, albeit in different ways. The dominant ideas in the present passage are those of greed and inequality, or, in a word, of distribution.

The complex and shifting conceptions of wealth and poverty that are put into play throughout the comedy may, then, be analytically resolved into two primary conceptions or topics: unequal distribution, and scarcity versus plenty. But the movement from one conception to the other is accomplished so smoothly that the work retains its apparent unity. In part, the trick lies with the representation of Plutus himself, who has two distinct symbolic aspects in the play. In the first place, and most obviously, there is the feature of his sight or blindness, which is the characteristic immediately relevant to the theme of equitable distribution: when Plutus does not see, he rewards the vicious as well as—or rather, instead of—the virtuous; when he does see, he visits the just rather than the wicked. In the second place, and this is less apparent, there is simply the presence or absence of Plutus, and this is related essentially to the theme of scarcity and plenty: when Plutus is at hand, he brings prosperity, when he is away, there is want. These two properties—vision and presence, with their negations—are so neatly intertwined that it takes a moment's reflection to realize that they operate in quite distinct ways and contexts.

The story begins simply with the appearance of Plutus, whom Chremylus is following at the instruction of Apollo's oracle. Logically, this should suffice for Chremylus, since all he has to do now is bring the god into his home, and wealth will be his.[24] Or, if loyalty demands that he share with his friends, he can take Plutus round to the homes of his fellow demesmen, those of them who are poor and honest. This is not to suggest that Aristophanes' fanstasy need be constrained by the rules of logic; I am merely exposing the places where it takes flight. For within a hundred lines of the beginning of the play, and less than twenty lines from the moment when he discovers the identity of the god, Chremylus begins to conceive of the plan that goes beyond anything Apollo had intimated, that is, to restore Plutus' sight. Chremylus' statement (212–14) that Apollo is aware of what is happening cannot mean that he told it directly to Chremylus, for otherwise Chremylus would not have been ignorant at first of who Plutus was. Not that there is some implied contrast between Chremylus' initiative and the message of the oracle. The point is simply that the whole issue of Plutus' blindness enters into the action independently of his first appearance on stage. There is a reason for this: Aristophanes wants the god on the scene, but he does not want the fact of his presence to resolve at once the problem of injustice that drove Chremylus to consult the oracle to begin with. This will rather be accomplished by enabling him to see again, so that he can visit good men and avoid bad. Thus, the god's arrival is engineered in a more or less mysterious way; the moment he is identified, attention is drawn to his blindness, and the idea of healing it is broached. But this does not mean that the matter of the god's presence is no longer of relevance to the play. On the contrary, it can now be reserved for quite another function, which will be exploited in the latter half of the comedy, when Plutus has his real epiphany; then his presence will signal a new age of prosperity for all.

Having once been explicitly articulated, the association of Plutus' vision with justice remains thematic, and is now and again reaffirmed throughout the play, as when Chremylus reveals to Blepsidemus (and, for the first time, to the audience) his intention of bringing Plutus to the precinct of Asclepius (400–412), or, much more emphatically, in the debate with Penia.[25] And yet, over and above this association, the restoration of Plutus' vision takes on another meaning in the context of

Zeus' opposition. Plutus is, as we have seen, in terror of Zeus, and must be made to realize his power. But asserting his power is one and the same thing as daring to see again. After Chremylus and Cario have given witness to the fact that all things turn on Wealth, Plutus reveals that he still has only one anxiety: "This power that you say I have," he asks, "how can I become master of it?" Chremylus remarks that Plutus is truly the greatest of cowards, as people say, and then reassures him that if Plutus throws himself into the business, then he, Chremylus, will have him seeing better than Lynceus (199–203, 208–10). The word for power here, *dunamis*, is pivotal: it looks back to the signs of Plutus' potency in the world, the fact that he alone is responsible, as Chremylus says, for all things good and bad; to which Plutus responds, "Am I, one person, capable [*dunatos*] of doing all this?" (186). Looking forward, however, *dunamis* must refer to the power of sight; the way that Plutus will become master of his own potency is to regain his vision. His sight, then, is his power. To put it another way, Plutus' blindness is an emblem of his powerlessness, and his healing is synonymous with the realization of his puissance in the world. From this point of view, the story of Plutus' recovery of vision is in the tradition of tales about the healing of magical or symbolic wounds, by which a fallen god or hero is restored to excellence or authority.[26]

The healing of the god, then, serves a double function in the play: on the one hand, it is emblematic of fairness in the distribution of wealth; on the other hand, it is a token of the god's return to power, a theme that is fully realized in the final scenes. This double function has a palpable effect on the plot. At the end of the episode in which Chremylus and Cario persuade Plutus to undertake the cure, Chremylus invites the god, as has been seen, into his house, and, after assurances that Chremylus is neither a miser nor a spendthrift, but a man of the middle sort (245), the god consents (251). From this point forward, Chremylus is rich, and Blepsidemus hastens to his house because rumors of his good fortune are already abroad (335–39). Chremylus explains his sudden prosperity by revealing that he has the god; he is inside, "with me" "With you?" "Absolutely." "Damn! Plutus with you?" "I swear it" (393–94). The presence of the god confers the blessing of wealth. Blepsidemus naturally enough asks whether Chremylus will send him now to his friends (398), to which Chremylus replies, rather inconsequentially, that this is not the problem: it is necessary to make him see (399–401). Blepsidemus falls in at once with the plan, so that the audience has no time to wonder why it is so important; Blepsidemus' own suggestion, after all, would appear as good. The action is now interrupted by the arrival of Penia, which is followed by the long dialogue between

Cario and Chremylus' wife, in which the slave reports, with comic embroidery, the healing of the god in the temple of Asclepius (641–770). When at last we see Plutus again, he is escorted by a great procession (750–59) and he proclaims his new dispensation to the world (774–81, esp. 779). After this, Cario reemerges from the house with the jubilant description of wealth blossoming within (802–22).

This arrangement of the action conveys the inescapable impression that the luxury within the house is the consequence of Plutus' vision, although we already know that it came about simply as the result of his presence inside. Plutus' own words help confirm the impression, when he says that it is inappropriate for him to take anything out, rather he must bring things into Chremylus' house—now that he can see (792–93). The point is surely not that he is now for the first time aware that Chremylus is really a just man; rather, the fact of his sight is here a token of the unstinting liberality of his new regime. This same suggestion hangs about the remark of Hermes, to which attention has already been called: "From the time when Plutus began to see again, no one sacrifices any longer to us gods, no incense, no laurel, no barley cake, no animal, no nothing" (1113–16). There is no particular connection between Plutus' sight and fairness here; everybody is rich, and the return of the god's vision is the sign of his supremacy over the Olympian pantheon (cf. also 1173–74, with 1178, where again Plutus' vision is the condition for universal prosperity).

The odd but deliberate confusion over whether it is the god's presence or the god's vision that is the cause of Chremylus' prosperity—a confusion generated by the postponement of Cario's description of the opulence within until after the healing of Plutus—is abetted in two earlier passages. In Chremylus' exchange with Blepsidemus, his friend inquires whether he is really rich, as people say. Chremylus replies: "I shall be right away, if the god pleases" (347). He adds that there is a certain danger in the matter. From what follows, it is clear that Chremylus must be referring to the problem of curing the god, and that his own financial success depends on it.[27] Since, however, the actual proposal to restore the god's vision is not mentioned for some fifty verses, it is natural to think that Chremylus' reservations about his wealth point vaguely to some delay in the god's efficacy. The second passage is Cario's announcement that the god has been healed, uttered to the chorus and following immediately upon the scene with Penia. Cario exclaims: "My master has been most fortunate, or rather, Plutus himself has been; for instead of being blind he has his sight altogether back and his pupils are shining for he found Asclepius the healer well-disposed" (633–36). Plainly, Chremylus' fortunes are equated with

Plutus' own. For the one, it is a matter of wealth, for the other, of vision. The god's vision is the condition for his efficacy.

The double function of Plutus' sight is the means of converting the plot of the play from the issue of distribution to that of the golden age. The device of the procession celebrating the healing of Plutus' eyes permits Aristophanes to fuse the themes of vision and epiphany, and thus to move from the idea of the cure and its associations (above all with the distribution theme) to the idea of Plutus' presence and power in the world. The transition can be observed. Cario concludes his account of the healing work of Asclepius with a peroration that incorporates symbols of regeneration into the account of the process: "Even before you, my mistress, could guzzle ten cups of wine, Plutus stood up and saw" (737–38). Cario awoke his master, as he tells it, and all those in the temple spent the whole night rejoicing in the god until the day shone; Cario himself praised Asclepius for making Plutus see, and Neocleides blind.[28] Chremylus' wife adds her word of admiration for Asclepius, and then inquires: "But tell me, where is Plutus?" (749), to which Cario replies, "He's coming." Later, Cario notes that the procession is getting close (767). The arrival and installation of the god in the house of Chremylus (actually a second installation) coincide with the restoration of his vision.

The association and, to a degree, confusion between several distinct versions of the problem of wealth and poverty are familiar. It is not difficult to discover in popular literature today such a welter of opinions existing side by side concerning the causes of economic distress: the corruption of a few parasites, a general decline in social morality, the scarcity of natural resources. By the fanciful device of introducing Wealth personified into his cast of characters, playing off the double function of Wealth's blindness as a source of error and as a sign of weakness, and mixing up the meaning of Wealth's presence with that of his restored vision, Aristophanes holds the several views together in a single tableau, while at the same time effecting a broad transition from a social conception, in which poverty is a consequence of injustice, to a natural conception, in which poverty is a function of scarcity to be remedied by a general and spontaneous bounty. This deflection in the play's themes serves to dissolve the issue of exploitation and inequality into a vague nostalgia for a golden age, a nostalgia that is catered to with comic exuberance in the utopian finale of the play.[29]

Essentially, Aristophanes' strategy is conservative, or at best apolitical. He displaces the real antagonisms generated by social conflicts within the ancient city-state with a vision of communal solidarity and well-being. As a solution to the problems of growing inequality between the wealthy and the poor in the aftermath of the Peloponnesian War, the further development of class divisions, the increasing significance of a state apparatus represented by the informal institutions of the sycophant and the orator or demagogue, Aristophanes offers the ancient dream of limitless bounty, which is the answer to a different question.[30] The historical Athens of the early fourth century B.C. with its living social contradictions departs the stage, or rather is subsumed under an ideal community of smallholders who share alike the burden of eking their livelihood from a stingy land and are granted the collective wish of universal prosperity. To work, such a transformation must appear natural. Analysis reveals how it is accomplished in *Wealth*.

The inconsistencies and contradictions among the complex of themes relating to poverty and plenty in Aristophanes' *Wealth* have not been treated as flaws. Rather, here, as in the four earlier plays of Aristophanes examined in the preceding chapters, ranging from the opening years of the Peloponnesian War through the glory days of imperial ambition and on to the Sicilian disaster and Athens' ultimate defeat, the specifically literary operation of the work has been located precisely in the overdetermination of the characters' motivations and social positions, and in the hiatuses or seams in the surface narrative, which have been taken as the signs of tensions immanent in ideology and social reality that are overcome factitiously in the production of the unified text. As Pierre Macherey writes:

> We understand then what we must seek in texts: not signs of their cohesion and of their autonomy but the material contradictions which produce them and which are reproduced there in the form of conflicts. ... Literature expresses these conflicts and adds to them an imaginary resolution; but these solutions, these compromises which are finally the texts, continue to bear the mark of the divisions which give theme a real base, a reality, and also an interest.[31]

We experience *Wealth* as a single work; but we know it as a complex and active intervention into the ideological instabilities of the Athenian city-state.

II

MENANDREAN
COMEDY:
SEX AND STATUS

6

Grouch

Menandrean drama differs from the Old Comedy produced by Aristophanes and his contemporaries in its concentration on the domestic world, and above all on the vicissitudes of youthful passion—the passion, that is, of young men who are blocked by stern fathers, rich rivals, or greedy masters from attaining the women they desire, and must rely on intrigue or luck to gain them.[1] Thus Plutarch observed that *erōs* played a role in all of Menander's comedies, and the rule holds for the plays of which we have any knowledge, including *Duskolos*, or *Grouch* (an alternative title is *Misanthrope*), which was produced in 316 B.C. when Menander was about twenty-five years old, just over a century after Aristophanes produced *Wasps*.[2] *Grouch* was recovered on papyrus in 1959, and is the only original play by Menander, or indeed by any Greek playwright in the New Comic tradition, that survives complete. In it, Sostratus, a young and elegant city lad who is the son of a well-to-do father (39–40), has fallen in love with the daughter (unnamed) of the title character, a harsh-tempered, antisocial old fellow named Cnemo. The problem for Sostratus is to break down Cnemo's resistance to a marriage for his daughter.

The function of *erōs* in *Grouch*, however, is exceptional for New Comedy, since it is rarely the case that a maiden girl known to be a citizen, and thus eligible for a legitimate marriage, is represented as the object of passionate desire.[3] Indeed, Menander seems at pains to call attention to the unusual character of Sostratus' infatuation in the opening scene of the play. Sostratus comes on stage accompanied by an officious friend called Chaereas, his hunting partner on the previous day

(42, 48), when he first caught sight of Cnemo's daughter as she was plac-
ing garlands in a precinct sacred to the Nymphs.[4] Sostratus has evidently
surprised his friend by revealing that he has conceived an erotic desire
(*erōn*, 52) for a free or well-bred girl (*eleutheran*, 50). Chaereas, who has
a reputation as a useful counselor (56), explains, a shade pretentiously:

> In these matters, Sostratus, here's how I am: if one of my friends calls
> on me because he's in love [*erōn*] with a courtesan, I immediately seize
> her and carry her off, I get drunk, set fire, brook no argument whatso-
> ever—before even finding out who she is, one must catch her, for delay
> greatly magnifies love, but with quick action it's possible to end it
> quickly. If someone mentions marriage, however, and a free girl
> [*eleutheran*], here I'm someone else: I inquire about her family, live-
> lihood, character. For all time to come I am leaving a reminder with
> my friend of how I manage in these things. (57–68)

Chaereas draws a sharp contrast between two kinds of affair. The passion (*erōs*) inspired by a courtesan or *hetaira* calls for quick action in
order to keep the infatuation under control. In the case of a free-born
maiden, on the contrary, it is assumed that the young man's intention
is marriage, which demands good sense and a careful investigation of
the girl's background.[5] Chaereas is appalled to learn that Sostratus has
already sent a slave to make contact with her family. His desire has the
impetuous urgency characteristic of the passion normally felt for courtesans.

The audience has been prepared for Sostratus' erotic interest in
Cnemo's daughter by Pan, who speaks the prologue. The god explains
that he is responsible for making Sostratus madly in love with the girl
(44).[6] He has a special concern for her thanks to her diligent care for the
Nymphs, who share their shrine with Pan. As Sostratus enters, Pan
points him out as "the one in love" (48).[7] Pan's intervention, and the
obvious good will toward Cnemo's daughter that inspires it, softens the
picture of an upper-class youth taking an amorous interest in a poor but
respectable citizen girl, since it is manifestly part of a divine and benevolent plan.[8]

Later in the play, Sostratus' father, Callipides, grants that there is a
place for erotic attraction in the choice of a wife (786–90): "I wish you
to take the girl you love, and insist that you should. . . . By the gods, I
do, since I know that a marriage is made stable for a young man if he is
moved to undertake it on account of love [*erōs*]." There is no suggestion of the conflict characteristic of New Comedy between a young
man's transgressive passion for a girl of improper status and the practical concerns of the father.[9] Love is simply acknowledged as an ingredi-

ent in marriage. As Gomme and Sandbach remark, Callipides' "sentiment would be more striking to a fourth-century audience than it is
today."[10] As will be seen, however, Callipides is not wholly indifferent
to the relative advantages of a conjugal alliance, and this will give rise
to a momentary tension between him and Sostratus.

The action of *Grouch*, then, in conformity with all of Menander's
plays, is motivated by passionate desire, but differs from the usual type
in that Sostratus is infatuated with a free maiden, and his aim, accordingly, is marriage. *Erōs* is harnessed to a plot based on a straightforward
proposal of wedlock, and Sostratus acts at once to seek out the girl's
family in order to ask for her hand. His father raises no objections, and
only the misanthropy of Cnemo stands in the way of the intended union.
His fierce temperament is thus pivotal to the story.

Cnemo, who wants nothing to do with his neighbors and fellow
citizens, lives on a remote rural property which he farms himself, with
only his daughter for company and an elderly slave who keeps house
for him. He is so shy of people that he has abandoned tilling a portion
of his land near the public road in order to avoid encounters with strangers. He is disposed to assault with clods and stones anyone who tres-
passes on his domain, and he can scarcely endure to be civil to the image of Pan in the shrine that borders on his estate, as the god tells us in
the prologue (10–12). Though his property is fairly large and his worth
is not negligible, Cnemo is stingy as well as misanthropic, and the prologue explains that his wife has left him in order to move in with her
son from a former marriage, whose house is next door to Cnemo's.

Cnemo's fierce isolationism renders him akin to the "humors" of
renaissance comedy, like Morose in Ben Jonson's *Epicene*, who are dominated by a single trait or passion magnified to the degree of absurdity.[11]
Formally, Cnemo's function in obstructing the desire of a young man
for a girl under his authority is analogous to that of other stock types in
New Comedy who are in a position of power over the beloved and
thereby serve as blocking figures, for example the villainous brothel
keeper in Plautus' *Pseudolus*, or the arrogant mercenary soldier in
Plautus' *Braggart Soldier* (*Miles Gloriosus*), who own or have contracted
for the girl in question.[12] It is comically effective to caricature the foibles
or fixations of such characters, in contrast with the wan fecklessness
of the protagonist, and the particular quality of the humor occasionally lends the play its title, as in the case of *Grouch* and *Braggart Soldier*, which is based on a Greek original called *Boaster* (*Alazōn*). Because
the hero of *Grouch* is in love with a citizen girl and, as the conventions
of the genre require, has marriage as his object rather than a casual
liaison, the blocking figure is not an owner or master but an adult male

relative, who is responsible for bestowing the intended bride in wedlock.

The father of the girl in the capacity of a humor seems especially
suited to the narrative formula of *Grouch*, in which an Athenian youth
is enamored of an eligible citizen girl. Where the boy's father obstructs
his son's affair in New Comedy, he is ordinarily moved by considerations of policy, and seeks to prevent a liaison with an expensive courtesan or with an impoverished woman of dubious citizen credentials,
which might damage the family's social standing or constitute an in-
fraction of civic norms. (Personal rivalries or antagonisms between families, of the sort dramatized in *Romeo and Juliet*, do not seem to have
been a motif in New Comedy.) Sostratus' father, Callipides, has no practical reasons for objecting to the match, nor does he, in the event. The
wishes of the girl herself, it may be remarked, are not much taken into
account on the New Comic stage; wedding arrangements are negotiated between the prospective groom and the male who has responsibility for the intended bride.[13] Indeed, citizen maidens normally have no
speaking role in the genre (the few lines assigned to Cnemo's daughter
are the kind of exception that proves the rule). The role of blocking
character is thus left to Cnemo, but since he, too, has no reasonable
grounds for preventing the match, his resistance is reduced to a pure
quirk of character, like that of the miser Euclio in Plautus' *Aulularia*
(possibly based on a Menandrean original), whose stinginess in the
matter of a dowry prevents his daughter from finding a suitable husband.[14]

The development of the plot in *Grouch* depends centrally on overcoming the misanthrope's obsession with privacy and hostility to his
fellows, and this part of the action proceeds straightforwardly. Sostratus
sets out to earn the confidence of the old man in order to gain his consent.[15] To this end, he dresses in country clothing and acquires an out-
door tan as he tries his hand at the hoe, but he fails to encounter Cnemo
at his chores and his efforts are thus to no effect. Cnemo's resistance is
broken only after he accidentally falls down his own well in pursuit of
a bucket that has dropped from a rotten cord, and has to rely on the help
of his stepson Gorgias, assisted by Sostratus, to haul him back out.
Cnemo discovers the speciousness of his pretended self-sufficiency,
realizing belatedly that he must rely on the kindness of neighbors and
that not all people are scoundrels. He commits his daughter to the authority of Gorgias, who gladly gives his approval to the intended marriage. In addition, he consigns to Gorgias half his property, leaving it
to him to arrange the dowry and the wedding between the girl and
Sostratus. Cnemo is now prepared to withdraw into solitude, but his

humiliation is completed by the antics of a cook and slave who had suffered earlier from his ill temper: they tease and manhandle him while he is still weak and battered from his fall, oblige him to dance, and, finally, force him, despite his protestations, to join in the festivities that are under way in the shrine of the Nymphs, where Sostratus' parents are offering a sacrifice. The final scene, which is something of a coda to the main action, is performed in a lyrical meter to the accompaniment of a flute (there is a stage direction in the papyrus after verse 879), and the spirit is bright and farcical.[16]

The humbling of the ogre-like Cnemo has a fairy-tale quality. As Gomme and Sandbach observe in reference to the finale, "Knemon and his unsocial way of life must be shown as defeated by the normal view that takes man to be a social animal."[17] To be sure, Cnemo's capitulation in joining the party is grudging and superficial—Gomme and Sandbach charge Menander with a want of strict consistency in suggesting, by means of the exuberant conclusion, a simple happy ending to the play—but the issue of the drama is not, in the first instance, Cnemo's personal transformation. It resides rather in Cnemo's role as head of household and his relationship in this capacity to his fellow citizens.

Marriage in classical Athens was not a wholly personal matter; it was also part of the nexus of social relations that bound into a community the discrete citizen households of which the city-state was constituted.[18] Since the law sponsored by Pericles almost a century and a half earlier (451 B.C.), marriage for Athenians was effectively restricted to those who were descended from citizen parents on both the father's and the mother's side.[19] Because Cnemo obstructs a marriage for his daughter (a stance that reproduces his own estrangement from his wife), his isolation cuts his household off from the network of connubial relations that underwrites membership in the polity. Sostratus' desire to marry the girl thus strikes directly at the social meaning of Cnemo's withdrawal from human interaction.

As a consequence of his misanthropy, Cnemo fails to provide for the future of his daughter and abdicates his responsibility for the continuation of his household. The theme of authority is broached early in the play, when Sostratus informs Chaereas that he has already sent his slave to seek out the girl's father or, he adds, "whoever it may be who is in charge of the household" (73–74). The person in charge is, in Greek, the *kurios*, who in Attic law is an adult male citizen with authority over his wife, children, and any other dependents, such as an unmarried sister, who are not otherwise in the care of a responsible party. At this point in the action, of course, Sostratus does not know who the girl's *kurios* happens to be, since he is unfamiliar with her family, but his remark perhaps hints at an ambiguity over who is in fact responsible for the girl.

Soon afterward, Sostratus encounters Cnemo's daughter (it is the only scene in which she appears), as she emerges from her house to fill a jug with water from the shrine of the Nymphs, since Cnemo's bucket has by now fallen into the well. Sostratus offers to fetch some for her, and the two engage in a brief dialogue. Davus, a slave of Gorgias who has overheard the exchange, curses Cnemo for his carelessness in allowing a virtuous young girl to go out by herself, without a woman to serve as chaperone (223).[20] He decides to report the matter at once to Gorgias, so that they at least can assume the care of her (226–29). When Gorgias appears, at the beginning of the second act, he reproaches the slave for having stood by like a stranger (238). One may not, he says, run away from relationship, employing here a word (*oikeiotēs*, 240) whose normal sense, according to an ancient lexicographer, denotes ties by marriage, although Menander used it loosely for blood relations.[21] Her father, Gorgias continues, wishes to be a stranger toward them, but they must not imitate his churlishness.

In the end, after his tumble into the well, Cnemo himself acknowledges his failure as head of household when he accepts Gorgias as his son and places him in charge of his estate and his daughter, entrusting him with the responsibility of finding a husband for her, since no suitor, he realizes, is likely to find favor with him (729–35; cf. 737–39). Gorgias agrees, and at once gives his consent to his half-sister's marriage to Sostratus, after a dutiful attempt to elicit Cnemo's approval for the match (748–60).

At this point in the play, with the girl formally betrothed by Gorgias to Sostratus (761–63) and Callipides about to bestow his blessing on the union (761, 786–87), the social disorder caused by Cnemo's misanthropy has been resolved.[22] Cnemo's household is liberated from the constraints of his irascible nature and is restored to the community of families that make up the city-state. For good measure, Sostratus gains his father's consent to a marriage between his sister and Gorgias (813–20). Cnemo himself, to be sure, remains aloof from the new arrangements, disclaiming any interest in the man his daughter is to marry (752) and demanding for himself and his wife simply provision for their support (739). His intransigence may seem a blemish on the spirit of comic resolution, although a facile conversion of the misanthrope would undercut the representation of his character. "He is not," as Gomme and Sandbach observe, "an admirable character, and he has no intention of behaving amiably or co-operatively in his retirement" (p. 268). The crucial thing, however, is that the social effects of his crankiness are now undone. The hilarity of the final episode may be taken as a sign of the festive reintegration of Cnemo's family—his daughter and newly adopted son— into the citizen community.

The function of Sostratus' passion for Cnemo's daughter is, on this view, to draw Cnemo's household back into the society constituted as a closed conjugal group in which Athenians marry Athenians and strangers are strictly excluded from connubial relations with citizens. By his opposition to any possible suitor for his daughter, Cnemo had threatened to sever the ties between his house and the citizen community. Sostratus' love is thus a manifestation of the city-state's claim on Cnemo's household: it dissolves the barrier represented by the misanthrope's secession, and in this respect Sostratus' passion in *Grouch* is akin to *erōs* in New Comedy generally, where it is typically a transgressive desire across status boundaries. Cnemo's misanthropy and the love interest, then, are associated not only on the level of the plot, where the curmudgeon is, as we have seen, the adversary of choice for a lover who aspires to legitimate wedlock, but also on the level of the theme, where the integrative quality of *erōs* complements the centrifugal force of Cnemo's withdrawal.

After he has been rescued from the well, largely through the efforts of Gorgias with the distracted assistance of Sostratus, Cnemo, not wholly repentant, delivers, along with his confession that man needs the help of others and cannot be independent of everyone, an explanation and an apologia for his ways.[23] Having observed, he says, the calculating greed of human beings, he had imagined that no one was really considerate of anyone else (718–21). The example of Gorgias, especially in light of Cnemo's former treatment of him, upsets this judgment. But still he ventures in his own defense: "If everyone were like me, there would be no courts, they would not be taking each other off to jail, there would be no war, and each would be content with his fair share" (743–45). The sentiment is a Greek commonplace: trouble starts when people stop minding their own business.[24] Nevertheless, it is a fine moment. One critic observes: "It is Menander's considerable achievement that after spending three acts building Knemon into a monster (a comic monster, maybe, but one for whom the audience's sympathy is not invited for a moment), he is able to transform him into a human being whose ill-guided attempt to live without assistance from others, *autos autarkēs* (714), is not merely touching but has a trace of nobility about it."[25]

While Cnemo's bid for a sympathetic understanding of his way of life comes as a surprise, there are several adumbrations of a virtuous side to his fierce temperament. Early in the action, when Sostratus' slave

returns breathless from his unfortunate interview with Cnemo, Sostratus himself ventures, if not a defense, at least a more generous interpretation of Cnemo's surliness: "A poor farmer is a bitter sort, not only
this one, but practically all of them" (120–31). Sostratus' own courage
deserts him when Cnemo arrives in person, but the suggestion that
Cnemo represents a general type of tough, hard-working peasant is
echoed later when Gorgias observes that Cnemo's vehemence is directed
against the idle lives that people lead (355–57). Cnemo himself confirms
this ethical interpretation of his solitariness: when Sostratus' mother,
inspired by a dream (412–18), leads a party to prepare an elaborate sacrifice to Pan in the shrine of the Nymphs next door to his house, Cnemo
mutters that people indulge in lavish displays of piety for their own
sakes, not the gods': the god himself would be content with some ritual
cake and incense, while the roasted animals cater to mortal gluttony
(448–53).[26] As Gomme and Sandbach remark, Cnemo's speech "introduces a new point: his dislike of his fellow men is rooted in a belief in
their selfishness."[27]

There are other indications of the virtue of Cnemo's ways. In the
prologue, the god Pan describes Cnemo's daughter as "like her breeding,
ignorant of pettiness" (35–36). The implied approval of Cnemo's household has seemed anomalous enough that some editors have elected to
emend the text (thus reading "*unlike* her breeding"), but Sostratus himself speaks later of the somehow liberal or decent rearing (*eleutherōs*,
387) the girl enjoyed in the company of her boorish father, which sheltered her from the corrupting influence of nannies, and when he speaks
with her he is struck at once by the liberal style of her rusticity (201–2).[28]

It has been suggested that the faults of Cnemo are patterned not
only on the type of the misanthrope proper but on that of the rude rustic as well, the "unattractive *agroikos* of Theophrastos or Aristotle,"
and that Menander "has used him to portray an excess of rustic harshness."[29] But the image of the rustic cuts both ways, carrying connota-
tions of sturdy independence, straightforwardness, hard work, and honesty alongside those of taciturn or uncouth unsociability. In the words
of a scholar who reveres Menander for his ethics and didacticism, "Rusticity is a fault in Theophrastus. In Menander it is coupled with noble
independence and innocence."[30]

In the view of some critics, the complexity of Cnemo's character,
especially as it is evoked in the latter part of the comedy, disrupts the
love story proper. Michael Anderson, for example, notes a conflict between "the romantic love interest (involving Sostratos and Knemon's
daughter) demanded of New Comedy, and a character-study of the misanthropic Knemon."[31] Anderson summarizes the thesis developed by

Armin Schäfer in his excellent monograph on the play: "Menander comes near to a solution . . . but these two elements are basically irreconcilable, and the play consequently fails to achieve complete unity of action."[32] While there is indeed a tension in the development of *Grouch*, Schäfer has, I think, located it in the wrong place. It is not that the interest in Cnemo's character interrupts the romantic strand of the plot. Rather, the two sides of Cnemo's gruffness—his bogeyman prickliness and the uncompromising self-reliance that has about it air of old-fashioned virtue—answer to two distinct elements in the amatory narrative.

Corresponding to the picture of Cnemo as an honest if hard-bitten farmer is the representation of Sostratus as something of an urban fop. Toward the end of the prologue, when Pan turns from his portrait of Cnemo to Sostratus, he calls him citified in his pursuits (41) and immediately illustrates the point by mentioning that he has been out hunting (42), an occupation characteristic of the idle rich.[33] New Comedy eschewed the representation of young rakes seducing innocent maidens, and Sostratus' intentions have indeed been honorable from the moment he laid eyes on the girl. But Gorgias' slave Davus is instantly suspicious when he finds Sostratus chatting with the girl, and he imagines that the lad has "sneaked in" to try his luck because he knows she is unprotected (224–26). When Gorgias catches sight of him, the first thing he notes is Sostratus' fancy cloak (257); then he adds that he has the look of a scoundrel.[34] Gorgias delivers a homily on the dangers of relying on good fortune and cautions Sostratus against contempt for indigent folk like himself (285). The commentators note Gorgias' overearnest manner and a certain want of logic, but his bluster may conceal a real anxiety over confronting a wealthy young man.[35] He explicitly denounces Sostratus for intending to corrupt a free maiden (*parthenon eleutheran*, 290–91), exploiting his own leisure to the harm of those who must labor, and he adds that a beggar wronged is the most churlish of men: the term is *duskolōtaton* (296), used elsewhere only of Cnemo (as in the title of the play), and while Gomme and Sandbach dismiss the occurrence here as accidental,[36] it is plausible that Menander is deliberately associating Gorgias' hostile reaction to Sostratus with the kind of misanthropy that Cnemo shares, as we have seen, with all poor farmers.

Sostratus replies that he is in love with the girl and that he has come to approach not her but her father (305–6), since he is ready to take her as his wife.[37] Gorgias insists that it is a hopeless ambition, in view of Cnemo's nature. "You've never been in love with anyone," says Sostratus (341), and Gorgias replies that he does not have the time: *erōs* is evidently conceived as the province of the well-to-do. When Sostratus persists, Gorgias advises him that Cnemo will not bear the sight of him at leisure and in luxury (357), and at Davus' suggestion, Sostratus doffs his cloak and takes up a mattock in order to give the impression of a poor farmer (369–70).

Gomme and Sandbach comment: "Here Menander employs the common dramatic device of laying a false trail; the suggested event does not occur, Knemon and Sostratos never meet in the fields, and Knemon never listens to Sostratos. But at a later stage they meet and Gorgias tries to introduce Sostratos as a hard-working farmer; Knemon shows no interest, and it is no longer necessary that he should."[38] Gorgias will then insist that Sostratus is not given to luxury (755) or to spending the day in idleness, and Cnemo concludes from Sostratus' sunburned complexion that he is indeed a farmer (754). While Cnemo appears to take no notice, Sostratus' good will in playing the farmer has gone down well with Gorgias, at all events. Gorgias gets Cnemo's attention briefly when he identifies Sostratus as the one who helped rescue him from the well (753), and the two dramatic devices aimed at softening Cnemo's intransigence momentarily intersect.

Just as Sostratus the lover challenges Cnemo's breach with society, forcing the old man to give up control over his daughter and estate, so Sostratus the upper-class sportsman comes into conflict with Gorgias' persona, and Cnemo's too, as a hardworking tiller of the soil. Cnemo's tumble into the well is the means of resolving the dramatic tension in the first scenario; Sostratus' gesture in playing the farmer points to a resolution in the second. The plan to represent Sostratus as a farmer is not simply an abortive scheme, to be displaced by Cnemo's fall. Rather, it coexists with the latter device and finds its place in a distinct moment in the complex action of the drama, the paradigm of class antagonism between the leisured rich and the toiling poor, just as the scene at the well answers to the issue of isolationism and exaggerated autarky. Cnemo's character is ambiguous because it is overdetermined by the double theme of *Grouch* and is fitted simultaneously to both narrative paradigms.

A second element in what may be called the paradigm of class conflict in *Grouch* involves Callipides, Sostratus' father, who is identified in the prologue as "a man who farms possessions in this area worth many talents" (40–41).[39] When Gorgias learns that Sostratus is Callipides' son, he is impressed: "he's a wealthy man, by Zeus, and justly so, since he's an incomparable farmer (775). Callipides consents graciously to Sostratus' marriage with Cnemo's daughter, as has been said, but balks momentarily at the demand, raised abruptly at the beginning of act 5, that he give his own daughter in matrimony to Gorgias: "I do not want to accept both a bride and a groom who are paupers: one is enough for me" (795–96). Sostratus caps his plea with a high-minded lecture on the right use of wealth, over which, he says, one is master (806; cf. 800) for a brief span of years; the noble thing is to assist all, and thereby render as many as one may prosperous through one's efforts. Such generosity, he adds, is immortal, and from it benefits will return in time of need (805–10). Sostratus' little sermon is reminiscent of Gorgias' moralizing speech at his first encounter with Sostratus and shows him to have taken Gorgias' lesson to heart. Callipides hears this earnest lecture with respect and kindly amusement and gives in at once, gently reminding his son: "You know me, Sostratus" (813).[40]

Callipides' resistance, perfunctory as it is, to the union of his daughter with Gorgias casts him in the role of blocking figure, and provides a counterweight to the function of Cnemo as an obstacle to the union of the two households. Implicitly, the scene justifies Gorgias' wariness toward the rich and may partially redeem Cnemo's surliness. His rudeness, at all events, is not the only barrier to full and free ties of kinship among all citizens.

Having brought his father round on the union between his sister and Gorgias, Sostratus must next overcome Gorgias' own inhibitions over marrying into a wealthy family (823–34). With both sides reconciled, rich and poor are joined by domestic bonds. As Sostratus says to Gorgias, who is still shy of mixing with the women inside the shrine: "You must now regard all this as family (873)." Sostratus marries for love, but Gorgias accepts Callipides' daughter as wife on the grounds that it is a sensible match and will unite the two households. Personal affection does not enter into his decision. His demeanor testifies to the attitude of a poor farmer toward affairs of the heart, and the contrast with Sostratus' erotic motive is striking.

The complex characterization of Cnemo, who appears both as a caricature of an antisocial boor and as an example of the dour but honest manner of a poor farmer, corresponds to two distinct story lines that enter into the plot of Grouch, the one based on the folk-tale pattern of an individual who withdraws from the group and fails to manage on his own, the other on a class opposition that is resolved by intermarriage between the rich and the poor; the latter theme is largely, but not exclusively, carried by the figure of Gorgias.[41] To these two paradigms there corresponds a complex attitude toward erotic love. Sostratus, contrary to his friend Chaereas' expectations, is passionate for a free citizen girl, although her status requires that he aspire to marriage rather than a short-term sexual liaison. The force of his infatuation induces Sostratus to ignore the obstacle posed by Cnemo's uncompromising temperament, but his behavior in talking privately with the girl rouses the suspicions of Gorgias, who must be induced to believe that Sostratus' intentions are wholly honorable. The boy has something of the jeunnesse dorée in him, and, alongside his role in undermining Cnemo's secession from the world, which victimizes his own daughter and stepson as much as anyone else, he plays his part in the subordinate drama of class antagonisms in which the rich are perceived as potential predators upon the poor.

If Cnemo, then, is one more example of a comic humor, just waiting to be humbled in his monomaniacal obsession, he is also to some degree a typical product of the hard conditions endured by struggling farmers. His wild eccentricity, however, makes it easy to deflate him as a figure for lower-class resentment; besides, he is not in fact all that poor, and Gorgias is in a position to offer a dowry of one talent for his half sister (845), which stands up reasonably well against the three talents that Callipides proposes to give for his daughter (844). By representing Callipides as a generous and hardworking farmer, morally equivalent to Cnemo in his honesty and self-reliance, who in addition is willing to overlook differences of wealth in the choice of conjugal partners for his son and daughter, Menander deftly neutralizes the theme of class conflict, and the bonds of kinship override class divisions.

The Hellenistic epoch was a period of accelerating class differentiation. The Macedonians supported political changes in favor of large landowners, and the ancestral image of a community of citizen-farmers was becoming ever less actual.[42] In *Grouch*, Menander endorses a principle of generous regard for others, of *philanthrōpia* in the large sense which the Greek term possesses, to stand against the disintegrative misanthropy of Cnemo. One writer sums up his argument: "Menander, then, in the 'Dyskolos' has pictured very vividly for us the schism existing between city and country in Athens in the late fourth century B.C. At the same time he has shown us that the seeds of philanthropia which can solve this problem lie in the refinement of the city and the practical experience of the country. He shows us also the great binding influence that this feeling can have."[43]

Harmony between rich and poor is indeed a premise of New Comedy. A rich father does not unrelentingly oppose a marriage between his son and a poor girl on economic grounds alone. Correspondingly, the playwrights do not resolve the tension, when it arises, between a father's practical interest in a profitable alliance and his son's spontaneous passion for a beautiful but impecunious citizen girl through the device of a recognition, by which the girl turns out to be the daughter of well-to-do parents after all. A foreign girl, of course, is rendered eli-

gible for marriage in this way; there is no other option for the dramatist, since marriages across status lines, that is, between citizen and
noncitizen, were strictly forbidden in Athens. But to exploit the recognition formula in order to overcome a father's objections to a marriage
with a citizen girl, however impoverished her family, would suggest a
real social barrier between rich and poor, and this would violate the spirit
of communal solidarity that is celebrated in New Comedy.

Menander also resolves the class issue in *Grouch* by displacing it
onto the theme of the misanthrope's idiosyncratic unsociability. The
blame for the tension in the drama falls squarely on Cnemo, and his
humiliation, rather than the good will of Callipides, is represented as
the critical condition for the integration of his household into the larger
community. Thus the evocation of a real social conflict between classes
is conjured away through the humbling of a comic grotesque, whose
crankiness is the primary cause of difficulties for the romantic hero. In
this, Menander's strategy in *Grouch* resembles that of Aristophanes in
Wealth, where, as has been seen, the problem of unequal distribution
of riches gives way to a utopian vision of universal bounty. In each case,
a potential story of social inequality and tension is overridden by an
alternative narrative that is fanciful or wishful in character: in *Wealth*,
a cure for economic scarcity in the return to the abundance of the golden
age; in *Grouch*, a festive reintegration of the community over a killjoy's
refusal to participate in social life. In Aristophanes' *Wasps*, the complex characterization of Philocleon—as a poor man dependent, like the
chorus, on the fees earned as a juror and, at the same time, as a well-to-
do householder (his son is on easy terms with the Athenian aristocracy)
whose passion for the courts is a pure obsession—enables a slide from
issues of class to the problem of one man's peculiar mania. So, too, in
Grouch, the displacement of the narrative line based on class antagonism by the issue of Cnemo's individual eccentricity is facilitated by
the overdetermined representation of Cnemo as simultaneously a
gloomy spoilsport and a grim but sturdy farmer.

Just because Cnemo's misanthropy is represented as an exaggerated
version of a poor farmer's native testiness, it is easy to dismiss the fierce
independence of the countryman as a curious quirk or lack of refinement. But the vision of an autarkic household estate ran deep in the
ideology of the classical city-state. In Aristophanes' *Acharnians*, produced in 425 B.C., the hero, Dicaeopolis (whose name means "Just City"),
in disgust at the corruption of his fellow citizens who will do nothing
to secure an honorable peace with Sparta, withdraws to his own farm
in the country and signs a private peace treaty with the enemy. The
fantasy that follows is based on the notion that an individual house-

hold could function like a city, autonomous and self-sufficient. Aristophanes' hero succeeds brilliantly in his bold enterprise and has the Athenians begging for a share in his treaty. Menander's grouch is humbled and withdraws into an isolated retirement. The ideal of universal autarky to which he clings is already, perhaps, more an object of nostalgia than a vital element in the cultural repertoire of Athens. A smallholder could in principle support himself by his own labors, and Menander's picture of Cnemo's property and circumstances is in this respect probably a fair one.[44] But Cnemo's vision of general self-reliance seems at best quaint and irrelevant; at worst, it is merely a cover for his irrational hostility toward his fellow citizens.

There is something in the figure of the misanthrope that lends itself to a double representation, both as the antisocial recusant of communal life and as the moral critic of society's vices. In the latter function, the misanthrope readily represents an earlier and passé ideal of natural virtue against which to measure the decline of contemporary life; in the former, his indignation appears reduced to mere boorish ranting. Like Cnemo, both the Timon of Shakespeare's *Timon of Athens* and Alceste in Molière's *Le misanthrope*, for example, have this double aspect. Each, for all the violence of his humor, embodies the values of a traditional and passing way of life and earns a measure of respect and even obeisance from the society he abandons.[45] For the new social forms have about them, it appears, something that is morally lax, fragmented, and disordered, and each society seems to need and to court, in different ways, the authenticity of the misanthrope, for all his absurdity. But the critical force of the misanthrope's denunciations is compromised by his extreme rejection of social life. While Sostratus' and Callipides' behavior conveys a certain upper-class superciliousness, which Sostratus is at pains to disarm, Cnemo's violent spirit must be broken. After his fall in the well, he releases his hold on his daughter and his property. In the slapstick finale, however, when he is forced to join the party in spite of his resistance, the surly misanthrope is ultimately reduced to a ridiculous figure of fun.

7

Shorn Girl

Menander's *Shorn Girl (Perikeiromenē)* is very likely set in Corinth,[1] although one cannot rule out entirely some other location: not necessarily Athens,[2] but perhaps a city near Corinth, where marriage between a male citizen of Corinth and a free woman of the city in which the dramatic action takes place is not absolutely excluded.[3] Certainty is impossible, since the play survives in fragmentary condition and the opening scene is missing. Glycera, the "shorn girl" of the title, has been living as a concubine *(pallakē)* with Polemo, a mercenary soldier. In a house next door (or next door but one)[4] dwells her brother Moschio, who is being raised as the son of Myrrhine and her husband, a prosperous citizen couple. Moschio is ignorant of his foundling status and of his relationship to Glycera.[5] Glycera, however, was raised by the old woman who discovered her brother and her when they were abandoned as infants; this woman passed Glycera off as her own daughter (130–31) when she gave her over into the possession of the soldier.[6] Previous to her death, the old woman informed Glycera that she was a foundling and sister to Moschio, but Glycera kept this information secret in order to spare Moschio the painful knowledge of his true status (147–50), and she continues to do so, later in the play, in deference to the wishes of Myrrhine as well (790–91).[7] Her embrace with Moschio, which was the cause of Polemo's jealous rage in which he cut off her hair (whence the title of the play), probably occurred prior to the events dramatized on stage.[8] Polemo, in consternation, subsequently abandoned his home for the company of friends, where he is staying when the action begins.

107

After the prologue, which follows the opening scene, Glycera arranges to take refuge with Myrrhine. Davus, a slave of Moschio's, pretends that Glycera's move was inspired by an interest she has taken in the young man and boasts that he himself abetted the move by persuading Myrrhine to comply (271–75). Sosia, Polemo's slave, discovers the departure of Glycera (366–67) and confronts Davus threateningly with accusations of kidnapping and adultery (375–77; 370, 390), but Glycera's maid, Doris, explains the real reasons for Glycera's flight, and Sosia, in a lost segment of the play, departs to tell Polemo the news.

When Polemo appears in act 3, his friend Pataecus discourages him from physically attacking Myrrhine's house (the plan advised by Sosia) since he has no legal grounds for such an act of violence. But Glycera, in conversation with Pataecus, refuses to be reconciled with Polemo and begs him to retrieve some precious objects for her (including keepsakes from her real parents) from Polemo's house (742–44). Pataecus recognizes the tokens and discovers that Glycera is his own daughter, whom he had exposed after the death of his wife and the ruin of his fortunes at sea (803–9).[9] In the final act, Polemo, informed of the new state of affairs, returns to the stage, and Pataecus, after congratulating Glycera for agreeing at last to be reconciled (1006), formally betrothes her to Polemo (1013–15), with the warning that he must henceforward moderate his behavior. The surviving text ends with a reference to arrangements for a marriage for Moschio as well.[10]

On the basis of this bare outline, one may perceive an affinity between the plot of *Shorn Girl* and the story forms characteristic of New Comedy in general. Foundlings or otherwise misrecognized individuals discover their true citizen identity by means of an *anagnōrisis* (recognition), as in Terence's *Andria* or Plautus' *Cistellaria*, to take familiar examples based on Menandrean originals.[11] This in turn enables a legitimate union in wedlock, eliminating the obstacle of status that had divided the lovers. The status barrier may be seen as a variety of the formula of separation and reunion that informs every one of Menander's comedies.[12] Reunion and recognition are elegantly managed in *Shorn Girl*, because the separation between Glycera and Polemo is the means by which the birth tokens are produced and thus identified by Pataecus: just as the tension between the lovers appears to be leading to a decisive rupture, with the removal of Glycera's belongings from Polemo's house, those same possessions turn out to be the key to revealing her citizen status and her reconciliation with Polemo is thereby achieved.[13]

Still, the cleverness of the plot does not entirely conceal a certain inconsequentiality, for the breach between Polemo and Glycera was not caused by her want of citizen status, as in comedies in which status is the obstacle that divides the lovers.[14] Polemo has neither the wish nor the need to alter the basis of his association with Glycera. Their separation is rather a result of Polemo's fit of jealousy and his humiliating treatment of Glycera. While the revelation of her true identity explains the nature of her relationship with Moschio, and opens the way to Glycera's marriage with Polemo, it does not, in itself, do anything to heal the rift between them. To be sure, Polemo is terribly contrite, but Glycera is unwilling to pardon him on this account. It is only after, and apparently because of, the lucky accident of her restored status as a citizen that she consents to being reconciled (1006–08, 1023).[15]

The integration of the two strands or complications of the narrative—namely, that of the quarrel between Polemo and Glycera and that of the misapprehension of Glycera's and Moschio's true status (including her relationship to Moschio)—is thus to a certain extent factitious. While Glycera's estrangement from Polemo leads to the discovery of her identity through the exhibition of her birth tokens, that discovery does not resolve the problem that caused the separation in the first place. At the same time, Polemo's grief and regret, which might have been represented as influencing Glycera to be reconciled, fail to move her. Rephrasing the issue in terms of Menander's strategies of composition, the question may be posed: Why did Menander fuse the problem of misrecognized citizen status with the story of a lover's quarrel to which that problem is apparently irrelevant?

Comparing the structure of *Shorn Girl* with another comedy in which the separation between lovers results from the deliberate rejection of one by the other, rather than from circumstances beyond their control, will help put the problem in perspective. In Terence's *Mother-in-Law* (*Hecyra*), based on a Greek original by Apollodorus of Carystus who composed in the generation after Menander, Pamphilus rejects his wife after the early birth of a child proves her to have conceived before their wedding. Pamphilus accepts her again only when it is revealed that it was he himself who had violated her. The revelation of identity, which does not in this case entail an alteration in civic status but which does affect, according to the conventions of New Comedy, the woman's suitability for marriage, directly eliminates the obstacle, as Pamphilus sees it, to the union.[16]

There survive, to be sure, only parts of Menander's *Shorn Girl*, and it is possible that some closer connection between the recognition and Glycera's willingness to pardon Polemo's offense was adumbrated in a lost scene. But it is difficult to see how the main structure of the plot could have been much affected. The basis for the separation remains Polemo's assault on Glycera. Had she forgiven him this, and had the recognition of her identity come, accordingly, after the reconciliation, one might have read their marriage as the symbol and reward of Polemo's repentance and Glycera's generous or loving disposition. But it is clear from the text that the pardon follows the discovery that Glycera is Pataecus' daughter, and this is precisely what makes her gesture seem arbitrary, unless perhaps it is explicable, as Pataecus hints, as a display of truly Greek magnanimity on the part of one who is favored by good fortune (1007–8).

Before undertaking, however, to patch up the unity or consistency of *Shorn Girl* on the basis of Greek conceptions of justice or responsibility, it is best to examine the possible grounds of the tension identified in the plot, apart from judgments based on ideals of aesthetic form; an unsynthesizable duality in a text may be the expression of social or ideological contradictions that resurface, albeit indirectly or symptomatically, in literary representations of social life. To anticipate the conclusion: Glycera's rejection of Polemo after he has insulted her, indeed her very freedom or capacity to reject him, suggests a narrative trajectory that is different from the formula, conventional to New Comedy, based on citizenship and marriage. The convincing dramatization of a proud and independent woman, in this case one who has entered into a permanent relationship with a man as his *pallakē*, disrupts the movement toward the usual closure in a citizen marriage, in which such independence on the part of a citizen girl is foreclosed by Greek social and literary conventions. Menander indeed subjects the autonomy of the courtesan to the conditions of a respectable citizen marriage, but in so doing he has exposed a tension in the Athenian construction of women's roles that leaves its mark on the structure of his narrative.

To begin with, there is an apparent confusion in the description of Polemo's relation to Glycera. The relationship is, of course, concubinage, but it is at times spoken of as a proper marriage, and Polemo, for his part, openly insists at one point that he takes it to be such.[17] Thus, shortly after the prologue, when Doris complains that the woman is unfortunate who takes a professional soldier as her man (*andra*, 186), it is reasonable, as Gomme suggested, to understand the word "man" in its common meaning of "husband."[18] Sandbach remarks on the absence both of any special ceremonies to validate marriages and of their registration in a public record. Polemo's and Glycera's "marriage" would of course be invalid in the sense that any children issuing from the union would not have the rights of citizens, but there were no particular formal requirements or practices to mark a difference between validly married couples and those living together on a permanent basis but without the possibility of transmitting citizen privileges to their offspring.[19]

The same attitude characterizes Sosia's conception of Moschio as a *moikhos* (adulterer, 357, 370, 390). When he learns that Glycera has moved into the house of Myrrhine, he accuses Davus and his master (the verbs at 375–77 are plural) of forcibly detaining a free woman against the will of her *kurios*, or legal guardian. Sandbach inquires: "Was the 'husband' of a *pallakē* in fact her *kurios*?" There is no evidence that he was, as Sandbach observes.[20] The point is that Sosia, in part no doubt to magnify the enormity of Davus' and Moschio's behavior, as he understands it, in part also because he shares his master's conception of Polemo's relation to Glycera, speaks of Glycera as though she were a legal wife. It is doubtless as "wife" that we must understand "woman" (*gunaika*) in verse 376.[21] The same idea informs Sosia's subsequent effort to intimidate Davus with the prospect of legal action, for it is with a view to the courts that Sosia demands a confession from Daos that he and Moschio are actually in possession of the girl ("You admit—tell me—that you have her?" 383–84, repeated, with mention of a witness, in 385). It is only after he has established the justice of his position— again, according to his understanding of the case—that Sosia threatens to attack Moschio's house physically.[22] In response to Davus' abuse, Sosia indignantly reminds him that they are living in a city (*polis*, 394), where laws, he implies, obtain. Here Davus appears momentarily disconcerted: at all events, he declares that they do not have the girl (395), which, if it is not an outright evasion, perhaps looks to the fact that she voluntarily moved in with Myrrhine, and so she is neither being held against her will, nor is she, strictly, in the possession of Moschio. With this, Davus withdraws.

Returning with Polemo in act 3, Sosia is eager for battle, but is dismissed by Pataecus (480), who counsels Polemo that he has no case. Pataecus acknowledges that the situation would be different if Glycera were Polemo's lawful wife (*gametēn gunaika*, 487), as Polemo and his household enjoy pretending (cf. 486).[23] Polemo objects that he for his part considers Glycera his wedded wife (489; *egō* is emphatic), to which Pataecus logically replies: "Who, then, is it who gave her to you?" (490). "Who?" exclaims Polemo; "She herself." "Great," says Pataecus; "She liked you then, no doubt; now she does not" (490–91).[24] The point is: if Glycera was free to give herself to Polemo, she is free to break the tie when it no longer pleases her. At no time was she bound in a legal marriage, which would have required that a proper guardian (*kurios*) had authorized the union. An informal, or self-arranged, relation, such as Polemo had enjoyed with Glycera, depends on sentiment, not law or custom.[25] Since Polemo had, as Pataecus said, mistreated Glycera, she is free to withdraw from the liaison.

Polemo, who is slow to appreciate his powerlessness, momentarily seeks to dodge the issue by pretending innocence, alleging that Pataecus' charge of ill treatment has wounded him beyond all else (493–94). Pataecus is not, however, distracted from the problem at hand: what Polemo is doing now is mad (496). He has nowhere to turn, for Glycera is her own mistress (*heautēs est' ekeinē kuria*, 497). If he still loves her, all that is left for Polemo to try is persuasion.

It is worth pausing here to consider the implications of Pataecus' argument. In describing Glycera as mistress of herself, he does not mean to suggest that she has the legal rights or status that pertain to an Athenian.[26] As Gomme and Sandbach remark, "she would be completely without standing in a court of law, since she had no man to represent her." There is no question here of her having given herself to Polemo with full legal authority, which would have meant, among other things (and *per impossibile*), that she would have been able to transfer power over herself to Polemo, who, as her husband, would have become her *kurios*.[27] Pataecus' expression, striking as it is, means simply that Glycera is independent, without a *kurios* at all.[28] It is precisely this independence that makes Polemo's treatment of her the decisive issue in their association.[29]

This is the sense in which Glycera may be said to be free (cf. *eleutheran*, 375). It is not that she has the free status of a citizen, as Sosia had implied;[30] that is a freedom which, for a woman, depends on the authority of another (cf. 376). Glycera's freedom is rather the reverse of this status-dependent type: it is the capacity to act independently and without obstacle—a freedom she lacks, for example, in respect to her brother, toward whom it was not possible for her to behave freely (*eleutherōs poiein*, 161) as long as she was obliged to keep her relation with him secret. Menander has portrayed Glycera's independence precisely in contrast with the free status that legal marriage would have represented, under which Polemo would have had the right at law to claim Glycera back from a neighbor who had given her refuge. To leave Polemo, as Gomme and Sandbach observe, "against his will, she would have had to be transferred to the guardianship of a male relative with the knowledge of the archon basileus [an Athenian official]."[31] Glycera's ability to leave Polemo explodes his pretensions to a legal marriage. That he had construed his relationship with her in such a manner contributes to the tension and pathos of the scene, no doubt, but, more than that, it structures the opposition between Glycera's personal independence as a *pallakē* and the dependent condition of a legally wedded Athenian woman.

Polemo, in the scene we have been examining, ventures a last legal gambit, pretending that Moschio has wronged him insofar as he has corrupted Glycera (498–99). Pataecus replies that Polemo is in a position to lodge a complaint concerning Moschio's conduct, but that he will certainly lose his case if he tries force, for the offense in question does not allow for private revenge (*timōrian*, 503), as adultery would, but only for complaint (*enkalēma*)—presumably, an informal complaint, since, as Gomme and Sandbach note, "no form of action for enticing away a *pallakē* is known, and it is improbable that any existed at Athens."[32]

Polemo, at last convinced of his helplessness, is desperate to the point of contemplating suicide. Sosia's earlier description of the intensity of Polemo's suffering (172–74) is visibly confirmed, and one may suppose that it aroused the sympathy of the audience, as it did Sosia's (356–60).[33] The sincerity of Polemo's regret, and of his love for Glycera, is not in doubt. It is, rather, represented as being so profound as to induce the expectation that he may be forgiven when Pataecus, at his earnest request, agrees to intercede for him with Glycera (506–13). We are informed that Pataecus knows her well (508) and can therefore speak freely with her. What is more, Polemo concedes his error (514) and promises to behave honorably in the future (515). Finally, the contrast between Polemo's humility and Moschio's fatuous and triumphant air when he comes on the scene, preening as though Polemo had departed in fear of him (526–29), may also have disposed the audience to empathize with the genuine emotion of Polemo.[34]

If any such expectations were nourished in this scene, or in what followed it in the original play, they are disappointed when Glycera herself appears in the fourth act. The papyrus resumes in the middle of her speech to Pataecus, after his attempt to mediate the quarrel in behalf of Polemo. Glycera begins—rather, the surviving text begins—with an indignant dismissal of the idea that she might have sought a liaison with Moschio.[35] She remains, however, absolutely firm in her rejection of Polemo. The text is very poorly preserved here, but Glycera clearly lets it be understood that she will not submit to Polemo's *hubris* (assault or violent conduct, 723), and that she regards his behavior as having been impious (724). To Pataecus' appeal for a more all-sided view of the case, Glycera replies that she best knows her own concerns (749; again, *egō* is emphatic), and she persists in demanding the return of her personal effects from Polemo's house. A last effort by Pataecus to implore her reconsideration falls on deaf ears (752–53), and her possessions, including, of course, the birth tokens, are brought forth, to be recognized, in due course, by Pataecus (824). Moschio discovers that he is Glycera's brother and Pataecus' son, and here again the papyrus is interrupted.

Although the focus of the scene shifts from the matter of reconciliation between Polemo and Glycera to that of the recognition of her
identity, Glycera's imperviousness to Pataecus' appeals in Polemo's
behalf seems well established. Her firmness looks like the mark of her
strong character and deep sense of injury.[36] Gomme and Sandbach comment on the scene in which she first appears: "Many modern writers
testify to the vivid impression made by Glykera," and they add: "it is
remarkable that it rests mainly on the following 18 mutilated lines."
Indeed, in these few lines (though she will have more to say in the course
of the recognition scene itself), one may agree with the judgment of
Gomme and Sandbach that "her indignation at being misjudged and still
more at the treatment received from Polemon, which she regards as
unforgiveable, are excellently portrayed."[37] Nevertheless, such a course
will prevent the happy conclusion of the comedy unless some means
are found to circumvent it. Sympathy for Polemo may dispose an audience favorably toward a final resolution of the quarrel, but that resolution will not be a function of Glycera's personal magnanimity or gracious-
ness. Her independence requires that she not compromise on the insult
she has suffered, and she is accordingly immune to sentimentality.

In the final act, Polemo, having learned of Glycera's and Moschio's
new situation, is overcome with shame and remorse, and at Doris' advice prepares a sacrifice in honor of Glycera's good luck, the better to
impress her and Pataecus with his honest intentions.[38] Pataecus emerges
from the house commending Glycera for her willingness to be reconciled, the more so in that she shows a generosity which is the sign, he
says, of the true Greek character (1006–8).[39] Pataecus proceeds with
startling suddenness to pronounce the regular formula for giving a
daughter in marriage and to stipulate the size of the dowry (1013–15),
which Polemo accepts with alacrity. Pataecus adds that Polemo's irrational behavior was the source or cause of a good outcome, and that it
is on this account that he has received pardon (1023).

Precisely why forgiveness should follow on the lucky event has been
discussed by scholars who have sought to explain, by reference to the
theories of Aristotle or other Greek notions, the logic of Glycera's
change of heart. William Fortenbaugh explains it best: "Forgiveness is
justified solely on the grounds that Polemon's act has been a source of
blessings. This justification is to be taken at face value. The blessings
resulting from Polemon's act simply nullify any possible moral indignation Glykera may have felt and at the same time remove from the
spectator any serious concern with fine distinctions between misfortunes, errors, and injustices."[40] To Fortenbaugh's analysis I would add
only that Menander's decision to neglect Aristotelian or other grounds

of forgiveness in favor of, as Fortenbaugh calls it, a "carefree pardon" indicates his indifference to overcoming the division between Glycera and Polemo on grounds pertinent to their quarrel, whether the grounds be sentimental or philosophical. While such a resolution was available to Menander, he did not elect to adopt it.

In the last scene of the play as it exists, there is, as Gomme and Sandbach have convincingly demonstrated and contrary to the opinions of most previous editors, no speaking part for Glycera.[41] Gomme and Sandbach argue first of all that such a part would require, uniquely in the surviving drama of Menander, a fourth actor for its performance. They support the plausibility of their view, which requires that they ignore the assignment of parts by a second hand in the margins of the papyrus, with an appeal to dramatic considerations as well: "It is conceivable that [Glycera] kept a modest silence and, like a respectable Greek girl, let her father speak for her. That he was not misrepresenting her sentiments would be known from 1006."[42] It is of course conventional in New Comedy that Athenian citizen maidens speak publicly, if at all, only under exceptional conditions: an example is Cnemo's daughter in *Grouch*, whose appearance alone in public, where she is engaged in conversation by a strange man, is regarded by her half-brother as a scandalous testimony to the laxity occasioned by her father's selfish ways.[43] What is striking about Glycera's silence in the conclusion to *Shorn Girl* is the contrast with the forthright speech and sure sense of her own interests and capabilities that had been hers till now. Her deferential silence, if indeed she maintained it throughout the final act of the play, appears as the sign of her new citizen status and the marriage that it brings. The role of Athenian wife thus deprives her of the very traits that have, as Gomme and Sandbach remarked, made "a vivid impression" upon modern readers and critics of the play. As Nicole Loraux writes of the marriage of Athenian women generally: "Once they have crossed the threshold of marriage, the husband becomes the provider and the wife earns the right to be quiet."[44] Glycera's change in status, imposing as it does a silence that is the sign of dutiful obedience, cancels the independence she had enjoyed as a concubine.

Certainly, the marriage to which Glycera consents (1006), and her father entrusts her, is one in which Polemo will have learned, and learned well, the lesson of his jealous rage. He magnanimously refuses to blame Glycera for her actions (1019–20, as restored) and implores her only to be reconciled. This will be a marriage with a history, and one may imagine, if one wishes, that this history will abide as a reminder of Glycera's dignity and her resentment of unjustified abuse.[45] Pataecus' admonition to Polemo on this score underlines the message, and Polemo's contrition will presumably have taught him self-control. Fortenbaugh, noting that such a change of character is not Aristotelian, remarks: "We are not meant to scrutinize Pataikos' injunction in terms of a consistent theory of human personality."[46]

Nevertheless, it is Pataecus, the father, who extracts Polemo's promise of good conduct and Pataecus who issues the warning. This is natural, insofar as, henceforward, it will fall to Pataecus to receive Glycera back under his authority or *kurieia* in the event that further troubles should threaten the marriage. For Glycera is no longer *heautēs kuria* (her own mistress), and she cannot act, or speak, in her own right and with her former freedom.[47]

Shorn Girl in its present state gives no evidence for any constraint on Glycera's decision to accept Polemo, but by the conventions of New Comedy, at least, Glycera had no choice but to marry him, once her citizenship was established, if, at all events, she was ever to marry at all. For the genre had it that a young woman must either be a virgin upon marriage, or else have known carnally only the man who will be her husband. To this rule there appear to be no exceptions, although citizen women who had been sexually violated could contemplate concealing the offense and entering wedlock.[48] Since citizen girls in New Comedy are expected to marry, the discovery of Glycera's true identity entails, under the circumstances of the play, that she will wed Polemo. Thus, the two themes or strands of the comedy—the recognition of Glycera's identity and the resolution of her quarrel with Polemo—need to be connected by no stronger tie of logic or necessity than that Glycera's good fortune in the matter of her birth inspire in turn a sentiment of good will toward a relationship with Polemo.

The tacit assumption of a connection between citizenship and marriage, manifested in the postponement of the reconciliation with Polemo until the question of Glycera's status has been resolved, may also be read as the sign of an elision in the play, which passes over in silence the problem of Glycera's submission to her new role as wife and citizen, sans voice and sans autonomy. Having granted it to Glycera to say that she knew best her own interests or concerns (749), Menander reduces her to the silent dependency of an Athenian wife by the commonplace device of a recognition, without further explanation of her change of heart or her adaptability to her new role. The peculiarity remains that, whereas in other comedies in the genre the recognition is the means of overcoming a status barrier to the relationship between lovers, here it contributes only incidentally to the resolution of Glycera's anger, and to her personal consent to a reconciliation with Polemo.[49]

While the focus of *Shorn Girl* is on the status of Glycera and its implications for the representation of her autonomy, there is also the suggestion of a more general transformation of roles mediated by the plot, in such a way that all the figures who stand in a more or less marginal relation to the city-state society are subsumed or normalized within it. The classical Athenian conception of the marriage transaction involves three parties: a man who gives the bride in marriage, a man who receives her, and the bride herself. The giver, whether he is the father, brother, or a close male relative of the bride, is her *kurios;* the receiver, upon utterance of the performative connubial formula, and conveyance of the woman to his own house, becomes her *kurios.* The woman is without *kurieia* or authority over anything in this exhange, including herself. In the initial conditions, so to speak, of *Shorn Girl,* the signs indicating the presence or absence of *kurieia* among the three parties appear to be reversed: Glycera is mistress of herself; Polemo, although he lives with her as her husband, is without authority over her; and there is no man to give Glycera in marriage—neither her father nor her brother is in a position to assume the responsibility of *kurieia* in respect to her. The effect of the recognition scene will be to restore the proper values to each member of the triad. Pataecus assumes his role as father, with the power to bestow his daughter in marriage; Polemo will assume the role of husband, with *kurieia* over Glycera; and Glycera is correspondingly deprived of authority over herself. The social normalization of Glycera's role, considered within the context of the city-state ideology, is part of a transformation involving all three agents in the marriage exchange.

What is more, each of the agents at the beginning of the play, when the normal signs of authority are inverted, is marked by a function that is in some sense beyond or outside the conventional ideal of the household-based society of the ancient city-state. In the case of Glycera, the mark is her apparent noncitizen status, combined with her role as concubine, which prevents her from entering into the system of social reproduction defined by the household. Polemo, for his part, is marked as a mercenary soldier, who operates not in the citizen army of his own community but as a hired officer in the service of foreign powers. Whether or not he was in fact a citizen of the city in which the dramatic action of *Shorn Girl* was located, his connection with the local society is volatile. Thus, he is bidden to forget he is a soldier (1016) as the condition for entering into the civic relation of marriage.

Finally, Pataecus is normalized as a father and head of household, securing his line and the bonds of kinship between households by engaging both his children in marriage. T.B.L. Webster has observed that "Menander apparently disapproved of wealthy bachelors," citing Micio in Terence's *Brothers* and Megadorus in Plautus' *Aulularia* along with Pataecus of *Shorn Girl*.[50] There may, however, be another respect in which Pataecus is reincorporated into the closed world of the city-state, as it is idealized in New Comedy. Pataecus, as we have seen, exposed his children when he lost his fortunes at sea (808–9). Consider, in this connection, the following remarks by Sally Humphreys on the nature of the classical Athenian economy:

> The *oikos* [household] tradition of economic activity was one of care-ful supervision and management, self-sufficiency, production for pri-vate consumption, mortgaging land if necessary to raise money for liturgies [i.e., public benefactions], for loans to friends or for family expenses such as dowries and funerals. . . . But interaction between the market and the *oikos* as a production unit was always impeded by the reluctance of *oikos*-heads to involve themselves in market transactions. . . . Land and slaves belonged to the *ousia*—"being," the identity of the *oikos*. Money and goods exchanged in the market were *chremata*—"things," transitory possessions. Transactions in the *oikos* sphere were part of a lasting pattern of social relationships—kinship, affinity, friendship. Market transactions were contractual and ephem-eral. . . . Citizens should maintain their political integrity and their status difference [from metics or slaves] by keeping to the traditional pattern of the landed *oikos*.[51]

There is no evidence in our text of *Shorn Girl* that Pataecus' current income is derived from land rather than from the kind of mercantile investments that had cost him his fortune at the time when his chil-dren were born.[52] But perhaps Pataecus' earlier involvement with the high-risk economy of foreign trade serves as a sign of his problematic relation to the city-state society, in the way that Glycera and Polemo are marked by their roles as concubine and mercenary soldier.[53]

The reassertion of communal roles for all the principals in the drama affirms the solidarity of the civic group. By uniting the concubine and former soldier in marriage, the play abolishes the obstacles of status in much the way that the marriages at the end of *Grouch* collapse distinc-tions of wealth within the city. With the shift in identities comes a transformation in character, in accord with which the self-reliant Glycera becomes a silently obedient wife while the volatile soldier promises to be a kind and dutiful husband. The personae in *Shorn Girl* are thus sequentially overdetermined in their motivations and social positions: the incompatible traits are distributed over separate moments in the action. As the agents are metamorphosed from one position to another, their natures are adjusted accordingly. But the problem of soldier's rage and Glycera's indignation is thereby left hanging, and the displacement of their quarrel through the discovery of Glycera's identity finesses the matter of the quality of social relations at the margins of the civic community. Polemo may have been convinced that Glycera was a legitimate wife to him even before the revelation of her citizen status, but no stable and approved relationship turns out to be available to the couple until Glycera's civic position is restored. Polemo's jealous anger and Glycera's desertion of his house discredit their bond and open the way to a resolution predicated on a citizen marriage. But the complex plot bears traces of alternative solutions and possibilities that have been suppressed by the ideological labor of the text.

8

Self-Tormentor

In New Comedy, a bride is presumed to be a virgin at the time of marriage (or, more accurately, at the time of her first marriage); if she has been violated, it is by the man who is destined to become her husband. A courtesan, on the contrary, has relations with several men, and this renders her ineligible as a conjugal partner.[1] For the courtesan, moreover, love is a business, and whatever the romantic feelings that may occasionally be attributed to her, her relationships with men are in the first instance commercial. This is the basis for the common characterization of the hetaera as greedy.[2] Marriage stands outside such mercantile transactions. Far from being acquisitive, the marriageable woman seems almost to be devoid of motives altogether. She is the object of another's desire, and it is she who is transferred from one party to another in the conjugal transaction. The courtesan engages as an agent in the sphere of economic circulation, selling the use of herself to a purchaser, while the bride is passively given, along with a dowry, by her father or nearest male relative to the authority of her husband.[3]

In addition to the contrast between the passive, virginal bride and the experienced, mercenary courtesan, New Comedy also installs a status difference between the two roles. Women eligible to become wives of Athenian citizens are of the citizen order, as they had to be after the legislation sponsored by Pericles in 451 B.C., while courtesans are represented as foreign, perhaps as resident aliens.[4] A citizen woman might presumably have adopted the career of courtesan, but in New Comedy they do not: such an occupation would render her unmarriageable, and place her effectively outside the citizen com-

120

munity, which is constituted by access to the network of conjugal relations.[5]

Professional courtesans are thus represented as both personally and socially ineligible for marriage with a citizen. Their occupation is an index of their status, and both simultaneously remove them from the sphere of connubial exchange. Contrariwise, marriageable women are doubly determined both as citizens and as virgins (apart from the case of women who marry the man who has violated them, and of widows). To put it simply: in New Comedy, citizenship implies chastity in a young woman, while multiple sexual experience entails noncitizen status.

Within this opposition between courtesan and wife, the figure of the concubine occupies an intermediate position and is particularly available to a complex and overdetermined representation. In contrast to marriageable women, the concubine is imagined as a noncitizen, ineligible for conjugal union with an Athenian. However, the relationship between a concubine and her partner is not conventionally treated as a commercial affair. Hers is a long-term attachment, and the material rewards she derives from the association, such as shelter, clothes, or jewelry, are not conceived of as profit on a business venture, any more than are they in the case of legitimate marriage.[6] Like a wife, the concubine too takes part in a household, where the transfer of resources assumes the symbolic form of sharing rather than payment, as opposed to the purely profit-oriented association characteristic of the courtesan. Eva Cantarella remarks that, despite the tripartition of women's roles that finds expression in the speech *Against Neaera* (attributed to Demosthenes), "in ordinary practice a relationship with a *pallakē* . . . was essentially the same as one with a wife," which may often have been the case, apart from the matter of her status.[7]

In New Comedy, then, the concubine is associated with the hetaera by the foreclosure of any possibility of marriage, on the basis of her civic status; and she is associated with the wife in her participation in a household, represented as a unique association free of mercenary motives. Where the deficiency in status is insuperable, the concubine has no hope of becoming a wife. An example is Menander's *Samian Woman* (*Samia*). The plot turns on a misapprehension on the part of Demea, who learns upon his return from a trip abroad that his concubine, Chrysis, is nursing a baby,[8] which he naturally supposes to be his own. It is in fact the child of Demea's adopted son, Moschio, and Plango, a neighbor's daughter whom Moschio had raped during the festival of the Adonia. Chrysis had generously agreed to conceal the affair by pretending that Moschio's child was hers.

Demea's initial reaction is indignation that Chrysis should put herself in the position of a wife by presuming to introduce a child into his household: "I did not realize," he says, "that I had a properly married courtesan" (*gametēn hetairan*, 130). Because Chrysis is not a citizen, she cannot produce a legitimate heir as opposed to a *nothos* (bastard, 136), that is, a child without a citizen's rights of inheritance.[9] Later, Demea discovers that the child is actually Moschio's, and, still thinking that Chrysis is the mother, decides to expel her from his home (352–54): "In the city you'll see," he tells her, "exactly who you are," hustling ten-drachma handouts at drunken parties (390–97).

Of course, Chrysis has in fact been faithful to Demea, and will, when the truth is out, again be received into his house. But her status as a Samian, rather than Athenian, means that she can never assume the position of wife, and her previous career as courtesan forecloses that possibility as well. For his part, Demea, a man of mature years who has an adult son and heir, has no need to take a legitimate wife. Both his situation and hers are conformable to a relationship of concubinage.

If, however, a young and inexperienced woman is associated as concubine with a man who does not have children of his own, nothing but a fault of citizenship prevents the conversion of her position to that of wife. This is a barrier that New Comedy is preeminently equipped to eliminate by means of its favored device, the *anagnōrisis* (recognition). In plays of this type, which include Menander's *Shorn Girl*, there is commonly a sharp contrast between the concubine and the professional hetaera; since the concubine will ultimately be revealed as a citizen, her behavior must not be incompatible with the station of a legitimately married woman.[10]

The plot of Terence's *Self-Tormenter* (*Heautontimorumenos*), based on a Menandrean original, reflects symptomatically the tensions in the ideological construction of the roles of courtesan, concubine, and wife. Menedemus has taken to hard labor on his country estate in Attica as a way of atoning for his strictness with his son over an affair with a Corinthian girl, which has caused the boy to depart for Asia as a mercenary soldier. The fact is that, unbeknownst to his father, Clinia has already returned to Athens at the beginning of the dramatic action, and has moved in with his friend Clitipho, the son of Menedemus' officious neighbor Chremes. Chremes, in conversation with his son, decides not to reveal to him Menedemus' change of heart, on the grounds that some fear in the boy may still be useful in amending his behavior; instead, he lectures Clitipho on the foolishness of young men who complain about obstacles to a trivial passion and cannot appreciate their good fortune in all other respects (199–210). Chremes does not know, however, that Clitipho is himself in love with a courtesan, in this case a full-blown professional type whose only demands are "Give me!" and "Bring me!" (223). In a monologue, Clitipho contrasts his case with that of Clinia, whose girlfriend is "decently brought up, and innocent of the courtesan's arts" (226). Clinia then enters muttering worriedly that his Antiphila may have been corrupted while he was away and will not have been faithful to him. Her mother, he fears, may have pressured her to adopt the courtesan's trade in order to accumulate wealth (230–34). At this point, the slaves whom Clinia and Clitipho had sent to fetch Antiphila (191) return, commenting in wonder on the crowd of slave girls, the heaps of gold and clothing that are bringing up the rear.[11]

Clinia at once concludes that his worst fears about Antiphila have proved true (256). His father was right, he concedes, when he expatiated on the morals of these women (*harum mores*, 260). Clinia readily includes Antiphila in the same class as courtesans in general. She had differed only in that she was still at the beginning of her career; in her first affair, her motives might still be pure.[12] Clinia's doubts are cut short by the intervention of the slave Syrus, who perceives Clinia's mistake and assures him that Antiphila has maintained the same way of life and the same feelings toward him (265). Syrus explains also that the old woman who was said to be her mother is dead (270). The knowing spectator will recognize the cue in "said to be": Antiphila will prove to be of citizen status. The maid, gold, and vestments that Syrus has in train turn out to be the property of Bacchis, Clitipho's courtesan, who is approaching along with Antiphila.[13] Syrus plans to pass Bacchis off as Clinia's girl (332–33) and give Antiphila over to the care of Clitipho's mother. At this point, Bacchis and Antiphila enter, deep in conversation.

Bacchis, rather surprisingly, is discoursing on the good fortune of women such as Antiphila: "I really admire you," she says, "and think you are lucky, in that you have taken care to have your character conform to your good looks. No wonder, bless me, that everyone wants you for his own" (381–83). Bacchis explains that women like herself must rely exclusively on their beauty, and are obliged to store up wealth against the day when it will fade. "For your kind [*vobis*], however, once you've decided to spend your life with one man [*viro*], whose character is just like your own, they attach themselves to you, and thanks to this you are each truly bound to the other so that no misfortune can ever befall your love." To this, Antiphila modestly answers: "I don't know about the rest; I do know that I, at least, have always made sure that my interests depended on his" (392–97).

This is all very sweet and edifying, but just what relation between

Antiphila and Clinia is being imagined here? Who are the women like
Antiphila, praised and envied by Bacchis? Not citizen brides, surely,
though one might be forgiven for thinking so, and translating *viro* as
"husband" rather than as "man."[14] The permanent, secure bond between man and woman envisaged by Bacchis certainly suggests wedlock. But the dialogue does not square with the picture of a citizen bride,
at least as the role is represented in New Comedy. Citizen girls depend
on a male *kurios* to arrange a marriage for them. Beautiful they may be,
but their good comportment is merely taken for granted, a product of
their secluded life and careful rearing, not of some special grace or effort of their own. Antiphila, on the contrary, is perceived by Bacchis as
a girl to whom another way of life might have been available, but who
has freely chosen virtue and fidelity to one man. Her reply suggests the
same: no mention of any male figure of authority, only her own resolve
to join her interests with those of Clinia. She has counted on this to
win and hold him, and it does. A moment later, when she catches sight
of Clinia, she nearly faints with emotion (403–5). It is her own feelings,
nothing else, that govern her commitment to her lover.[15]

It is not just the personal independence of Antiphila that marks her
off from the image of a citizen wife. She is also a Corinthian, to all appearances (96). Marriage between her and an Athenian is out of the
question, even if Clinia adores her to such an extent that he more or
less thinks of her as a wife, as Menedemus puts it (*prope iam ut pro
uxore haberet*, 98).[16] Just what is the lasting union to which Bacchis
has been referring, then? The only possible arrangement is concubinage,
and while the example of *Samia* indicates that a long-term partnership
of this sort is within the conventional repertoire of New Comedy, it
seems to have been a form specific to a mature couple, for the reasons
that have been set forth above. Surely at some point Clinia must have
been expected to produce legitimate heirs, which he cannot have done
with a Corinthian.

There is thus an air of unreality about Bacchis' speech. Whatever
the hopes that women in Antiphila's position might have entertained
about their future, and about the undying loyalty promised by their
lovers (Selenium in *Cistellaria* is a case in point), surely an experienced
hetaera like Bacchis would not be under the illusion that a course such
as Antiphila's was in general a practical route to a stable and secure
relationship. Yet Bacchis speaks not of Antiphila's unique good fortune
in finding one such as Clinia, but of the whole class of women who,
like her, prepare themselves for an enduring love through a strict practice of virtue (cf. *omnium vostrarum*, 366; *vos*, 387; *vobis* vs. *nos*, 388;
vobis, 392; *vostrum, vos*, 393; *utrique*, 394; *vostro*, 395). There can

hardly have been, in reality or on the stage, such a category of novice concubines, grooming themselves for a happy life among the world of Athenian citizens.

Reasoning along entirely different lines, A. J. Brothers has argued that the scene with Bacchis and Antiphila, and also a later scene involving Bacchis alone, were added to the Menandrean original of *Self-Tormentor* by Terence, whether freely composed or lifted from some other Greek comedy.[17] Brothers's arguments are congenial: Bacchis, the calculating courtesan, is not the woman to deliver a moralizing lecture on the advantages of Antiphila's position, who is still the concubine she was at the beginning of the play. Antiphila's naive confidence in Clinia and his intense passion for her remain the sole basis of their relation. The confused and confusing conception that Bacchis entertains of the contrast between her own condition and that of Antiphila, whom she seems to regard more as wife than concubine, looks like the work of the Roman dramatist, writing for an audience that would not be so conscious as Menander's would of the absolute status barrier between an Athenian and a Corinthian. For Terence, the mutual love between Clinia and Antiphila, together with her constancy and simplicity of life, may have been enough to motivate an extreme opposition between Antiphila and the professional courtesan, in which virtue is rewarded with a happy and lasting union, irrespective of the problem of citizenship, while women who sell their favors for profit are doomed to a lonely old age. But if the apparent assimilation of concubine to the position of legitimate wife betrays the hand of the Roman poet (without the Greek text, absolute certainty is impossible), Terence was nevertheless, as I shall argue, faithful to the spirit of Menander's original *Self-Tormentor*.

It will be recalled that Chremes, the father of Clitipho, has refrained from revealing to his son Menedemus' change of heart concerning Clinia's affair with Antiphila. The following morning, convinced that Bacchis really is Clinia's girlfriend, Chremes informs Menedemus of his son's return. Menedemus is eager to forgive all, but Chremes urges him not to go to the opposite extreme. Formerly, he points out, Menedemus drove his son to the point of leaving home rather than overlook his visits to a certain little lady (*mulierculam*, 444) who was at that time happy with anything she received. Now, thanks to Clinia's behavior, she has turned professional, as Chremes supposes, and demands enough to ruin a satrap, much less Menedemus. Here again one may note the light in which an Athenian naturally views a woman of Antiphila's station. Chremes offers some details of the previous night's festivities, but Menedemus replies: "Let her do whatever she pleases, take, consume, destroy, I'm determined to endure it if only I can have him back"

(464–66). Given what is known of Antiphila, and the extreme difference between her character and that of Bacchis, Menedemus' attitude here seems not so much indulgent as thoroughly irresponsible, and Chremes wisely warns him at least to make a show of paternal authority. If the boy must have money, let him think he has tricked his father out of it rather than live utterly without a sense of restraint. Menedemus sees the sense in this, and agrees (490, 495–97, 507).

It is easy to feel superior to Chremes here. He is a trifle pompous and sententiously advises his neighbor, unaware that it is his own son who is enamored of the high-priced courtesan. But, given the facts as both Chremes and Menedemus perceive them, Chremes is absolutely right, and Menedemus knows it. Antiphila was one thing; Bacchis is quite another. The one affair was an affordable indiscretion, but a courtesan like Bacchis spells sheer calamity. To Chremes' way of thinking, and also to Menedemus', the contrast between the two reduces pretty much to cost. The inexperienced young woman comes cheaper than the services of the hardened professional. For the audience, however—which is aware of the intensity of feeling between Clinia and Antiphila, and the profound integrity of her character—the distinction drawn by Chremes goes further. Menedemus seems wrong to have opposed his son's affair, not simply because it was still financially manageable, but because it was different in kind from the relation between a youth and a courtesan, as illustrated by Clitipho's infatuation. In the case of a woman like Bacchis, it is right and necessary to dissolve the attachment by whatever means possible, but the evident contrast between such a relation and that between Clinia and Antiphila—brought out most vividly in the scene inserted by Terence, if one is right in attributing it to him—allows one to disapprove of Menedemus' earlier strictness on quite different grounds. It was not simply that he had overreacted to a lesser danger, as Chremes puts it. Rather, he had been severe with his son when, as it must now seem, there was no danger at all, over an affair that was decent and deserving of a lasting commitment, as Bacchis herself affirms. Menedemus is unarguably foolish to welcome Bacchis into his house, but Antiphila appears to be another matter altogether.

If our sympathies for Antiphila extend this far, then we, too, like Bacchis in her curious and rather poignant speech, are neglecting the social barrier that consigns Antiphila forever to the position of concubine: that is, we are implicitly allowing a sense of her virtue to cancel the deficiency in her status. If Menedemus' new leniency toward his son looks like approval for a real and enduring bond, not with a Bacchis, to be sure, but with a woman as good and loyal as Antiphila, then it poses a challenge to the status rules by which the citizen community of the Athenian city-state was defined.

When Chremes discovers how he has been hoodwinked, he is beside himself with rage. Menedemus reminds him of his own unfortunate example (919–20), but Chremes is not mollified: "If I continue to meet her expenses, Menedemus," he says, "my situation will really be back to the hoe" (931).[18] Chremes evidently means to contrast the genuine necessity of hard labor that he foresees for himself with Menedemus' self-imposed punishment of toiling in his own fields. He is quite right that his estate cannot bear the costs of a hetaera such as Bacchis, and his case is clearly different from that which Menedemus faced earlier when he stubbornly opposed Clinia's liaison with Antiphila. It is again easy to laugh at Chremes here as a man ready with advice for others but blind to his own faults, but there is nothing to suggest that Chremes should or could support a courtesan in his house. Chremes quickly and cleverly devises a way out of the difficulty. He will pretend to offer his entire estate as dowry for Antiphila (940–42), who has been revealed as his own daughter, in order to bring Clitipho to his senses. It is a perfect object lesson, and Chremes' success in beating the younger generation at its own game is a turn everyone must have enjoyed—all the more so inasmuch as he is terminating an intolerable association for the good of all concerned. Clitipho is humbled, and Chremes finally relents (though he may have been just acting all along; cf. *simulato*, 943),[19] on the condition that Clitipho take a wife (1056, 1059).

The denouement has been discussed at some length, because it is important to assess Chremes' role correctly. If we simply judge him to have gone from one extreme to the other, and to have behaved just like Menedemus the moment the problem strikes home, we shall miss the crucial difference in the nature of Clinia's association with Antiphila, and in Clitipho's with Bacchis, as they have been represented throughout the play and above all in the dialogue between Bacchis and Antiphila that may be the work of Terence. The fact is that Chremes has not shifted ground at all. He is undoubtedly something of a meddler, but his advice to Menedemus is consistently sound. He counsels a middle course: one may wink at an affair with an innocent foreigner, but entertaining an expensive courtesan is another matter entirely. On this latter score, he again takes his own advice, not in a spirit of dumb obstinacy, but with a clever stratagem that weans his son from his folly by demonstrating what it means to squander one's fortune. Everyone, including Clitipho, concedes that he is right.

This interpretation of Chremes' role, which is closely connected with the distinction between the situation of the hetaera and that of the young concubine in this play and in Menandrean comedy generally, runs counter to the view of Chremes that largely prevails in current scholarship. Dante Nardo, for example, writes:

> Chremes is the only character to emerge from the play completely and irremediably defeated: as father, as husband, as *sapiens*. Thus his every word—beginning precisely with *homo sum*—and, in general, everything that bears upon his character and his personal "philosophy," his *ars vivendi*, must be interpreted in the light of this resounding failure, toward which the old man proceeds the more shamelessly as the net that he himself has cast entangles him; and his failure paradoxically proclaims the "inhumanity" of this self-declared "human being."[20]

There is no need to resurrect the view, which goes back to Cicero and Seneca's *Epistulae Morales*, of Chremes as a paragon of enlightened or humane sentiment.[21] He is certainly an object of fun in Terence's play. His officiousness, however, does not compromise the value of his advice or the logic of his conduct. The leniency he urges on Menedemus early in the play is not available to him as a response to his own son's affair. One must take not only the characters, but also the situation into account. Bacchis is one thing, Antiphila another. But what is Antiphila? Until we learn otherwise, she is a noncitizen resident at Athens, whose relation to Clinia can at best be that of concubine.

To recapitulate: Menedemus regrets his harshness toward his son's affair with a young foreign woman or concubine. The opposition between father and son caused by this amour is thus resolved at the very beginning of the action by a change of heart on the part of Menedemus. That might have been the end of it, had New Comedy permitted a permanent bond of this sort between young lovers, but it did not. Hence, a further resolution occurs when Antiphila proves to be a citizen. There is a wrinkle, however, after Antiphila's true status is discovered. Clinia pretends for his friend's sake to be involved with Bacchis rather than with Antiphila. It is extraordinary that Menedemus consents to this, too. Prodded by Chremes, he acknowledges his error here, even though he is too cowed by the fear that his son may again leave home to oppose him openly.

Chremes really does have a hetaera relation on his hands, namely his son's involvement with Bacchis. When he realizes this, he responds with the dowry trick, thus obliging Clitipho to give up Bacchis and accept a legitimate marriage. There is no question but that Chremes' reaction is entirely justified within the logic of the play. The son must ultimately submit to his father's wishes, even if he is granted the liberty of a brief fling at his father's expense.

Menedemus relents in the case of Clinia and Antiphila, and because the contrast between the courtesan and concubine is drawn so sharply in this comedy, Menedemus seems right to have done so. Antiphila's character and way of life, as opposed to Bacchis', compel sympathy irrespective of her status, though in the end her status is, as it must be, converted to that of citizen. Menedemus' sentimental reasons for forgiving his son are thus congenial; only when he abandons all paternal responsibility even in the case of a woman like Bacchis is it apparent that he has gone too far.

By the conventions of New Comedy, however, an enduring relation between a young citizen and a concubine is no more acceptable than one with a courtesan. That is why the relation with Antiphila must be converted into legitimate wedlock. It is easy to approve of a sincere and decent association such as that between Antiphila and Clinia, but this is not the same thing as endorsing marriage across status lines. Terence, if indeed it was he who interpolated the dialogue between Bacchis and Antiphila, has muddied the issue by suggesting that women like Antiphila might count on an enduring bond with a citizen youth.

Yet the Terentian version preserves the tension that is built into the structure of Menander's play, in which an association across status boundaries is valorized even as it is displaced, in accord with the demands of the genre, by a resolution that regularizes the relationship as marriage between citizens. The dislocation in the narrative development of *Self-Tormentor*, whereby an affair that is tolerated at best for reasons of expediency (Antiphila is undemanding) appears justified sentimentally by the character of the girl (inconsequentially confirmed by the revelation of her true status), is analogous to the shift in the plot of *Shorn Girl*, in which the recognition of Glycera's identity and the marriage that ensues seem extraneous to the quality of the prior relationship between her and the soldier Polemo.[22] As noncitizens, both Glycera and Antiphila are represented as subjects of an autonomous desire that is constitutive of a mutual bond with their lovers. This autonomy is submerged in the wedding arrangements at the denouement of the play.

The condition of concubine lends itself to an overdetermined representation, according to which a noncitizen woman is simultaneously excluded from marital ties by virtue of her status and endowed with qualities that are characteristically the virtues of a citizen bride. Distinct narrative lines intersect as a function of this complex characterization. Thus, as a potential courtesan, Antiphila is barred from an enduring relationship with Clinia, and Chremes' strictures against

Menedemus' leniency at the end of the comedy conform in this respect to Antiphila's situation. Because she will be revealed to be a citizen, however, Antiphila is represented as opposite in type to the professional courtesan, and Chremes' unsentimental appraisal of her claims, together with his remonstrances against Menedemus' self-reproaches, cast him as the heavy in the piece. The plot makes a gesture toward a universal inclusiveness in the depiction of Antiphila as virtuous and thus a fit partner to Clinia, but it is canceled by her conversion to citizen status, which validates the marriage on different grounds.

The social basis for the tension within the narrative is the contradiction between an exclusive conception of citizenship as the condition of connubial relations and a sense of Greek identity grounded in common values. Erotic passion is by nature transgressive. With sexual desire installed at the heart of New Comedy, Menander had a ready-made vehicle for utopian impulses to universal community. Love between individuals of different status, neatly facilitated by the ambiguous position of the novice courtesan or concubine, thus performed the function of imagined political or social solidarity in the plays of Aristophanes. By exploiting clever turns of plot and the device of the recognition, however, New Comedy simultaneously acknowledged the constraints of local identity and reproduced the ideology of the citizen household.

9

Eunuch

Like *Self-Tormentor* and the two other comedies (*Woman of Andros*, *Brothers*) that Terence adapted from Menandrean originals, *Eunuch* has a double plot. The frame story is based on a rivalry between two lovers enamored of a courtesan. One of these is a more or less sympathetic young man, the other a vainglorious mercenary soldier. There is some question whether this latter role derives from Menander's *Eunuch*, the primary model for Terence's adaptation. Terence mentions in his preface that he imported the soldier, and also his calculating flatterer, from another play by Menander, and it is just possible that the rival in the original *Eunuch* was a different figure.[1] In Terence's version, at all events, the youth contends with a soldier for the attentions of the courtesan, who is a free woman of noncitizen status (she has recently moved to Athens) and, in accord with Athenian social institutions, is therefore ineligible for marriage with a citizen.

The competition between the two lovers initially takes the form of gifts. The soldier, Thraso, sends an attractive and cultivated young maid, whose name is Pamphila, while Phaedria delivers a decrepit slave woman and also a eunuch. The eunuch is a pretty poor specimen himself, and the soldier thus has a distinct advantage. But Phaedria's younger brother, Chaerea, has fallen in love with Pamphila, and he takes the place of the eunuch so that he can follow her inside the house of the courtesan. There he rapes her. Pamphila proves, however, to be a citizen and when Chaerea is subsequently unmasked, the way is open to marriage between two citizens, which is duly arranged.

Thus the gifts—maid and eunuch—turn out to have their own story. There is, however, an additional wrinkle. Pamphila is not only a free citizen. Having lost her parents as a child, she had been reared by Thais' mother as a kind of foster sister to the courtesan. Thais, then, has a personal interest in recovering authority over Pamphila, and this automatically gives Thraso the edge over Phaedria, whatever the market value of their gifts. But if Thais' motives are not narrowly avaricious, then Phaedria also has an advantage, namely, love—always the prerogative of the young citizen against the foreign mercenary in comedy. For even though she is a professional, Thais is represented as harboring a tender feeling for the young man.

The gift-giving competition between Thraso and Phaedria thus looks to two different sides of Thais. As a form of bidding for her favors, which is how the two rivals treat their respective offers, the gifts are addressed to Thais the businesswoman. But Thais is also motivated by personal feelings both for Pamphila and for Phaedria. In this respect, she is obliged to choose between compulsion—the need to ingratiate Thraso so that she can obtain possession of the girl—and love. A double aspect is thus built into the rivalry between the lovers.

What follows is an attempt to tease out the ideological implications of this division inscribed in the role of the courtesan. The double determination of the figure of the courtesan was undoubtedly central also to the structure of the original *Eunuch* by Menander, and the results of the analysis will illuminate the operations of Greek ideological production. Once again, moreover, as in the study of *Self-Tormentor* in Chapter 8, it may be possible to identify ways in which the Terentian adaptation develops and probes tensions implicit in the plot of the Greek model.

The play begins with the entrance of Phaedria, who is debating with himself whether to respond to a summons from Thais (similar lines are quoted from Menander's *Eunuch*, which evidently opened in the same way).[2] Phaedria is resentful because on the previous day Thais had barred him from her house. Phaedria's slave, Parmeno, counsels him against a show of independence, and goes on to explain Thais' mercurial behavior as follows: "A thing that has neither sense nor measure you cannot control by sense. In love, these are all inbred vices: insults, suspicions, hostilities, truces, war, peace again; when you insist on making such unstable things stable by means of reason, it's exactly like trying to be rationally insane" (57–63). Now, the equation of love with madness was proverbial and is captured in a Latin jingle that goes back as far as Plautus: *amans amens*.[3] Nevertheless, it is worth eliciting the precise sense of Parmeno's words. Parmeno contrasts the mutability of passion

with the fixed and constant nature of reasoned dispositions. Passionate states are unstable (*incerta*); reason cannot endow them with its own
characteristic firmness. Associations based on reason or calculation
(*ratio*) are not disrupted by arbitrary quarrels, any more than enmities
are ended by sudden reconciliations. Rational behavior is settled and
determinate. Love, however, is the reverse: fights do not mean that love
is over, they are simply part of the syndrome, as much as making up
again. It is in just this compatibility of opposites, this collapse of sustained discriminations, that the irrationality of love consists. That is
why it is fruitless to resist Thais' summons as long as Phaedria is in
love.[4]

To this advice, Phaedria replies: "What a shameful business. Now
I realize that she is evil and I am miserable. I am fed up and yet I am
burning with passion; conscious and aware, alive and alert, I am dying,
and I do not know what I'm doing" (70–73). Superficially, Phaedria's
outburst would seem to illustrate Parmeno's theory.[5] But in fact
Phaedria takes a different line. His complaint is not about the instabil-
ity of passion. In his view, love is stubborn rather than mutable. The
problem is that he is in love with a wicked woman, as he supposes. Love
is thus not so much changeable as blind. While Parmeno identifies an
opposition between passion and rationality (*ratio, consilium*), Phaedria
points to an inconsistency between love and good sense (*prudentia,
scientia*). For Parmeno, Phaedria's indignation at Thais' behavior is a
vestigial scruple of reason that does more harm than good. He counsels
his master to buy himself off as cheaply as possible, and not to add to
love's miseries; "those that it possesses, bear properly" (78).

At this moment, Thais emerges from her house. Parmeno notes her
entrance with a metaphor drawn from agriculture that is likely to be
Terence's own touch: "There she comes, that blight on our property"
(79).[6] This charge strikes the note that was merely latent in Phaedria's
complaint. Thais is, after all, a professional courtesan. For her, it is a
question not of passion but of business, or, as the lover inevitably perceives it, of greed. Thais' fickleness is not a symptom of love's irrationality, nor of a change of heart, but simply a matter of profit and loss. If
she has turned him away, it is because another customer, still flush, is
on the scene. Now the truth, as I have already revealed, is that Thais is
not as mercenary as that (in the Greek original, the information about
Pamphila may have been disclosed in a prologue).[7] But the passage shows
how Terence, in the thirty-five verses of the opening dialogue, sketches
in the complex of motives, mercantile and amatory, that inheres in
the double aspect of the rivals' gifts. All this very likely goes back to
Menander.

Thais makes her appearance worrying aloud that Phaedria may have misconstrued his exclusion from her house the previous day. By this, she undercuts both explanations of her behavior, whether as whimsicality or as avarice. Phaedria begins by complaining about the inequality in his and Thais' feelings, as a result of which he is wounded by rejection while she remains indifferent (91–94). Thais explains in turn that she did not turn Phaedria out because of love for anyone else, but rather because it was necessary (*faciundum fuit*, 97). Her object now is to reconcile Phaedria to this necessity without offense to his role as lover. She proceeds matter-of-factly, describing Pamphila's history to the time when the soldier acquired possession of her. She adds that Thraso has become suspicious of her relation with Phaedria, and asks Phaedria to grant her several days to be devoted exclusively to the soldier, so that she can ensure the transfer of the girl.

Phaedria is outraged. He pretends that the whole story is a fabrication, that Thais loves the soldier and fears Pamphila as a rival. There is a momentary standoff, but Phaedria deflects the argument by asking: "Is he the only one who gives?" (163), and he specifies the cost of his own presents at twenty minae. Thais then makes a bold move: rather than have Phaedria as an enemy, she will do as he bids, despite her own wishes. To which Phaedria replies: "If only you said that from the heart (*ex animo*) and honestly, 'rather than have you as an enemy'! If I could believe that was sincerely said, I could endure anything" (175–77).

This is the crucial turn. Phaedria has demanded sincerity. With that, he can allow Thais her freedom of action. The language is very careful here, and repays attention. Phaedria puts his faith in Thais' words: *utinam istuc verbum diceres* (If only you said those words . . .), Phaedria says, and the slave Parmeno picks it up with the remark: "How quickly he collapses, conquered by a single word." It is a matter of belief: do Thais' words reveal what is truly in her heart or mind, her *animus*? Phaedria solves the problem of submitting to his rival by opening up a space between act and feeling. It is the only solution that will preserve both the claims of love and a frank acknowledgment of his rival's power. Thais at once assures Phaedria that she is speaking *ex animo*, citing her previous favors for him as evidence. Phaedria consents to two days apart.

"For these two days, Thais," Phaedria says, "good-bye." Thais responds with the conventional Latin interrogative formula of leave-taking, "Want anything else?", which requires no answer, but Phaedria answers: "What do I want? That when you are with that soldier of yours, you not be with him [*praesens absens ut sies*]; that day and night you love me, miss me, dream of me, wait for me, think of me, hope for me, rejoice in me, be totally with me—to sum it up, become my soul [*animus*], since I am yours" (191–96).

These lines, together with his earlier expostulation about mutuality and sincerity, have established Phaedria as a figure of deep feeling. Readers have found difficulty in reconciling such an emotion with the cross-bidding for Thais' favors represented in the offer of gifts (recall that Phaedria mentions their cash value). It has been suggested, for example, that the Roman comedians failed to understand the refined relations that Greeks might enjoy with a hetaera or courtesan. There was no comparable institution at Rome, and the rough Latin equivalent, *meretrix*, always retained the base connotation of whore, *scortum* in Latin or *pornē* in Greek—quite a different thing from the *hetaira*.[8] Alternatively, the modern reader has been warned against sentimentalizing the courtesan, who for Greeks and Romans alike remained a woman for hire.[9] The controversy erupts dramatically over the final scenes of *Eunuch*, where Phaedria unexpectedly consents to an arrangement in which he will share Thais with the soldier, on the condition that Thraso foot the bills—a denouement that is startling and, to some scholars, objectionable, not because such arrangements are unheard of in Greece or Rome—for that is not the case—but because it appears degrading to Thais, who is taken to be a good-hearted courtesan (*bona meretrix*), and inconsistent with the nature of Phaedria's love, for which the evidence is precisely the passages that have been under examination.[10] This extraordinary conclusion will be discussed shortly, along with the controversial question of its attribution to Menander or to Terence. Here it may be noted that Phaedria has only a limited part in the rest of the action. He quits the stage to isolate himself for the two-day interval he has pledged to Thais, and while he in fact returns almost at once, his hands will then be full with the problem caused by his brother Chaerea. He has no further meetings with Thais, and encounters the soldier only in the finale.

It has been seen that a tension between Thais' role as lover and as professional courtesan is written into the opening scene of *Eunuch*, and that this tension is subsequently displaced by the alternative conflict within the courtesan herself between her love for Phaedria and her need to oblige Thraso, not out of frivolousness or greed, but for the purpose of redeeming Pamphila. This latter opposition is mediated by a distinction that Phaedria draws between interior feeling and exterior behavior, so that he can both believe in her love and allow her to submit to Thraso, if only temporarily, as she has already done on the previous day. If Phaedria is to believe in Thais' love, he must in this case detach act from feeling.[11]

When Phaedria completes his impassioned speech, he exits without waiting for a reply from Thais. She, with the stage to herself, delivers a brief monologue: "Wretched me," she repeats;[12] "perhaps he has little faith in me and is judging me by the characters of other women. But I am conscious and know for certain that I have not invented any lies and that no one is dearer to my heart [*cordi*] than Phaedria" (197–201).

There is some reason to think that this monologue, and also perhaps the outburst of Phaedria that immediately precedes it, are the work of Terence, though the question cannot be settled with certainty. The use of soliloquy here deserves notice. Thais asserts that she has acted entirely in the interest of Pamphila and adds that she is expecting the imminent arrival of Pamphila's brother, which would clinch the case for her citizenship. Thus, the monologue as a vehicle for Thais' inner feelings takes on an expository function, such as customarily belonged to Greek prologues. This may, then, be an indication of Terence's workmanship, since he regularly replaced the prologue proper with a preface on literary matters, and so was obliged to transfer certain kinds of preliminary information to the body of the drama.[13] Thais' brief monologue also responds formally to Phaedria's demand for sincerity, and the language in which she expresses her own certainty and self-awareness (*certo scio*, 199) appears to echo the earlier dialogue (*incerta*, 61; *scio*, 73).[14]

If the impassioned utterances concerning true or sincere love are possibly interpolations by Terence—and the reader must here be warned how tentative such inferences necessarily are—there is some indication in the text as to how Menander's courtesan might have appeased the jealous Phaedria without recourse to such sentimental lyricism. Recall the words of Thais that elicit Phaedria's initial outburst: "rather than have you as an enemy (*inimicum*, 174)," she says. Thais has a practical cast of mind. She confesses freely to Phaedria that her interest in Pamphila is not solely a philanthropic one: she hopes to provide herself with useful friends (*amicos*, 149) by the service (*beneficium*) of restoring Pamphila to her family. For an independent, noncitizen woman in Athens, with no status before the law, this would have been a consideration of the first importance. Later, after Phaedria grants Thais her two days with the soldier, she says: "I love you for good reason, you do me kindness" (186). There is a range of meaning in Thais' phrase *bene facis* that is difficult to capture, for it recalls the word *beneficium*, favor or service, which Thais had earlier employed in connection with her plan for Pamphila.[15] It is plausible that Menander's Phaedria was as attentive to Thais' practical needs as to her protestations of love for him and did not inquire further into the truth or honesty of her feelings.

There is another exchange, by general consensus an interpolation by Terence himself, where love and hire are seen to interpenetrate.[16] The soldier's first entrance at the beginning of act 3, is with customary braggadocio. Then, with an abrupt change of subject, he inquires of Gnatho—a hanger-on of Thraso's—whether he ought to clear himself before Thais of the suspicion that he is in love with Pamphila (434–35). Gnatho counsels that it is better to keep Thais jealous in order to have a weapon against Phaedria. To this, Thraso submits a curiously modest and sober objection: "If she really loved me, then that would help, Gnatho" (446). Gnatho replies: "Since she looks forward to and loves what you give her, she has long since loved you, it has long since been easy to hurt her. She is constantly afraid that the profit she now reaps you may angrily bestow elsewhere." "You're right," says Thraso; "that hadn't occurred to me." "Ridiculous," answers Gnatho, "you just weren't thinking" (447–52). This blunt equation of avarice and love passes with the soldier, who is vain and dim enough to miss, or want to miss, the paradox. But the problem concerning love and money is not confined to Thraso. Phaedria too gives presents and wants love in return. If in his case the contradiction is muted, it is because the audience is allowed to imagine that Thais not only needs Phaedria but in addition loves him, and loves him sincerely at that. In the dialogue between the soldier and his parasite, Terence unmasks the problem.

When Thais comes out to greet the soldier, he puts Gnatho's theory to work: "My Thais, my pet, what's up? Do you love me on account of that harp girl?" (455–57). Thraso's formulation is softer than the parasite's; he suggests that an appreciation of gifts is the cause of love, not love itself. But the coarseness is noticed by Parmeno, who is on hand with his own presents: "How charming! What a start he's off to" (455–58). Yet such delicacy does not prevent Parmeno from competing on the same terms: "Whenever you're ready, the gifts from Phaedria are here" (464–65; cf. 282–85). Parmeno also turns Phaedria's absence to advantage, representing it as a sign of suave superiority that his master makes no exclusive claims upon the courtesan (480–81, 484–85). Perhaps Parmeno is simply making a virtue of necessity,[17] but Menander's Phaedria may have had a debonair streak, and so, too, may Terence's.

Chremes, the brother of Pamphila, at last arrives at Thais' house, where Thais produces the birth tokens. Chremes does not recognize them and prepares to summon his old nurse. (At this point, he encounters Thraso, who arrives with a small army of slaves and cooks.) The postponement of the recognition is thematic, since Chaerea has by this time (unbeknownst to Thais) raped Pamphila; thus, she will no longer make an acceptable wife by the conventions of New Comedy, and

Chremes would presumably have no interest in establishing his connection with her.[18] Only marriage with Chaerea can now restore her to
her original status, and this is achieved by the unmasking of Chaerea
and the corroboration of Pamphila's identity.

A bare seventy verses from the end of the play, a lovesick and mostly
humbled Thraso slips back again. Two brief scenes more, and he meets
Phaedria for the denouement. This is engineered by Gnatho. Thraso has
understood that he is defeated. He has lost Pamphila and learned that
Chaerea will marry her with his father's consent. The old man has also
agreed to take Thais under his protection, which Terence expresses in
terms of the Roman relationship of patron and client (1039–40).[19] Thais
is wholly Phaedria's. But Thraso's love increases with his despair (1053),
and he appeals pathetically to Gnatho for help. Gnatho's strategy is to
recommend to Phaedria that he share Thais with the soldier, and he
persuades him with three arguments: Thraso will cover the expenses;
his silly self-importance will be a source of amusement; and there is
no chance that Thais can fall in love with him. Thraso, gratified, remarks that everyone loves him. "Just what you promised," says Phaedria
to Gnatho in the final line of the play.

This scene, as has been said, is unpalatable to many critics, and it
has often been explained away as Terence's rather than Menander's.[20]
The evidence is scarcely conclusive. The scene seems like a coda to the
theme of commercial love that has been in the air since the beginning
of the play. The courtesan is in business.[21] But the customer is a lover,
and wishes to be loved. It has been seen how Phaedria found refuge from
this dilemma in the idea of sincerity, which presupposes a division
between outward behavior and one's true or inner self. On this interpretation, which may owe something to Terence's hand, Thais yielded
to Thraso out of necessity, but her heart was Phaedria's. At the end of
the play, Phaedria has possession of Thais, but this does not alter the
contradictory basis of their association. There can, for example, be no
question of marriage, both because of Thais' profession and because of
her alien status, which absolutely prohibits such a union with a citizen. As a young man still under the authority of his father, Phaedria is
also in no position to take her as his concubine; in any case, he will, in
the natural course of events, be expected to take a wife for the production of legitimate heirs.[22] A permanent union, then, between Thais and
Phaedria is out of the question. Yet their mutual love seems to call for
such a solution.

The idea of love—Thais' love for Phaedria—is reimported into
the discussion by the cynical Gnatho to mark a distinction between
Phaedria and Thraso (1080). The opposition between love and hire,

which Gnatho himself had collapsed earlier to reassure Thraso of Thais' favor, is exploited here to relax Phaedria's possessiveness. The new terms with Thraso will be profitable to Phaedria and, at the same time, will not threaten the idea that Thais' love is exclusively his. If there is any echo here of Phaedria's earlier plea for sincerity, it does not undercut Gnatho's scheme but gives it its logic. Only now, instead of being the solace for a compromised relation, the notion of true love makes it possible for everyone to benefit. As for Thais, such a conception of love is not only compatible with the life of a courtesan, it is essential to it if she is to negotiate the claims of business and affection.

Before considering the implications of the arrangement between Phaedria, Thraso, and Thais (who, it may be observed, is not consulted on the matter), we may take brief notice of the subplot involving Chaerea and Pamphila.[23] Upon being discovered, Chaerea declares that he violated the girl "not for pride's sake, but for love" (877–78). He is happy to take Pamphila as his wife, on condition that she is a citizen (890; cf. 1036). Pamphila's feelings are not sounded: by the conventions of the genre, she has no other hope of respectability. In any case, marriage is the concern of her guardian. But it is not a question of options: sex between citizens is coded as marriage. Without marriage, sex expels Pamphila from the citizen community, precisely as though Chremes had been unable to recognize her (which is just what happens prior to Chaerea's offer of marriage). In Chaerea's case, the question of reciprocal love is entirely unproblematic, since his relation to Pamphila is reducible to a function of status.

If for Chaerea the two possible relations with Pamphila (depending on her status) are rape and marriage, Phaedria's association with Thais appears as a third term: a voluntary relation with a free noncitizen woman that depends on mutual assent and affection. But, as has been noted repeatedly, that relation is not a simple one. In the courtesan's role, sincere love stands in tension with the necessity of earning a living by the commerce of her body.[24] It has frequently been observed that the practice of arranged marriages and the relative seclusion of Athenian women inhibited free romantic attachments among citizens in Athens and that such sentiments accordingly found expression in liaisons with hetaerae.[25] But these were not associations among equals, and the image of the courtesan as a professional engaged in business exposes her essential degradation behind the appearance of a voluntary association.

In Terence's Eunuch, the simultaneous presence of both aspects of the courtesan's role invites a further inflection in the idea of love, which opens onto the idea of sincerity. Love is represented as mutual and by consent, but assent in the courtesan is etherealized as an inward reflex of the mind, while the body is subject to the constraints of money or other forms of power. This division is symbolized by the bargain struck between Phaedria and Thraso in the finale of the play. The ideal of sincerity masks the contradiction between sentiment and compulsion in erotic relations with courtesans.[26]

It is impossible to say with certainty what in *Eunuch* is Terence's and what Menander's, but the tension between true and purchased love seems most in evidence in those passages that may be plausibly assigned to Terence, independently of the provenience of the last scene.[27] It may be that because Rome had no institutionalized role comparable to that of the Greek hetaera, what was a customary relationship in Greece was more transparently complex and contradictory in the context of a Latin adaptation.[28]

In the concluding scene of Menander's *Grouch*, the misanthropic Cnemo is obliged to dance and join the party that is going on inside the shrine to Pan and the Nymphs. The ideological tensions that inform the plots of New Comedy are frequently sublimated in a scene of festive exuberance in which distinctions of class and status are submerged in the general hilarity.[29] By the end of *Eunuch*, everyone will be inside Thais' house: Pamphila and Chaerea, Chaerea's father, who came to the rescue of his son when he learned that he had raped a free woman, and now Phaedria and Thraso as well.[30] All conflict dissolves in the pleasure-mansion of the courtesan. If, despite the antic flavor of the finale, Thais nevertheless remains, as she does for many critics, an individual of personal worth who is demeaned by such a merry arrangement,[31] this is perhaps because the contradictions in the role of the hetaera are not entirely canceled in *Eunuch*. In the end, neither the carnival spirit nor a nascent ideology of sincere love fully masks the tensions inherent in erotic relations of exploitation.

10

Arbitrants

As the preceding chapters have indicated, the dramatic tension in Menandrean comedy characteristically takes the form of a conflict between a young man's erotic passion, which binds him to a woman irrespective of barriers of class or status, and the exclusive codes and institutions of the Greek city-state. The opposition between the transgressive movement of desire and the ideological constructions of difference generates a complex narrative situation, with a double impulse toward utopian inclusiveness and the reassertion of conventional social boundaries. The motivations of the characters in the dramas are correspondingly overdetermined, answering simultaneously to the multiple possibilities projected by the contradictions in social values. These ideological stresses leave their traces in lapses in the logic of the plot and in consistency of characterization.

Menander's *Arbitrants* (*Epitrepontes*) depicts a situation in which a husband discovers that his wife has been raped prior to their marriage. This is the only form in which citizen women are represented in New Comedy as having a sexual experience outside of marriage, since they are not normally constructed as autonomous subjects of erotic desire. The tension in this case resides not in the negotiation of class or status positions, but in the codes that define connubial eligibility in the city-state. *Arbitrants* thus centers on the conditions for relations between the genders as such and on the unequal expectations that constitute the social differences between the sexes. More specifically, the play, properly understood, provides a unique glimpse into the nature of male anxiety in classical Greece over the premarital sexual experience of women.

Although the first act of *Arbitrants* is severely mutilated, it is evident from scraps and fragments that the opening of the play dramatized the essential facts of Charisius' estrangement from his wife, Pamphila.[1] Five months after their marriage, while Charisius was away on a business trip, Pamphila bore a child, which she exposed with the assistance of her nurse. Onesimus, a slave of Charisius, has informed his master of Pamphila's actions, with the result that Charisius has abandoned his own home and taken residence at the house of his friend and neighbor, Chaerestratus, where he has, in addition, hired a courtesan named Habrotonum at twelve drachmas a day to entertain and distract him (136–37).[2] Humor is provided by Pamphila's father, Smicrines, a miserly codger who arrives on the scene to complain equally about the plight of his daughter and the extravagance of Charisius' entertainments.

In the second act, the audience learns that a slave shepherd named Davus has found the exposed infant, and taken it home to rear, along with a necklace and other keepsakes adorning it. But the baby proves burdensome, and he gladly hands it over to a charcoal burner and slave of Chaerestratus, Syriscus (or Syrus) by name, who is eager to raise it since he and his wife have but recently lost a child of their own. Later, Syriscus learns that Davus has retained possession of the trinkets left with the abandoned baby and demands them as the property of the child. Davus claims them as his own lucky find, and the two slaves turn to a bystander, who happens to be Pamphila's father, Smicrines, in order to arbitrate the issue (it is this scene that gives the play its title). Among other arguments, Syriscus appeals to the possibility that the jewelry may serve as recognition tokens (303, 331, 341), citing mythological exempla to corroborate that exposed children have been rescued from humble obscurity and restored to their original free status thanks to items of this sort. An audience familiar with the conventions of New Comedy will have readily perceived that the tokens will serve just such a purpose in this case as well, and may also infer, if the facts have not already been set forth in a prologue (none survives), that the baby in question is none other than the child of Pamphila and indeed of Charisius as well. That Smicrines, the child's grandfather, is judging the case adds an elegant touch of irony. Smicrines decides in favor of Syriscus, and before he exits he makes sure that the grumbling Davus hands over the ornaments.

Alone with his wife, Syriscus inspects the jewelry and has just begun examining an engraved ring as Onesimus, Charisius' slave, comes on stage. Onesimus identifies the ring as belonging to his master, and snatches it away. Both men enter Chaerestratus' house, with the intention of putting the matter before Charisius on the following day.

Onesimus, however, shrinks from showing his master the ring, since he fears it will stir up Charisius' regrets over the separation from his wife, for which he is inclined to blame Onesimus' tattling; Onesimus even hints at the possibility of a reconciliation between husband and wife that would leave him out in the cold (425–27). When Syriscus takes him to task for stalling, Onesimus explains how Charisius lost the ring at a nighttime women's festival and surmises that he must have raped the girl who was the mother of the exposed child and who left the ring among the trinkets in its possession. The problem is that the girl is unknown. The courtesan Habrotonum, however, has overheard the conversation and reveals that she chanced to witness just such an assault at the very same festival among a group of girls she was attending as a kithara player. She is confident she can recognize the unfortunate woman, who was of a wealthy family, and counsels Onesimus to make a clean breast of it with Charisius, since if the mother of the child is of free status, there will be no cause for concealing the event (495–96). As Gomme and Sandbach explain: "Habrotonon will have it in mind that he might wish to repudiate Pamphile . . . and marry the other girl, obtaining what was always important to a Greek, a male heir."[3] Habrotonum declines to help find the girl, however, as long as she is uncertain of the identity of her attacker; while she accepts that the ring is Charisius', she has no way of being sure that he had not lent or lost it to some other man who then committed the rape, and she does not wish to upset the girl's family in such ambiguous circumstances. Instead, she proposes to wear the ring herself in the presence of Charisius, and then pretend that it was she who was raped and who seized the ring on the fateful night. If Charisius confesses to the deed, then that will be the time to seek out the true mother. Act 3 ends with Smicrines still grumbling about the goings on at Chaerestratus' house—he seems to believe that his son-in-law has had a child by Habrotonum—and threatening vaguely to take his daughter home with him, dissolving the marriage with Charisius.[4]

We come now to the crucial scenes. Smicrines pleads with his daughter to leave Charisius, but Pamphila, in a badly damaged passage, defends her loyalty to her husband.[5] Habrotonum then emerges with the baby and recognizes Pamphila as the woman who was raped at the night festival (859–60), while Pamphila simultaneously notices a familiar token on the infant (865–66). Since Habrotonum has securely identified Charisius as the father of the child, the women are now aware of its true parentage, and Habrotonum leads Pamphila indoors in order to go over the story in detail. At this point, Onesimus bursts on stage, excitedly remarking on his master's irrational behavior. I quote extensively here his monologue, along with that of Charisius which follows, since they contain the nub of the issue we are considering (the translation is that of Geoffrey Arnott in the Loeb Library edition).[6] Onesimus explains that Charisius overheard the dialogue between Pamphila and her father, and as he listened:

> "O my love, to speak
> Such words," he cried, and punched himself hard on
> His head. (898–90)

Onesimus continues reporting the reactions of his master:

> "What a wife
> I've married, and I'm in this wretched mess!"
> When finally he'd heard the whole tale out,
> He fled indoors. Then—wailing, tearing of
> Hair, raging lunacy within. He went
> On saying, "Look at me, the villain. I
> Myself commit a crime like this, and am
> The father of a bastard child. Yet I
> Felt not a scrap of mercy, showed none to
> That woman in the same sad fortune. I'm
> A heartless brute." Fiercely he damns himself,
> Eyes bloodshot, overwrought. (890–900)

Onesimus is again in terror that Charisius will hold him to blame for denouncing Pamphila, and he withdraws as Charisius emerges. I quote his words up to the point at which the text becomes too mutilated to follow:

> A faultless man, eyes fixed on his good name,
> A judge of what is right and what is wrong
> In his own life pure and beyond reproach—
> My image, which some power above has well
> And quite correctly shattered. Here I showed
> That I was human. "Wretched worm (Charisius imagines the
>   *daimonion* saying), in pose
> And talk so bumptious, you won't tolerate
> A woman's forced misfortune. I shall show
> That you have stumbled just the same yourself.
> Then *she* will treat you tenderly, while *you*
> Insult her. You'll appear unlucky, rude,
> A heartless brute, too, all at once." (Then in his own voice:) Did she
> Address her father then [as] you'd have done?

"I'm here," [she said (?)], "to share his life. Mishaps
Occur. I mustn't run away." (To himself:) You're too
Superior . . . (908–922)

Charisius' speech has appeared remarkable, and rightly so, for the way
in which he seems here to judge himself by the same standard he has
applied to Pamphila, and finds himself wanting in humanity. Some
scholars have seen in Charisius' attitude a sign of Menander's self-
conscious feminism. Thus P. Fossatoro, writing in 1915: "It is a feminist thesis: a lapse in a woman must not be judged according to a different norm from a sensual offense on the part of a man."[7] And again,
K. Stavenhagen, in a seminal article published in 1910: "Here for the
first time a man treats his transgression as standing on the same plane
as the fault of a girl."[8] More recently, Dario del Corno remarks in his
edition and translation of the plays of Menander (1966): "In an ethical
sense, the real resolution, in fact, of the crisis occurs when Charisius
decides to return to his wife while he is still in ignorance of the happy
twist of fortune that has intended that the child that she conceived
should be his own."[9]

Wilamowitz, in his 1925 edition of the play, adopts a more sober
tone:

> A few generations ago, one would have asked about his [i.e., Menan-
> der's] meaning and have found it no doubt in this, that man and woman
> are measured pretty much by the same gauge. . . . But Charisius draws
> no universally valid conclusion whatsoever [concerning the similar-
> ity of his situation to that of his wife], and we are not inclined to ask
> how he would have turned out in the long run, if he had had to for-
> give his wife a real fault.[10]

Other critics, however, have challenged the idea that there is anything resembling an egalitarian stance in Charisius' self-reproach. Thus,
Alain Blanchard, in 1983: "What used to be seen in the *Arbitration* was
the expression of a feminist thesis: a fault in a woman must not be
judged in a different manner from one in a man. Strange feminism, when
one knows that Charisius' fault is to have violated in the past the woman
who subsequently became his wife, while the fault of the latter is simply the misfortune of having been violated."[11]

The crux of the matter has turned on Charisius' conception of himself as the victim of misfortune (*atukhēma*), as in the lines that he puts
in the mouth of his imaginary *daimonion*: "You won't tolerate a woman's
[or your wife's] forced misfortune [*akousion atukhēma*]. I shall show
that you have stumbled just the same yourself [*eis homoi' eptaikota,*

literally: have stumbled into the same things or situation]" (914–15). Thus Wilamowitz remarks: "It was considered very much from the man's point of view, since his guilt was supposed to be merely an *atukhēma*, which is what had really happened to Pamphila."[12] Earlier, Charisius speaks of his own wretched misfortune (*ētukhēka*, 891), though he has so fine a wife (Arnott translates: "I'm in this wretched mess"), and then berates himself for hard-heartedness toward "that woman in the same sad misfortune" (*atukhousēi taut' ekeinēi*, 898) as his own. Edward Capps comments that "Pamphila was the victim of the same outrage that he had committed—as he supposes—, upon another girl,"[13] in an apparent attempt to exonerate Charisius at least here from his habit of self-exculpation by importing, quite gratuitously, a reference to the fortune of the girl he thinks he has raped.

Sandbach takes a sterner view. Of the first passage, he remarks: "Probably *atukhein* is here used euphemistically for *hamartanein* [to err]"; that is, Charisius tries to gloss over his offense as a mere accident. Of the second passage, Sandbach observes: "Again the euphemistic use of *atukhein* may be present. Charisios can conceive of his crime in getting Habrotonon with child (as he thinks) as an *atukhēma*: whereas Pamphile had no responsibility for her motherhood, which was an *atukhēma* in the proper sense of the word." Finally, on the passage which we mentioned first, Sandbach notes (on the word *eptaikota*): "'To have stumbled'; Charisios must use a somewhat euphemistic word since he is representing himself, as he did in 898, as being in the same position as his wife. He had had bad luck, like her, and she, as appears in 921, was prepared to treat his situation as a misfortune, not a crime."[14]

Menander was perfectly well aware of the difference between an *atukhēma* and an *adikēma*, as fr. 359 Körte-Thierfelder clearly demonstrates ("There is a difference between a misfortune [*atukhēma*] and a crime [*adikēma*]: the one occurs by accident [*dia tukhēn*], the other by choice"),[15] and a suggestion on the part of Charisius' that his rape of a woman was an "involuntary misfortune" sounds not so much euphemistic as downright hypocritical.[16] But is this, in fact, what Charisius is claiming? Let us look once again at his words, as quoted by Onesimus; I translate lines 895–98 literally: "Having done such a deed myself, and become the father of a bastard child [*paidiou nothou*], I did not have or give a portion of forgiveness to her who was unfortunate in this same respect." Charisius is comparing his situation as the father of a *nothos*, as he supposes, with that of Pamphila, who gave birth to a child as a result of the rape.[17] This is the misfortune of which he speaks, both in reference to her plight and to his his own. Throughout, *atukhein* and *atukhēma* refer to the circumstance of producing an illegitimate off-

spring, and this can, both in the case of Pamphila and of Charisius himself, be described perfectly reasonably as an unintended piece of bad
luck.

Indeed, Charisius cannot very well mean at this point in the play
to compare his rape of Habrotonum, as he supposes, with the fact that
Pamphila has been raped. After all, he has known from the very beginning that he had raped *someone*, and there is no reason why at this
moment he should suddenly be moved to recognize the analogy between
his wife's circumstance as a victim of sexual violence and his own active
commission of the very same crime.[18] Besides, the entire complicated
plot of this play, which was recounted at the beginning of this chapter,
seems to have been constructed precisely in order to bring about the
relatively unusual situation in which Charisius knows (1) that his wife
has borne a *nothos* (bastard) and (2) that he has been responsible for the
birth of a *nothos*, without however yet being aware (3) that the two
nothoi are one and the same.[19] This is the consequence of the extraordinary maneuver by which Habrotonum pretends that the baby is hers,
on the grounds that she wants to be absolutely sure that Charisius,
rather than someone else who had somehow acquired his ring, was the
rapist. The action seems organized simply to allow Charisius to recognize the identity of circumstance between his wife and himself in the
fact of their both being parents of an illegitimate child, and his monologue is indeed, as del Corno observed, the ethical climax of the plot.

If this, however, is the plain meaning of the text, and if in addition
the focus on the *nothos* both follows from the structure of the story and
makes clear sense of the repeated use of the expression *atukhēma* in
reference to Charisius as well as to Pamphila, why have so many excellent scholars missed the point, and taken Charisius' words as at best
a self-exculpating euphemism for the act of rape? One may venture a
plausible answer to this question. At the beginning of the play, Charisius
abandoned his wife because he had found out what had befallen her; in
act 4, he perceives that he is in the same boat and prepares to return to
her. If he left Pamphila because she had been sexually violated, then
the reason he subsequently changes his mind must be that he has come
to take a more charitable view of such a misfortune in a woman, and
this will be the result of reflection on his own wanton behavior. Whatever pain it causes him to think that she has been tainted by a prior
sexual experience, he manages forgiveness because he can see his own
responsibility as an aggressor. Such is the logic, it appears, that has
induced critics to read Charisius' change of heart as a newfound capacity, however transient, to accept his wife despite her violated condition,
a capacity that is helped along by the equation, albeit self-serving, of

her experience with his own violent action in the past as involuntary misfortunes.

This line of reasoning is sound enough, if in fact Charisius can be said to have deserted his home because Pamphila had been raped. But was this his reason? Since the reversal in the drama centers, as has been seen, on Charisius' recognition that Pamphila's misfortune is analogous to his own, and that this misfortune is precisely that of having been responsible for the birth of a *nothos*, it is reasonable to suppose that the problem corresponds to the solution, and that Charisius left his wife not because she had been raped as such, but rather because she had produced a bastard child, which is, after all, exactly what he learned from his slave Onesimus. If it is understood that it is the fact of a *nothos* that moved Charisius to abandon Pamphila, the climactic scene as it has been interpreted here makes perfect sense. What is more, Charisius' capacity to see the equivalence between his wife's misfortune in producing an illegitimate child and his own case no longer appears as a dishonest evasion of his responsibility for rape, but rather as an extraordinary rejection of the usual Athenian double standard for women and men in the sphere of sex and reproduction. On this reading, then, it is possible to recover a sense of the sexually egalitarian implications of *Arbitrants* that Stavenhagen and Fossatoro perceived, although their failure to distinguish the question of rape or penetration from that of illegitimacy left Charisius' great speech, with its comparison between Pamphila's misfortune and his own, open to an ironic interpretation.

The issue between Charisius and Pamphila in *Arbitrants*, then, is that Pamphila has produced a *nothos*, not simply that she has been violated. It is the child, and not the idea, for example, that Pamphila has been polluted or contaminated by the sexual assault, that causes Charisius anguish in the first instance, and he is obliged to examine his reaction when he learns that he, too, is responsible for the birth of a bastard. Modern readers have mistakenly ascribed to Charisius a motive that is not his—namely, an anxiety that centers on sex rather than childbirth and legitimacy, and which views a woman who has had any kind of premarital sexual experience, whether voluntary or not, as marred or corrupted. On the evidence of *Arbitrants*, it seems that this was not how Menander expected his Greek audience to respond. Rather, the hero's feelings about the premarital assault on his wife constellate precisely around the issue of children and legitimacy. Anxieties about "damaged goods" and the like are irrelevant to his motivation.

Why critics today should have assumed that Charisius or Menander would be concerned primarily with the rape and sexual penetration of Pamphila, rather than with the issue of a *nothos*, may have to do with the nature of contemporary male anxiety over women's sexuality, which is not entirely congruent with the classical Athenian structure of feeling.[20] For example, the Greek term *parthenos*, commonly translated "virgin," does not refer exclusively to physical inviolateness. Rather, *parthenos* often indicates the status of an unmarried girl, who becomes a woman (*gunē*) when she is given to a citizen husband for the purpose of producing lawful heirs. A woman who had been raped might nevertheless be referred to as a *parthenos*, or "maiden," since she had not made the proper transition to the condition of *gunē*. Thus, the poetic hypothesis to Menander's *Hero* informs us that "a *parthenos*, having borne a male and female child together, gave them to a guardian to rear, then later married the man who had violated her" (1–3). There is no suggestion here of a virgin birth, of course; *parthenos* means an unwed citizen girl.[21]

Furthermore, the Greeks in classical antiquity seem not to have known of the existence of the hymen in women. Bleeding at the occasion of a woman's first experience of intercourse was explained as a result of the readier flow of menstrual blood, which was partly blocked up by the narrowness of the vaginal channel, until it was widened by penetration.[22] There was no tradition of exposing the wedding linens, or of digital testing, in order to determine the virginity of a bride, and Greek popular beliefs may not have focused so narrowly on physical virginity as modern attitudes suggest.

If a Greek girl had been violated, the chief evidence would normally be the birth of a child, since her family, and especially the women who would be most likely to be informed of the matter, would try to keep the event secret, as evidently happened in Pamphila's case. Nor does Charisius hold anyone to blame for having failed to inform him of the condition of Pamphila; his slave Onesimus is in constant terror he will become the object of Charisius' rage for having done precisely that. In Terence's *Mother-in-Law* (*Hecyra*), based on a Greek original by Apollodorus of Carystus that has obvious affinities with *Arbitrants*, the husband Pamphilus, who similarly rejects his wife when he discovers that she has borne a child conceived prior to wedlock, nevertheless agrees to keep the facts concealed so as not to compromise the girl's future chances at a respectable marriage (*Mother-in-Law* 395–402; the child of course turns out to be his own). In Plautus' *Pugnacious* (*Truculentus*), Callicles' daughter, who has been raped by Diniarchus, attempts to keep the birth of a child secret by having it exposed (797–98); her father has in the meantime betrothed her to a relative of his (848–49).[23] If the child can be concealed or disposed of, the fact of rape itself seems to pose no necessary obstacle to the girl's chances of finding a husband,[24] though

in practice such situations are always resolved in New Comedy through
the union of the original parents of the child.[25]

Conditions of Athenian social life may have discouraged an obses-
sive preoccupation with physical virginity at the time of marriage. There
is no inhibition in New Comedy with regard to marrying a widow, irrespective of whether she has had children; Cnemo, in *Grouch*, is a case
in point. Given the continual warfare that characterized the Greek city-
states, and the tendency for men to take brides much younger than
themselves, young mothers must commonly have been available as
potential brides, and bridegrooms may have learned to feel, in these
circumstances, a keen difference between women who had conceived
legitimate children in wedlock and those who had borne the offspring
of a dubious or unknown father.[26]

What is more, the ideology of pederasty entailed that Greek boys
were perceived by adult males as objects of love and sexual desire.[27] It
may be that, as a result, Greek men were less inclined to that mystification of female sexuality that informs modern male anxieties over
virginity and penetration.[28] Male anger over adultery or the violation
of a virgin girl seems to have been based as much on a sense of personal
or proprietary injury as on feelings of jealousy and insecurity. The easy
availability of courtesans, prostitutes, or slaves for the satisfaction of
sexual desire may have helped condition the prevailing Greek view of
sex as an appetite more or less like hunger, and comparable, when carried to excess, to gluttony.[29]

In Lysias' defense speech on the murder of Eratosthenes, the defen-
dant remarks that the law inscribed in the Areopagus "judged that men
who commit rape [*tous biazomenous*] deserve a lesser penalty than seducers [*tous peithontas*]." The reason alleged for this rule is that those
who employ violence are detested by their victims, while seducers "corrupt the soul in such a way as to make other men's wives [*allotrias
gunaikas*] care more for them than for their own husbands, and the whole
household comes to depend on them, and it is uncertain whether the
children are those of the husband or of the adulterer" (Lysias 1.32–33). The
speaker has an interest in making adultery appear the gravest kind of offense, but he evidently counts on the jurors to agree that the physical violation of his wife is less momentous in and of itself than the threat to the
integrity of his home and the legitimacy of his children (it is evidently
assumed that any issue resulting from rape will be exposed).[30] Analogously,
the tyrant in Xenophon's *Hiero* (3.3–4) remarks that adulterers are uni-
versally punished by death because they corrupt "the love [*philias*] of wives
for their husbands; for [*epei*] when a woman has sex as a result of some
mishap their husbands esteem them no less, provided that their love seems

to remain uncontaminated."[31] Here again, the emphasis is on the integrity of the family rather than on the pollution of the violated woman.

Whether Charisius was wholly indifferent to the sexual violation of Pamphila, apart from the birth of an illegitimate child, may be left moot. In *Eunuch* (867–70), Thais laments that the violation of Pamphila has foiled her plan to win her recognition as a citizen, presumably on the grounds that Pamphila's brother will have no interest in acknowledging her when he learns of her ruined condition. But whether the reason for her disqualification is that the rape has rendered her taboo or stained in the eyes of Athenian men is uncertain. One must again be wary of projecting onto the Greeks attitudes inveterate to modern culture. In *Arbitrants*, at all events, it is the issue of the child that is central to the play, and it displaces in Charisius' mind any consideration of Pamphila's technical virginity at the time of marriage.[32]

As many historians have argued in recent years, Greek law and custom were concerned above all to preserve the integrity of citizen households, in the first instance by ensuring the legitimacy of the heirs. At least since Pericles' legislation of 451 B.C., it was necessary that a child be the offspring of two citizen parents (that is, an *astos* and an *astē*) in order to inherit, and the Greek idea of the *nothos* refers not to the illegitimacy of a child borne out of wedlock, but to the civic status of the parents.[33] As long as the woman raped by Charisius proves to be a citizen, the child will be *gnēsios* (legitimate) rather than a *nothos* (at all events once the parents are wed and the child is acknowledged), irrespective of whether she turns out to be Pamphila or some other woman, as the play itself makes quite clear. Correspondingly, the reason Charisius believes that he has fathered a *nothos* is that Habrotonum is not an Athenian citizen, rather than that she is not his wife. In this context, then, it is natural that male feelings concerning the suitability of a citizen girl as wife, if she has been raped prior to marriage, should focus on the production of a child, whose status will, of course, be dubious. Charisius seems to have internalized just the set of responses necessary to sustain and reproduce the social code that sought to guarantee the citizen line and its exclusive access to landed property.[34]

Nevertheless, Charisius is not moved simply by a transparent desire to preserve the citizen status of his posterity. After all, he knows that Pamphila has exposed the child, and he has no reason to suspect that it will survive or be recognized as hers. Even if it were, he would not be obliged to treat it as his child, and it would be barred from inheriting in any case, since its father was unknown. Charisius' decision to leave Pamphila is not a gesture that sustains in a direct or rational way the structure of the Athenian city-state as a closed, consanguineous group.

But this does not mean that there is no connection between Charisius' motives and the values of the city-state. There is always a gap between the explicit formulation of a social code and the way in which the code is internalized and sustained in the motives of individuals: this dissonance is just the space that ideology inhabits.[35] Charisius was not worried for the purity of his line when he abandoned Pamphila; he was horrified at the thought that she had borne a *nothos*, and if this served, in the last analysis, to reproduce the *oikos* system of Athens, it was an incidental and unconscious consequence of Charisius' response.

Charisius' recognition of the equivalence between his situation and that of Pamphila, the content of which has been clarified by the preceding analysis, enables him to transcend, at least in the heat of the moment, one of the ideological inhibitions that support the exclusivity of Athenian citizenship and to accept his wife back even though she has borne a *nothos* (illegitimate child). His action depends on the ideological space between social function and individual motivation. Charisius responds to the condition of Pamphila not as a violation of a public protocol but as a personal betrayal, and he is able, through an honest appraisal of the likeness between her misfortune and his own, to bring his reaction under control and acknowledge Pamphila's innocence. His perception of the identity between male and female responsibility in the bearing of a *nothos* poses a utopian challenge to both the status and gender codes of the city-state.

Charisius' impulse, however, is compromised by the formulaic recognition (*anagnōrisis*) by which Charisius discovers that the woman he raped and his wife are one and the same. The dutiful resolution, which bows to the prohibition in New Comedy of marriage between a woman who has been violated and a citizen male unless he proves to be the author of the attack, has the quality of an afterthought, normalizing the relationship in accord with the conventions of the genre at the expense of the ethical significance of Charisius' decision to accept his wife independently of the discovery. In this split (*décallage*) between the moral trajectory of the narrative and the extrinsic solution to the stigma attaching to Pamphila, the structure of *Arbitrants* resembles that of other Menandrean comedies, including *Self-Tormentor* and *Shorn Girl*.[36] In these comedies the partial independence of the ethical dilemma in relation to the formal resolution required by the genre opens up a space in the text for the affirmation of the dignity and equality of women which they were denied in the civic world of the polis. The fissure in the structure of these plays testifies to the tension between women's (and men's) autonomy as moral agents and the constraints of status and sexual propriety by which they were bound.

11

The Miser

"The specificity of a foreign culture cannot be grasped without setting it off against others, or at all events one's own."[1] This observation by Christian Meier may serve as the justification for the final chapter of this book, which compares an ancient comedy with one of its descendants composed in the early modern era. The purpose is to set in relief the social distinctions and codes of the classical city-state as they inform New Comedy by determining how they are transformed in a work produced under the new social conditions of modern nation-states. Thus, the present concern is not primarily with questions of sources, dramatic technique, or aesthetic ideals. *The Miser (L'Avare)* by Molière and its model, Plautus' *Aulularia (The Play of the Pot)* have been selected for analysis because the contrasts are particularly illuminating in cases of imitation. This choice has also to do with literary historical considerations: Aristophanic comedy had a limited influence on European drama, and while New Comedy inaugurated a brilliant tradition, the plays of Menander and his contemporaries were unknown until the beginning of this century, apart from brief fragments, and their legacy was transmitted through the Latin versions by Plautus and Terence. The Greek antecedent for Plautus' *Aulularia* is not known, but the play bears a close resemblance to Menander's *Grouch,* and many scholars have unhesitatingly affirmed that the original must have been by Menander himself.[2]

The broad similarities between *Aulularia* and *The Miser* are evident. In both, an obsession with wealth on the part of the central figure is an obstacle to the marriage of his child (in the Latin play) or children

153

(in the French adaptation), in part because he is unwilling to provide a satisfactory dowry. The resolution, in each, depends on the discomfiture of the antisocial protagonist, brought about by the theft of his hidden treasure, with the consequent marriage of his offspring. The analogies with Menander's *Grouch* are also clear: the humbling of a monomaniacal figure, or humor, and the reintegration of his household into the communal order, symbolized by weddings and festivities in the denouement. In spite of the overall resemblances, however, *The Miser* not only differs in important details from the Plautine play, it systematically reverses the fundamental premises of its structure.[3]

It may be helpful to begin by reviewing *Aulularia*.[4] The prologue to the play informs the audience of two circumstances. First, it is reported that Euclio has discovered a pot of gold hidden beneath his hearth and that the safekeeping of this treasure has become his ruling passion. He affects a condition of extreme poverty, lest he be suspected of harboring secret wealth. Second, the prologue relates that Euclio's daughter, Phaedria, has been raped by a young man who knows her identity, although she does not know his; as a result, she has conceived a child. In the course of the play the cries induced by her birth pangs will be heard, at which moment Lyconides, the youth who had assaulted her, decides to reveal himself to her father and request her hand in marriage (682–96); according to the conventions of New Comedy, which have been noted in the previous chapter, Phaedria will not otherwise be marriageable. Before Lyconides can come clean, however, the miser's gold is stolen. In his anxiety for its safety, Euclio had removed the pot from his house. First, he reconnoitered the urban precinct of the goddess Fides, or Good Faith, but he rejected it as unreliable; he is then observed burying it in a grove outside the city walls sacred to the woodland deity Silvanus.

The stage is now set for an ingenious misunderstanding, which Molière could not resist lifting for his version. Lyconides approaches Euclio to confess to the violation of his daughter, but does so in terms so general that Euclio mistakenly supposes him to be referring to the theft of his gold. One cannot miss the implicit equation of the robbery and the rape as offenses against Euclio: Phaedria seems reduced to one more possession of her father's. In the next scene, Lyconides discovers that the miser's gold was pinched by his own slave. He is thus in a position both to restore Euclio's treasure and to redeem his daughter. While the conclusion to the play is mutilated, the evidence of the prologue makes it clear that Euclio will give at least a part of his gold as dowry for his daughter, and the play may have ended with some farcical business at the miser's expense, like the finale of *Grouch*.[5]

   The parallelism between the offense against the miser's property
and the assault on his daughter's honor has its roots in the social structure of the classical city-state. At Rome, the rights of commerce and of
marriage, encoded in the formula *ius conubii et commercii*, were constitutive of participation in the citizen community. Both these rights
depended on the capacity to enter into legal contracts, which was restricted to adult male citizens under their own authority (*in sua
potestate*). The obligation between contracting parties, in turn, was
represented as good faith (*fides*), the chief expression of reciprocity
among the community of citizens.[6] Outside the civic space, lawful
exchange in trade or matrimony, and the morality that sustains them,
are suspended. The territory beyond the city walls may be imagined as
a no-man's-land, where violent appropriation takes the place of the ethical relations that characterize the city-state. Rape displaces connubial
exchange in the domain of sexual relations, while theft stands in for
the reciprocal exchange of goods.
   The miser, who hoards his wealth and, by his stinginess, denies his
daughter the possibility of marriage, ruptures the ties that constitute
him as a member of the community and withdraws from the civic space.
By the implicit logic of New Comedy, he has rendered himself an out-
sider, with respect to whom the rules of the community are in abey-
ance. Thus, his daughter has been forcibly violated at a nighttime festival for the goddess Ceres (36), which was celebrated exclusively by
women on the model of the Greek Thesmophoria (this was perhaps the
festival indicated in the Greek original of *Aulularia*),[7] while his wealth
is stolen from its hiding place beyond the perimeter of the city, where
he chose to conceal it in preference to the temple of Fides. The figure
who, by his pathological fixation, has removed himself from the reciprocities of civic life, finds himself no longer sheltered by its norms.
   The resolution of the drama is achieved, as has been seen, by the
elementary mechanism of humbling the secessionist, thereby reaffirm-
ing the claims and integrity of the community. Euclio discovers his
vulnerability in two successive instants: losing both his gold and, by
the rape, the marriageability of his daughter. By this double expropria-
tion, he is unable to engage in either of the forms of exchange constitutive of membership in the citizen body, and his social position is brought
into conformity with his moral privatism. The social deficiency in his
daughter is exemplified when Lyconides' uncle, Megadorus, takes a
fancy to the girl and requests her hand, in ignorance of the rape and
pregnancy; when the truth is out, he yields to his nephew, who spontaneously acknowledges his responsibility, moved perhaps by the awareness that he now has a child.[8]

Once reduced to a state of utter deprivation, Euclio may recover his property, on two conditions: first, that his gold enter into circulation, specifically in the form of a dowry; and second, that his daughter be related by conjugal ties to another household. Thus, as in *Grouch*, the miser's imaginary autarky is abolished, and his estate rejoins the system of exchange that defines the community. Whether the miser's character was reformed in the lost finale of the play may be left moot; it is the fate of his household that matters.

To sum up the analysis of the social logic implicit in the plot: *Aulularia* presupposes rules of exchange in the domains of property and kinship—that is, the rights of commerce and marriage by which civic membership is constituted. The miser's hoarding of his gold and the consequent limitation on his daughter's access to the network of connubial relations mark a rupture in the system, which is mended after Euclio's discomfiture. In this schematic presentation, tensions or contradictions in the narrative have, to be sure, been neglected in the interest of exhibiting the matrix of reciprocity in goods and sex that underlies it.

Let us now turn from Rome to France. Molière dispenses with the convention of a prologue, introducing his play instead with a dialogue between the miser's daughter, Elise, and her suitor Valère, who has insinuated himself into Harpagon's household as a gentleman's man. Molière drew for this scene upon Ariosto's *I suppositi*, first produced between 1528 and 1531. Ariosto's play opens with a maiden revealing to her nurse that a servant in her household, with whom she has commenced, at the nurse's instigation, an erotic relationship, is in fact of noble birth; he is a visiting Sicilian (the setting is in Ferrara), who has exchanged identities with his serving man in order to take up a position near his beloved. The disguise permits the pair to get around the young lady's father, who has planned a match for his daughter with a doddering doctor. Like Ariosto, Molière portrays the romantic bond as mutual, and the woman as equally a subject of desire, even though he casts Elise as modest and hesitant in contrast to the frank affections of the Italian heroine. In Plautus' play, consistent with the conventions governing ancient New Comedy, Phaedria does not appear on stage; her only utterance is her inarticulate cry in the throes of childbirth. Never in the classical genre, as has been said, does a young woman known to be an Athenian citizen express love for a man; rather, she is treated exclusively as the object of a transaction between men, to be transferred from the house of her father to that of her husband.

To return to Molière, the next scene reveals that Elise's brother, Cléante, is also in love, with a poor but beautiful girl named Mariane who lives nearby with her mother. It has been remarked that in ancient New Comedy, the father typically blocks his son's liaison with a partner ineligible for marriage, for example a courtesan or foreigner, in favor of a legitimate and advantageous alliance with a respectable citizen family; in this way, he upholds the social norms, as in Plautus' *Cistellaria* and Terence's *Self-Tormentor* (both based on Menandrean originals), that the young man in his passion threatens to transgress. When the blocking figure is the father of the girl, as in *Aulularia* or *Grouch*, he does not oppose his daughter's desire, which is not represented in the genre, but prevents her marriage by virtue of his perverse nature, which repels all social ties. Doubling the romantic plot in Molière's play reflects the active role accorded to respectable women in Renaissance comedy, for example in Ariosto. It also allows Molière to place the focus on tensions within the miser's own household, thereby synthesizing the plot involving conflict between father and son with the paradigm based on the antisocial humor. Harpagon is simultaneously located within two distinct positions with respect to the plot forms of New Comedy.

On the one hand, Harpagon plays the part of the father who has arranged a marriage uncongenial to his son, and in this case to his daughter as well. The plot involves a conflict between passion and filial piety, which in Greek and Roman comedy is commonly resolved through a recognition—the girl proves to be of citizen status—that reconciles duty and desire. As a miser, however, Harpagon sheds the aura of social responsibility that attaches to a head of household. His children have both sentiment and respectability on their side, since his motives in arranging their marriages are not simply mercenary—a sober calculation of interests is compatible with a father's responsibilities—but absurdly greedy, and the alliances he proposes are insupportable.

The third scene of *The Miser* introduces Harpagon himself. In a dialogue with his son's servant, he reveals a morbid fear of being robbed. The exchange is modeled on a similarly paranoid outburst of Euclio against an old slave. In Molière's version, this conversation leads directly to the scheme to steal the miser's gold. Cléante and his servant take the parts of Lyconides and his slave in Plautus' play, except that Cléante is an active participant in the plot. The reason for Harpagon's anxiety is that he has just come into possession of a large sum which he has not yet had the opportunity to invest or lend out; hence he has resorted to the expedient of burying it in his garden, thereby leaving himself vulnerable to theft (1.4). Harpagon's meanness is calculating. He disapproves of his son's extravagance because he depends for his income on the risky business of gambling and then squanders it on wigs and sashes, instead of lending it at a profitable rate of interest. The contrast between the father's attitude toward money and that of the son will be exhibited most sharply in act 2, where Cléante, desperate for cash, secures a loan at an exorbitant rate, only to discover that the usurious lender is his own father. Harpagon is shocked that his son should contract such a debt, while Cléante is appalled at his father's shameful occupation. This scene, which is derived from a seventeenth-century French comedy, *La belle plaideuse*, by Boisrobert, has of course no counterpart in Plautus' *Aulularia*. Euclio never puts his gold to work. He keeps it concealed and inert, locked within his house or buried in a sacred precinct. His wealth earns nothing, just as it buys nothing. Nor does Euclio do anything to augment his treasure by other means. His passion for his gold is pure fetishism, the love of the thing for its symbolic value only, without reference to its use or function. Euclio's possessiveness is in a sense a violation of the very nature of the thing he treasures, since money withdrawn from circulation is no longer currency but worthless matter, even if that matter is precious metal. Euclio is, to be sure, represented as miserly, but his relation to his gold is not reducible to ordinary greed. He is enamored of the substance, not its value in the process of exchange. That is why his retentiveness may be construed as a breach with his society, which is based on principles of reciprocity. In a word, Euclio is less a miser than a hoarder.

Harpagon is the very reverse of Euclio. His rule is to keep his money in constant circulation, continually drawing a profit that is at once sent forth to earn again. It is the sheerest accident that he has, at the moment the action of the play commences, a large sum actually in his possession. Of course, this is so arranged in order that his stash may be vulnerable to theft, though Molière might equally well have humbled the old skinflint by, for example, representing a major borrower as forfeiting on his debt. In any case, Harpagon is no hoarder in the manner of Euclio. He does not store up wealth or rest content with keeping it secure. Money that is not earning money is wasted, on Harpagon's view, and he perpetually increases his income in the spirit of high finance. He is the opposite of retentive: his parsimony in the matter of fancy dinners, carriages, and the like is not mere niggardliness, but rather a means of converting all but the bare essentials of existence into the most mobile form of value, money. In the deal he had been arranging with his son, until the identities of the two parties became mutually known, Harpagon had insisted that the borrower accept as part of the loan old pieces of furniture and other bric-a-brac at inflated prices. Cléante regards this as a swindle, and rightly so, no doubt, but it also reveals that for Harpagon everything in his possession is negotiable tender. Harpagon is the miser as usurer or financier.

When Cléante and Elise attempt to broach with their father the topic of their respective enamorments, Harpagon forestalls them by revealing that he has in mind for them matrimonial arrangements of his own. As a match for Elise, he has decided on a wealthy old widower named Anselme, while Cléante is to be betrothed to a certain widow, on behalf of whom approaches had been made to Harpagon just that morning (1.4). To top it all off, Harpagon also announces his own intention to wed, and the object of his infatuation is none other than Mariane, Cléante's beloved. The plot thus takes a double turn. Elise is, as has been seen, in the typical situation of the enamored youth in ancient New Comedy, whose desire is obstructed by the father's contrary disposition. In the classical genre, as has been indicated, the conflict between father and son is usually based on a social difficulty: the boy loves without regard to the class or status of the young woman, while the father insists on a legitimate and practical union that will provide a lawful heir for the family estate and cement an alliance with a respectable citizen household. The parent may relent in the matter of class and accept as his daughter-in-law a woman of modest means. But the status barrier is absolute in New Comedy, and if the girl is not of citizen stock, nothing can save the situation except a recognition, by which her true citizenship is revealed.

The case of Elise is a variation on this format, since Valère's apparently humble station is not necessarily an insuperable obstacle. True, the audience learns at the very beginning that he has come to Paris in search of his parents and has adopted the disguise of a serving man only in order to be near his beloved. One is thus prepared for the disclosure of his true station, which is that of son and heir to Anselme, whom Harpagon had selected as his daughter's spouse. What barrier is it, however, that this recognition eliminates? Not one of civic status, since Anselme is not French but Neapolitan, and this distinction in nationality poses no difficulty to the union between his son and Harpagon's daughter. Rather, it is one of class, or, more particularly, of wealth, since Harpagon looks only to profit in the choice of a partner for his children. But Harpagon's interest in money is represented in *The Miser* not as a normal concern for material welfare but as a pathological fixation. The recognition seems, in this case, adapted not so much to the removal of a social obstacle to the union of the young couple as to the indulgence of the miser's idiosyncratic obsession. It is Harpagon's extreme greed, not the willful passions of his children, that is foregrounded as the problem for his family. With the recognition, it is almost as though the plot were making a gesture of deference toward the miser's preoccupation with wealth as a condition for all social ties, rather than chastening his perverse avarice.

There is a hilarious scene (1.5) in which Valère, whose love for Elise is still unknown to Harpagon, is summoned to offer his opinion on the suitability of a match with Anselme. All of Valère's insinuated objections to so unequal a marriage between an old man and a young woman are met with a single overriding argument: Anselme is prepared to accept the girl *sans dot* (without a dowry). The inspiration for this skit is a scene in Plautus' *Aulularia*, where Euclio's rich neighbor Megadorus offers to dispense with a dowry for the sake of his daughter's hand. Euclio's willingness to give his daughter away without a dowry is a sign of his mean temper and reveals the extent to which his preoccupation with his gold has extinguished his sense of pride and decency. Megadorus' offer is not only unseemly in itself, since it has something of the character of a bribe, but it is also, as the audience knows, futile, since Phaedria is compromised by her pregnancy, and in the end will be wedded to a suitably younger man. But marriage without a dowry for Euclio's daughter would have subverted the whole meaning of the comedy, since Euclio's reintegration into the community depends on the circulation of his gold, as well as the betrothal of his daughter. The two systems of exchange are coordinate, complementary, in *Aulularia*.

In the case of Harpagon, however, an inordinate concern with the dowry is not entirely in character. Harpagon, as has been seen, is not averse to parting with cash, provided he can secure a good return on it. There is no reason why he should not venture a respectable sum toward the marriage of his daughter with a wealthy, aged gentleman with no known heirs. He is acting the part of a hoarder, like Euclio who is his model here, rather than a usurer, which is his proper metier. To this point, he has been characterized as eager to make money, not to store it up uselessly. Like the accident by which Harpagon finds himself momentarily in physical possession of a strongbox full of money, the obsession over a dowerless wedding is a throwback to the classical prototype of the miser as he is represented in Plautus' play.

The parallel engagement of Cléante to a widow is displaced as an element in the plot by the news that Harpagon intends to take Mariane as his wife, and is thus cast as a rival to his son. This latter pattern is not unknown to ancient comedy: it is central to three of Plautus' plays.[9] In each case, the errant father is exposed and must submit to the indignation of his wife, thus clearing the field for his son. Harpagon, by contrast, is a widower and does not think to conceal his infatuation, since he plans a proper marriage with the girl. A different kind of pressure is required to secure his consent to his son's marriage with Mariane. This takes place in two stages. First, Mariane is revealed to be the sister of Valère and daughter of Anselme. Anselme prefers Cléante as the part-

ner for his daughter. Second, Cléante announces that his father's treasure is now in his possession and that he will return it only on the condition that Harpagon yield in the matter of matrimony with Mariane
(5.6). Under this double assault, Harpagon gives in, with the proviso that
Anselme will have to bear all the costs of both weddings.

In place of Anselme as his daughter's betrothed, Harpagon has
Anselme's own son and heir, and Mariane, in turn, no longer appears
as the child of an impoverished mother, but as a girl who will bring a
fortune as her dowry. Purely from the financial point of view, Harpagon
has realized his ambitions for his children's marriages, having secured
prosperous partners for both. That these arrangements come at the cost
of his own passion for Mariane is a separate matter. In fact, Harpagon's
infatuation with the poor young woman is something of an anomaly,
given his single-minded fixation on money. When Frosine, the go-
between, tries to paint Mariane's thrifty habits as a net gain in income,
Harpagon is not deceived: "It's a joke to have me count as dowry all the
costs she won't incur. I shall not allow for what I don't receive—I have
to lay my hands on something" (2.5). Frosine alludes to riches that
Mariane has laid up in foreign parts—a cue to the alert spectator of the
recognition to come—but Harpagon is skeptical and changes the subject to the problem of the difference between his age and that of his
intended. By introducing the rivalry theme between father and son,
Molière has had to endow the miser with a secondary motive—love as
opposed to greed—parallel to that of Cléante. True, a sentimental attachment to a young lady is less seemly in an old widower than in a boy,
and the sympathies of the audience will naturally be with the latter,
especially given the absurd figure that Harpagon cuts in the play.[10]

One might perhaps seek an analogy between Harpagon's amatory
disposition and his fixation on wealth: both may in some sense be imagined as erotic drives. In Molière's Dom Juan, the hero's passion for
women is represented as coordinate with the evasion of his debts. But
it is precisely the motility of Dom Juan's desire, the radical reduction
of all women to the single currency of sex, that renders his passion a
figure for the nascent capitalist's indiscriminate interest in commodities and in their common denominator, money. Harpagon's fixation on
an individual woman, on the contrary, is akin to his preoccupation with
his buried treasure or to his worries over his daughter's dowry. Just as
the latter two motifs are a survival from Plautus' version, in which the
miser is concerned to keep his particular cache of gold wholly intact,
rather than to increase it by investing it at interest, so too Harpagon's
desire for Mariane is a kind of fetishism, like all infatuation, by which
free libidinous energy is cathected onto a unique figure, a specific con-

gealed form of sexual capital. As a usurer, for whom money is never this or that bit of metal but cash value in the abstract, Harpagon should, if he is to be consistent in the sexual and the economic spheres, want not this or that woman, but sex in general.

However this may be, Harpagon clearly sacrifices his passion for gain in his choice of the apparently impecunious Mariane as his mate. With respect to his children, however, he acts entirely in character, putting them into circulation, as it were, to realize a profitable return. Whereas the essence of Euclio's behavior in Plautus' *Aulularia* had been withdrawal from the world of reciprocal exchange, rupturing the commercial and connubial network by which civic identity was constituted, Harpagon is busy contracting marriages for his children, just as he lets his money out on loan. Far from closing himself and his household off from society, Harpagon is the very spirit of social interaction, continually bonding his estate with others, both conjugally and economically. The problem with Harpagon is not secession, but an exploitative engagement with the world. In Molière's play, the issue is not the reintegration of the miser into society, but the transformation of the basis of his relations with others from profiteering into a kind of sentimental fair play. Harpagon, whose name, incidentally, suggests graspingness (from the Greek verb *harpagō*), overrides the ostensibly natural attraction between his children and partners both virtuous and coeval in his concern for a material advantage, just as he extracts a more than just return on his usurious transactions. This is a man from whom society must be protected, not one in need of closer commerce with his fellows.

In the denouement, Molière allows the audience to have it both ways. Elise and Cléante obtain their hearts' desire and secure a profitable match into the bargain. Harpagon, unlike Euclio, persists in denying his daughter a dowry, but it does not really matter in *The Miser*, since concern about the dowry is not, in this version, a symbol of the miser's isolation, but a mere tick in Harpagon's make-up, having nothing to do with his fundamental vice, that is, the unconstrained will to accumulation. Sentiment replaces financial calculation in the contracting of marital alliances, but it is worth noting that both principles— romantic attachments and economic exchange—are universal in Molière, as opposed to the localism characteristic of classical New Comedy. In Menandrean drama, the recognition serves to reconcile a young man with his father by legitimizing the object of his wayward passion. For Cléante and Elise, however, there is no civic obstacle to their amour encoded within the text, only the extreme acquisitiveness of their father. Thus, there is no necessary social function to the revelation that Valère and Mariane are of noble stock, just the sentimental motive of restoring the children to their father and rewarding their goodness with the inheritance that is their due. They need not be proven citizens of France, nor are they. The structure of social relations in Molière's France is not the parochial kinship pattern of the ancient city-state, or at least of Athens, in which the community extended only to those of citizen extraction in both the paternal and maternal lines. The reintegration of Euclio into the exchange network of his society is the other side of the coin to the ancient city's exclusivity, since the same rights of marriage and trade from which he threatens to isolate himself by his miserliness served as well to mark off from the civic community all who were not of citizen status. The plot of *The Miser*, by contrast, is predicated neither on individual withdrawal nor on the imperative of a narrow communal or ethnic integrity. The imagined basis of social transactions is the autonomous individual, stripped of substantial characteristics such as nationality or blood. The person appears to have the same abstract and universal being as money.

Molière's *Miser* precisely inverts the fundamental structure of Plautus' *Aulularia* in that it represents the miser, or more properly the usurer, as one who exploits the codes of economic and connubial exchange for the sake of exorbitant gain, whereas, in the Latin forerunner, the miser, or more properly the hoarder, cuts himself off from the forms of social reciprocity. Harpagon's offense is that he fails to appreciate the conventional ethical constraints on the free pursuit of profit— that is, lending at a fair rate of interest and taking into account personal sentiment in the creation of marriage alliances for one's children. In the nascent capitalist world of seventeenth-century France, the antisocial aspect of miserliness presents itself as a hypertrophy of the imperative to engage profitably in the processes of exchange, while in the agrarian economy of the classical city-state it takes the form of a deficient participation in the reciprocities of social life.

Nevertheless, as has been seen, Molière's miser retains traits of his model in the Plautine version that are at variance with his character as a single-minded profiteer. Harpagon is not a plausible representation of the moneylender's avarice, but a composite caricature of stinginess. This is only to be expected. Usury was not really the form in which the laws of merchant capitalism presented a threat to social morality, any more than hoarding was a danger to the emerging money economies of antiquity. The forms of exchange embedded in comic drama are nostalgic idealizations of the complex practices of social life. Or, rather, they are not mere idealizations but structures riven by contradictions and fissures, which reflect the labor of the text to present a coherent and unified system of motivations in a world marked by asymmetrical relations of power. The tools of poststructuralist criticism have encouraged critics to locate such gaps and inconsistencies in narratives. But the fault lines, so to speak, at which they occur are characteristic of the specific cultures in which the ideological structures, and the texts that bear them, are generated. The conditions of the production of such texts are intrinsic to their interpretation.

Conclusion

The premise of this book has been that Greek comedy reproduces in an altered register tensions that enter into the ideology of the ancient city-state, in which ideals of social harmony that are grounded in images of a golden age and other emblems of collectivity come into conflict with a system of competitive values and exclusionary practices based on class, status, and gender. As John Brenkman puts it: "The social dialectic of art does not arise from the conflict between a divided reality and a unified work, but rather takes the form of conflicts *within* the work, including the conflict between its unity and its division."[1] Drawing on Ernst Bloch's idea that utopian possibilities are latent in the everyday practices of social groups, Brenkman inquires how poetry in particular gives expression to aspirations that are projected from within and yet transcend the ideological constraints of a given society.[2] According to Herbert Marcuse, art necessarily evokes "the words, the images, the music of another reality, of another order repelled by the existing one and yet alive in memory and anticipation, alive in what happens to men and women, and their rebellion against it."[3] But it does so not in the form of an abstract vision of a better world, but in language that is charged and riven by the repertoire of historical meanings that are sedimented in ideology. Poetry works, as Brenkman expresses it, through "its concrete connections, as a language practice, with its relevant social contexts."[4]

The social context of Aristophanic comedy was the city-state at war and in the immediate aftermath of war, and the Peloponnesian War was waged ideologically as a struggle between classes as much as between cities or ethnicities. Issues of civic solidarity and identity in Athens were crossed with themes of panhellenic unity, and comic visions of peace and prosperity could put pressure on the restrictive codes of Athenian citizenship. In the political sphere, which class or party might successfully appropriate the nostalgic and perhaps anticipatory images of natural harmony was up for contention. In the plays of Aristophanes, integrative ideals tend to be associated with a politically moderate leadership representing the established families of Athens: the conservative and well-to-do Bdelycleon in *Wasps*, the sage and self-disciplined Lysistrata whose name evokes that of the contemporary priestess of Athena, and the aristocratic old Aeschylus in *Frogs*. The court-shy Pisthetaerus in *Birds* may also be of this stamp, despite his later adoption of tyrannical airs. In general, the utopian models were undergirded by an appeal to images of the common farmer celebrated in *Works and Days* of Hesiod and envisioned as the bedrock of traditional values in the polis. They were in turn contained by the exigencies of Athenian policy and the practical interests of the groups that exploited them. Aristophanes might construct a comic fantasy of a classless and borderless society, but he left intact the patterns of differentiation encoded in Athenian "language practice." Thus, women abandon the acropolis and return to their homes in *Lysistrata*, while the men carve up the Greek world figured as the body of a woman; family is valorized as the basis for citizenship in *Frogs*, even though slaves have earned the franchise for their military service to the state; the critique of the rich in *Wealth* is transposed into the genial ideal of a reign of plenty, which can be imagined at a cost to no one.[5]

During much of Menander's lifetime, Athenian policy was largely in the hands of leaders imposed or supported by foreign powers, and comedy retreated from explicit engagement with political themes. Strains in the civic ideology surfaced instead in a domestic context, centering on relations between men and women of different status or class, or else divided by codes of propriety that had their basis in the citizenship rules of the city-state. Although *Grouch* is in some respects analogous to Aristophanes' *Wealth* in its concern with relations between rich and poor, Menander's play is located in the remote countryside, far from the civic center of Athens, and there is no interest in controversial public roles like that of the sycophant.

It has been suggested that the preoccupation with civic status in Menander's comedies was prompted by Athens' loss of control over its citizenship criteria in the late fourth century B.C., and that his plots are contrived to allay anxieties over the accidental loss of status: in the end, true identities are reasurringly discovered.[6] The soothing atmosphere of New Comedy has been ascribed also to the conservative cast of the theater-going public. Geoffrey Arnott has argued that the composition of the audience had been "altered by the abolition of the state subsidy which previously enabled the poorest Athenians to attend theatrical performances." The prosperous or middle-class audiences of Menandrean comedy, Arnott suggests,

> wanted to turn their backs on the recurring disasters of life—public disasters like the bloody suppressions of uprisings in 303 and 295, the sieges of 304 and 296–4, famine in the 320's and the 290's; and the private disasters of death, disease and separation—and to be entertained instead by the consoling and idealised picture of stable, middle-class family life, where the problems of money and sexual desire, of misunderstandings and flawed relationships, were more limited in scale, always fathomable, and always resolved in the inevitable happy ending which celebrated and cemented family unity.[7]

But if the recognition of foreigners, resident aliens, foundlings, and slaves as Athenian citizens reaffirms local identity, it also suggests that people divided by barriers of status share a common nature. Menander seems to preserve in this way the ecumenical impulse of Old Comedy, although it is always recontained by the tricks of plot noted by Davies and Arnott. Despite the bland or conservative sentiments characteristic of Menander's personae,[8] the plays subtly undermine the comfortable acceptance of city-state exclusiveness and the privileges of class and point toward a wider conception of Greek identity.

Both Aristophanic and Menandrean comedy are products of a world of agrarian communities in which participation in the polity is constituted by access to property and kinship ties. Utopian gestures toward inclusiveness in spite of class and status are situated in the context of this underlying ideological structure. For all the differences between the forms of Old and New Comedy, the contradictions that they manifest in lapses of narrative coherence and the multiply determined motivations of characters are symptomatic of a shared problematic. Ancient comedy enacts the strains inherent in the corporate identity of the classical city-state.

The modern nation-state also seeks to ground civic status in principles of filiation, but its exclusionary tendencies are sapped by a capitalist ideology—and to a degree also a capitalist practice—predicated on the motility and equivalence of commodities, that informs all categories of social life, including personal identity.[9] In this context, ecumenical identification is not simply a liberating ideal but a potential inherent in economic relations that threatens to dissolve ties based on local loyalties.[10] Thus, for Molière, the moment of universal reciprocity is figured not in an antique reminiscence of a golden age or in the transgressive movement of passionate love across status lines but in the calculating greed of a usurer who reduces all forms of exchange to cash value. It is just this corrosive materialism that must be recontained by the sentimental denouement of the play.

Molière achieves the reintegration of the miser by subordinating the logic of his behavior to the form of classical New Comedy, which affirms the wisdom of erotic love against social obstacles of any sort. Jonathan Haynes, in a brilliant study of the theater of Ben Jonson, writes (borrowing an idea of Raymond Williams) that "some artistic forms, like the portrait or Greek drama, are created in and determined by specific historical circumstances, but become the general property of subsequent traditions."[11] The adaptability of the ancient genre is indeed remarkable, but so is the transformation of its function. If, as Walter Cohen observes, "the social basis for the recovery of antiquity in the theater was the gradual transition from feudalism to capitalism,"[12] capitalism in turn conditioned the ideological operations latent in the comic tradition of ancient Greece. With each appropriation of the classical forms, imperfect unities of plot and character are forged out of the complex values of cultures under pressure. In this book, I have sought to disclose the mechanisms of this ideological activity in the comic productions of the Athenian stage.

Notes

Introduction

1. Kassel and Austin 1983– will, upon completion, be the fundamental edition of Greek comedy, including the fragments. Translations of Aristophanes are widely available; for Menander, including the major fragments, see Miller 1987; for a translation of the fragments of Greek comedy (apart from Menander), see Rusten et al. (forthcoming).

2. An intermediate stage was known as Middle Comedy; for the division into Old, Middle, and New Comedy, with discussion of the ancient sources, see Nesselrath 1990.

3. For an introduction to the main features of Aristophanic comedy, see Dover 1972.

4. The best general introduction to New Comedy is Hunter 1985.

5. Though out of date and marred by a tendency to take comedy as an accurate reflection of contemporary realities, Ferguson 1911: 74–87 gives a good sense of the social concerns of New Comedy; cf. Gruen 1990: 124–57 for reflections of contemporary issues in Plautine comedy.

6. On the parabasis, see Hubbard 1991. It is possible that personal satire in Old Comedy was sometimes limited by public decree; for a recent discussion of the evidence, see Atkinson 1992.

7. On the relationship between narrative practices and social identity, cf. Bennington 1990: 132: "The idea of the nation is inseparable from its narration: that narration attempts, interminably, to constitute identity against difference, inside against outside, and the assumed superiority of inside over outside."

8. Frow 1986: 19.

9. Jameson 1981: 146.

10. On the symptomatic reading (*lecture symptomale*) of a text, see Althusser and Balibar 1970: 16; Smith 1984: 73, 75–82.

11. Bal 1987: 107–8. For the multiplicity of personae inhabiting Dicaeopolis, the protagonist of Aristophanes' *Acharnians*, see Fisher 1993: 44.

12. Macherey 1978: 79–80. Cf. Thompson 1984: 25: "The representation of unity in the context of restricted and mutable social relations thus implies the projection of an 'imaginary community' by means of which 'real' distinctions are portrayed as 'natural,' the historical is effaced in the atemporality of essence". See also Kavanagh 1981; Eagleton 1983: 81; Laclau 1977: 102–3: "In periods of stability, when the social formation tends to reproduce its relations following traditional channels and succeeds in neutralizing its contradictions by *displacements*, this is when the dominant bloc in the formation is able to absorb most of the contradictions and its ideological discourse tends to rest more on the purely implicit mechanisms of its unity." Marianetti 1992: 3 (cf. 18) discusses the contradictory elements in Aristophanes' *Clouds* as a function of social change, but sees them as a product of Aristophanes' "intention to portray diverse forces."

13. On the controversy over the political significance of Aristophanic comedy, see Edwards 1991: 178 n. 52.

14. Heath 1987: 43; cf. Gomme 1938; Halliwell 1984; Bremer 1993.

15. Heath 1987: 44, 50; cf. 45–46 (on *Frogs*), 53.

16. Goldhill 1991: 200; cf. 221. For Goldhill, comedy "tests . . . the possibilities of transgression" (188; cf. 194, 201); as a result, it is both conservative and critical, standing at the margin between accepted ideas and festive violation. Heath 1987: 40–41, on the contrary, denies any distance between the ideological content of the comedies and popular beliefs: "The plays are so nicely attuned to the prejudices and expectations of the majority of Aristophanes' audience that one would hesitate to affirm of anything in them that it was put there in order to express Aristophanes' own political views."

17. For recent discussions of Aristophanes' relationship to popular ideology, see especially Brock 1986; Edmunds 1987; and Henderson 1990 and the subtle analysis of the relationship between Aristophanes' political views and the nature of his comedies in Hubbard 1991.

18. Goldhill 1991: 194; cf. Loraux 1980–81: 150 and 1984: 195: "For laughter too answers to a history."

19. Calame 1989a discusses the way in which the use of masks in Old Comedy is a vehicle for unmasking social and political realities.

20. Rose 1992: 42.

21. Lefèvre 1973, 1978 argues forcefully the case for Terentian originality, but he has not won general assent; cf. Blanchard 1983: 264. It is possible to speak with a little more confidence of Plautus' technique in adapting Greek comedy thanks to the recent discovery of a papyrus fragment of Menander's *Double Deceiver* (*Dis Exapatōn*), the model for Plautus' *Bacchides*; for a recent and subtle discussion, see Goldberg 1990.

Chapter 1

1. On the comic hero, see Whitman 1964. Sutton 1980: 84–90 offers an Adlerian reading of the Aristophanic hero who is marked by a "superiority com-

plex" and an "omnipotence fantasy"; Carrière 1979: 85–110 sees in the structure of the Aristophanic comedy a motion from reality to utopia. See also Landfester 1977: 194 and Sifakis 1992 for a narratological analysis of the plots of Aristophanic comedy on the lines of Propp's morphology of the Russian folktale.

2. See Heberlein 1980.

3. See Händel 1963: 239–40, 253–56.

4. On the festive moment in comedy, see Stallybrass and White 1986: 6, who remark: "Everywhere in literary and cultural studies today we see carnival emerging as a model, as an ideal and as an analytic category." Cf. Plutarch *Life of Lucullus* 39.1: "One may recognize in the life of Lucullus, just as in Old Comedy, in the first part civil and military affairs, but in the end drinking and dining and all-night revels and torchlights and every kind of amusements," cited in Kunst 1919: title page. On the conclusion to *Wasps*, see Whitman 1964: 156; Kunst 1919: 33; Spatz 1978: 70; Lenz 1980: 17. The Dionysian character of the dancing contest in the finale is suggested by the slave's invocation of Dionysus at 1474, and by the puns on *trux* (wine dregs), at 1521 and 1537; cf. Reckford 1977: 302, 309–10.

5. On the utopian comedies, see Carrière 1979: 85–110; Händel 1963: 226–27; Reinhardt 1960 [1938]: 263–65; Richter, 1933; Zimmerman 1983.

6. See Hubbard 1991: 126, with bibliography in n. 29.

7. On the jack-in-the-box farce, see MacDowell 1971: 149 ad 139–229; *Wasps* is cited according to this edition unless otherwise indicated.

8. On disease, see 77, 80, 87, 114, 651; on madness, see 744. See also Dover 1972: 127; Lenz 1980: 39–40. Reckford 1987: 279 interprets the entire play as a "healing catharsis."

9. Jameson 1966: 10. See especially Ben Jonson's *Every Man in His Humour* (1599); Jonson labeled his early plays, in which the type of the humour was paramount, "comical satires."

10. In different ways, Schwinge 1975: 41–42 and Koch 1965: 74–79, have raised the question of the relationship between the critical or satirical thrust of Aristophanic drama and the autonomous comic elements in the plays. According to Schwinge, the mock conversion of Philocleon shifts the argument from a political critique of the jury system to the exemplification of the type of the buffoon, now reduced to an isolated and purely private figure. The pivotal moment is the *agōn*; after that, Bdelycleon can indulge his father's passion, now reduced to a private "tick," with the mock trial in his own home.

11. For the reversal, see Whitman 1964: 145.

12. Dover 1972: 122; the translation of 1351–59 that follows is Dover's. Starkie 1897 quotes the scholiast ad 1355: "old men are twice boys." Bowie 1987: 112–15 interprets the rejuventation of Philocleon as a reversal of the Athenian rite of passage to adulthood (*ephēbeia*).

13. There is no indication that Philocleon either does or is expected to mature again in the subsequent action; the choral interlude on the transformation in his character (1450–73) simply marks the end of his jurying days, as Philocleon himself testifies (1335–40), and is not an earnest comment on "Philokleon's probable development in years to come" (MacDowell 1971 ad

1450–73). This puts into question the suggestion of Whitman 1964: 144, followed by Vaio 1971: 335 and (most fully) Lenz 1980: 32–43, that the theme of the play is education.

14. For Bdelycleon's intentions, see 736–40, 1004–6; cf. 478–79, 506, 720–24; for Philocleon's refusal, see 341, cf. 612–18.

15. Cf. 784–85, where Philocleon consents to receiving his wages (*misthon*) from his son. On the Athenian attitude toward wages, see Ste. Croix 1981: 182–91; on surrender of authority or *kurieia*, see MacDowell 1971 ad 613.

16. See Dover 1972: 128.

17. See Lenz 1980: 25 for further discussion.

18. For Phrynichus the tragedian, see 219–20, 269–72, 1490, 1524 (on 1490, see Borthwick 1968: 44–45). For traditional art forms, see 318–19, 1479–81. For campaigns, cf. 236, where the action at Byzantium presumably evokes the Great War, especially in light of Xanthias' image of a Persian attack at 11–12. See also 355, for the subjugation of Naxos, which occurred somewhere around 470 B.C., and 439, where Philocleon laments his defeat at the hands of barbarians (his slaves are the immediate reference, but I suspect there is an implicit historical allusion as well). For the reference to Athens' role in repelling the barbarians, see 1077–1101. Note also the pun on the great king at 1124, Philocleon's suspicions of Persian attire at 1136–38, and Bdelycleon's reference to Marathon at 711.

19. These include *orgē* (and the verb *orgizō*), 223, 243, 404, 424, 425, 431, 560, 574, 646, 727, 883, 1083; *kholē* (bile), 403; *menos*,: 424; *thumos*, 567, 648. Cf. words or prefixes denoting acerbity (*oxus*, 226 and 407, of the wasps' sting; compounded with *thumos*, 406, 455, 501; with *kardia*, 430, see also 471, 1082, 1105, 1367; and *drimus*, 146, 277), toughness (*prinōdēs*, 383, cf. 877), and irascibility (*duskolia*, 882, 942, 1105; cf. 1356), images of knitted brows (655), looking daggers (literally "mustard," 455), eating one's heart out (283–87, etc.), barking outcries (198, 226, 415, 1311, cf. 596 of Cleon), and nettles (884). In general, see Taillardat 1965: 194–220; as Taillardat notes (211 n. 1), *Wasps* furnishes a particularly large number of illustrations in this category.

20. MacDowell 1971 glosses *orgē* here as spirit or courage; cf. the same claim in the same words a year later in the parabasis of *Peace* (752, with Platnauer 1964 ad loc.), and *Lysistrata* 550 and 1113 (*orgōntas*), with Rogers 1911 on the latter verse: "The word conveys no idea of anger."

21. The ambivalent nature of the wasps' aggressiveness is brought out clearly by Lenz 1980: 42–43.

22. At 57, 238, 354, 357, 363, 449, 554, 556, 759, 928, 933, 953, 958, 1101, 1200–1, 1227, 1345, 1369, 1447.

23. Dover 1972: 126–27.

24. Dover 1972: 127. On the motif of theft, see also Vaio 1971: 343. As a caution against too high-minded a condemnation of stealing in comedy, we may note that theft, particularly of food, seems to have been a feature of certain cultic practices and that there may have been certain gestures and dances in Old Comedy that represented such theft; see Lawler 1974: 79–80.

25. It is true that Bdelycleon, in exasperation, calls his father *ponēros* (192–93, 214; cf. 243) and even *miarōtatos* (most polluted, 397); also, the old man comically confesses to an urge for mischief (*kakon*, 322, 340; cf. 168).

26. This, I think, is the social basis for the quality of pathos that Silk 1987: 87–89, 110–11 brilliantly exhibits in the reminiscences of the chorus.

27. Compare also the uninhibited attitude of the old men toward sex and pleasure in general, as indicated by uses of the words *hēdonē* or *hēdomai* (e.g., 272, 510–12, 605, 1534, 1667; cf. 1006).

28. For the intertextual associations between *Wasps* and *Clouds*, see Hubbard 1991: 113–14, 125, 134–38.

29. Rau 1967: 154–55 argues that consistency in characterization is an aesthetic principle belonging only to later comedy than that of Aristophanes; see also Edmunds 1980: 25; Wilamowitz-Moellendorff 1935 [1911]: 312–13; Dover 1972: 61–63; Plebe 1952: 39–43, 51–59.

30. For the reading *neōn* in 343, see MacDowell 1971 ad loc.

31. For condemning the rich, see 575–76, cf. 626; for the change of gear, see 1168, 1171, 1309. On 1309, see Richter 1858 and Vaio 1971: 340.

32. See 417, 464–70, 474, 487; cf. 342–45, 411–14; Neil 1901 ad 235–36; Richter 1858 ad 417.

33. Philocleon's tastes, for example his suspicion of wine and kitharas (1253, 989; cf. 959), reflect simultaneously an old-fashioned ethic and a class hostility toward aristocratic symposia. The complex reference of such signifiers enables the cross-characterization of Philocleon. Markle 1985: 266–67 argues persuasively that "jury pay was sufficient to allow citizens who otherwise would have been compelled to work full time to support their households, to have leisure to serve on juries and attend the assemblies"; he observes that in the case of Philocleon, who is well-to-do despite his affectation of old-fashioned simplicity, "Aristophanes has drawn a caricature of the Athenian juror."

34. On the sleight of hand in Bdelycleon's argument, see Dover 1972: 129–30.

35. Note also Philocleon's instinctive association of writing with doing harm, 960–61.

36. Lenz 1980: 25.

37. On Xenophon's *Poroi (Ways and Means)*, see Austin and Vidal-Naquet 1977: 316–19.

38. For passages in which Aristophanes in one way or another mocks the courts, see Ste. Croix 1972: 362 nn. 8, 10.

39. Lateiner 1982: 4, 5, 7.

40. Lateiner 1982: 11. See also Connor 1971: 175–94; Lateiner 1981: 151–52, 158; Carter 1986: 50–51; Sinclair 1988.

41. Cf. *misodēmos* (473); *misopolis* (411); contrast, after the chorus has been persuaded by Bdelycleon's arguments, *ton dēmon philountos* (888–89) and *philopatrian* (1465).

42. *Wasps* announces itself as "a little argument that has judgment"; on this phrase, see Reckford 1977: 291, 299; Reckford 1987: 224. But argument

itself is deconstructed in the play: one of the words signifying persuasion, by which Philocleon acknowledges his submission to his son (*anapeithō*, 784), is employed also in the sense of "suborn" (101; cf. 278). On Derrida's conception of deconstruction and the irreducibility of ambiguous or contradictory terms, see Culler 1979; 1982: 180–225.

43. MacDowell 1971: 249, with apparent credence in the charge. For a rare and salutary reminder of the antidemocratic bias of our sources, see Jones 1953.

44. Note the contrast between "here" (*enthade*, 765), that is, in the house, and "there" (*ekeise*, 765; *ekei*, 767, 770), in the actual court; cf. MacDowell 1971 ad 765. On the metaphorical density of the scene, see Newiger 1957: 130. Gill 1985: 315 conceives of the scene as a kind of psychodrama designed to cure Philocleon of his disease (cf. 309–10). For Bowie 1987: 119, the location of the court in the doorway to the house (802, 871, 875) is a sign of its liminal function in Philocleon's rite of passage.

45. This point is brought out very well by Schwinge 1975: 41–42. See also Whitman 1964: 155: "Formerly, as a judge Philocleon had been part of society, not, as he thought, the main driving gear, but only a cog; still, a part." Xenophon *Oeconomicus* 11.21–24 reports that the conservative Ischomachus enoyed holding a mock court at home.

46. MacDowell 1971 ad 799 thinks it is invented by Aristophanes. The scholia suggest that Philocleon is here speaking to himself; cf. Green 1968 ad loc.

47. Vaio 1971: 339, quoting Ehrenberg 1961: 102. Cf. Vaio 1971: 335 n. 1 and 342 on motifs linking the first and second parts of the play. For the law court and the symposium as symbols of "opposing ways of life," cf. Banks 1980: 82. On the symposium in the life of the aristocracy, see Murray 1983: 264. Pellizer 1983: 29–41 notes the agonistic violence characteristic of the traditional symposium, while Lissarague 1990: 25–28 emphasizes its ritual character and sees in the ceremonial mixing of wine and water a symbol of its ideal equilibrium.

48. Banks 1980: 84.

49. Banks 1980: 83; Henderson 1975: 79. Cf. Whitman 1964: 157.

50. The mention at 1301–2 of other, more conservative participants in the symposium widens the scope of the satire and has sometimes been applauded as a sign that Aristophanes was above partisanship; see Carter 1986: 63–70 on the histories of these personalities, which include "political and nonpolitical figures" (p. 68). Hubbard 1991: 136 argues that Bdelycleon, who in the first part of the play is represented as an uncompromising opponent of Cleon and in this capacity stands for the views of Aristophanes himself (114), is transformed in the symposium scene into an ambitious and amoral figure no better than his father.

51. Cf. *kalos kagathos* (1256) and Ste. Croix 1972: 371–76 for full discussion of this idea with relevant bibliography; also pp. 358–59 on Aristophanes' use of political and moral terminology.

52. Ste. Croix 1972: 356. Cf. 357–58, 370–71; Henderson, 1980: 189.

53. Dover 1972: 131. Cf. Bowie 1987: 125.

54. On the Athenian *oikos* (household) and the ideal of autarky, see Lacey 1968: 15–24; Ste. Croix 1981: 116–17; Foley 1982: 18–19.

55. *Pais* was the common term of address to a slave, but here the content of the metaphor is laid bare: slaves are like children because they are vulnerable to corporal punishment without institutions of redress.

56. The offense is *hubris;* see MacDowell 1971 ad 1418.

57. For persuasion, see 116, 278, 471–72, 513, 668, 697, 713, 729, 743, 746–49, 760–61, 763, 784, 974, 1470, and, in an ironic context, 568, 573, 586.

Chapter 2

1. It is a city that they are seeking from the beginning (48, 121, 123, 127, 136); despite the phrase *topon apragmona* (troublefree place, 44), there is no suggestion of a pastoral ideal. When Alink 1983: 317 says that Pisthetaerus and Euelpides "are looking for another, non-city-like place to live," this is so only in the sense that they desire a place free of the litigiousness that accompanies city life, at all events in Athens. Heberlein 1980: 27–37 distinguishes the protagonists of Aristophanes' utopian plays, such as *Birds*, from the farmer-heroes of the peace plays (*Acharnians*, *Peace*), but the differences seem less compelling than the similarities.

2. For an exhaustive examination of this myth in relation to *Birds*, see Hofmann 1976: 72 ff., and with special reference to Sophocles' *Tereus* (produced ca. 431 B.C.), see Dobrov 1990a. Quirini 1987: 35–37 sees Tereus' Thracian origins as a sign of barbarism—dubious in light of his achievement in teaching the birds to speak Greek; on the ideological construction of Thrace as an emblem of barbarism in Athenian drama, see Hall 1989: 133–38.

3. Cf. Blaydes 1882: xiii: "Now, two things in this play seem above all to indicate [Aristophanes' intentions], that is, the departure of two Athenian citizens on account of the crooked condition of the city in the beginning of the play (30–48), and Peisetaerus' triumph and assumption of universal power in the end." There is an abrupt introduction of a new plan of action near the beginning of several of Aristophanes' plays—for example, the idea of restoring Plutus' sight in *Wealth* (discussed in Chapter 5 of this volume); of installing a communist regime in *Assemblywomen;* and of occupying the acropolis in *Lysistrata* (See Chapter 3 in this volume and Vaio 1973).

4. Henderson 1990: 8. Sommerstein 1987: 4 remarks more cautiously: "It is tempting, and may not be entirely mistaken, to see some association between this fantasy of total power and the popular mood at Athens in 415/4," though he distinguishes *Birds* from Aristophanes' other surviving fifth-century plays for "having no strong and obvious connection with a topical question of public interest" (p. 1). Hubbard 1991: 159 sees scant evidence in the play for "any systematic allegory concerning the Sicilian expedition"; he suggests instead that the rebellion against the gods evokes the recent desecration of the herms and profanation of the mysteries, and that the play "explores the consequences as well as the causes of such impiety" (p. 161); see also Craik 1987.

5. Suevern 1827; for an independent and eccentric interpretation along the lines of Suevern's, see Harman 1920.

6. Green 1879: 8.

7. See Hofmann 1976: 70; cf. Alink 1983: 250–57 for an overview of interpretations of *Birds*.

8. Green 1879: 8–9, 12. Köchly 1857, quoted from the summary in Green 1879: 10.

9. Arrowsmith 1973: 155.

10. Plutarch *Life of Alcibiades* 17.1, cited in Arrowsmith 1973: 141.

11. Schareika 1978: 104. See also Katz 1976.

12. Whitman 1964: 179, 169. Dover 1972: 145, cited in Schareika 1978: 61–62, remarks that *Birds* does not "direct the attention of the community towards any desirable policy or decision or any reform of its political habits."

13. Dobrov 1990b: 3–4.

14. See Introduction. Cf. Macherey and Balibar 1981: 80. "The *model*, the real referent 'outside' the discourse which both fiction and realism presuppose, has no function here as a non-literary, non-discursive anchoring point predating the text."

15. Edwards 1990: 54 observes that the "mimetic conception . . . obscures the genesis of the text, its production, the process of composition occurring in a social and political context."

16. Cf. Volosinov 1973: 10: "The domain of ideology coincides with the domain of signs," cited in Frow 1986: 64. Frow remarks that the sign "signifies only by virtue of a social consensus, and . . . where this consensus is founded on social relations which are contradictory, the symbolic order is necessarily involved in this contradiction."

17. Eco 1984: 1257 (my emphasis).

18. On *nomos*, see Ostwald 1969.

19. Alink 1983: 318.

20. The most conspicuous example is the second book, devoted almost in its entirety to the *nomoi* of the Egyptians.

21. There is a connection here with the nature of textuality as such; cf. Blumenberg 1979: 42: "Reality presents itself now as never before as a sort of text which takes on its particular form by obeying certain rules of internal consistency," cited in Gelley 1987: 28. In reference to the discussion of narrative by de Certeau 1980: 205–27, Gelley remarks: "Narrative practices . . . are conceived as establishing boundaries, creating an accredited 'theater' of action, a 'scene'" (p. 29).

22. This has something in common with the notion of leveling proposed by Donaldson 1970: 5–9; in the extreme case, however, an anomian place will be no place at all.

23. See Donaldson 1970 for the pattern of inversion; see Carrière 1979: 89–91 for inversion in connection with the golden age.

24. More 1910: 140: "Wherefore not Utopie, but rather rightly / My name is Eutopie: a place of felicity." On *eutopia*, see also González de Tobia 1994.

25. In the poem on Eutopia partially cited in the previous note, More writes: "Now am I like to Plato's city." On the customs of the Egyptians as the reverse of those of the Greeks, see Herodotus 2.35; Sophocles *Oedipus at Colonus* 337–43. On the cyclopes, see *Odyssey* 9.189 *athemistiaēidē*; 215 *oute dikas eu eidota oute themistas* (having no knowledge of just ways or sanctions). For Callicles, see Plato's *Gorgias*; for Thrasymachus, see *Republic* 1.

26. The reference to a cockfight at 70–71 may suggest that aggression and domination among the birds arises through contact with human society.

27. Cf. 20, 51, etc.; in *Knights*, the sausage-seller refers to Athens as "the city of the Gapenians" (*tēi Kekhēnaiōn polei*, 1263); Arrowsmith 1973: 138 n. 10.

28. Cf. *Frogs* 692. In Sophocles' *Antigone* 1069, the correct interpretation of *atimōs* is "without civic status," as Kells 1963: 57 demonstrates; contra, e.g., Jebb 1928 ad loc., who translates "ruthlessly" (I owe this reference to Diane Juffras, personal communication). In general, see Harrison 1971: 82–83.

29. Cf. Toynbee 1981: 40: "The Hellenic and the nomad ways of life were at opposite poles."

30. Cf. Slater 1990: 42–43, who examines the implications for staging the scene.

31. See *Odyssey* 1.22–24. Gelzer 1976: 2–3 sees the indeterminate locale of the opening scenes as a means of exciting the audience's curiosity and preparing for surprise effects; cf. his analysis of the playful punning on *polos* and *polis* (p. 7).

32. The visitors to Cloudcuckooland in the "exemplificatory" scenes in the latter half of *Birds* appear to fall into three groups of three. The first group consists of the priest (851), the poet (904), and the oraclemonger (959); all have or pretend to some role in the foundation of the city. The second group consists of Meton the geometer (992), the inspector (1021), and the decree salesman (1035); they arrive before the city is fully established, and offer laws or principles of order. Finally, after a choral interlude and visits from Iris and messengers, a would-be parricide (1337), a dithyrambic poet (1372), and a sycophant or informer (1410) arrive; by now, the city of the birds has its constitution and subjects each of these visitors to its own discipline. For a different analysis, which collapses the first six visits (801–1055) into one group focused on the foundation ceremony of the city, see Gelzer 1976: 10; the point of demarcation is 1118: "Our sacrifices are favorable, O birds." For the division of Aristophanic comedy into the creation of the utopian dispensation followed by scenes illustrating the consequences of the new conditions, see Zimmerman 1987: 50.

33. See Carrière 1979: 88.

34. I derive this last expression from Wolf 1982.

35. Dorfman 1983: 26; for a model analysis of colonialist discourse in Shakespeare's *Tempest*, see Brown 1985: 48–71. Quirini 1987: 87 acknowledges that the city of the birds lacks the negative features of Athens, but he argues that by this very circumstance it is "populated by monstrous and am-

biguous figures" who are "worthy denizens" of so ridiculous a place; to reject the life of the polis, even for its vices, entails an escape from history to a universe that is still inchoate and monstrous, a state of origins "that *must* rather be closed off once and for all" (150). I do not see as a major theme in the play the dread of primal formlessness.

36. Romer 1990 shows how the new theogony promulgated in *Birds* reproduces the hierarchical structure of power, and more specifically the inequality between the genders, that is authorized by Hesiod's *Theogony*. For the role of Eros or passionate desire in Orphic cosmogony and its relation to myth expounded in *Birds*, see Calame 1991: 229–31. It may be noted also that, with respect to the birds, Pisthetaerus plays a role like that of Prometheus in the development of human beings, especially as represented in *Prometheus Bound* attributed to Aeschylus; this may in part explain the appearance of Prometheus in Cloudcuckooland later in the comedy.

37. On the parthenon in Athens, four conflicts were represented on the metopes: between gods and giants, Lapiths and centaurs, Greeks and amazons, and Greeks and Trojans. Barbarians, women, beasts, and primordial deities stand in as antagonistic others, whose aspiration to power is conceived as a challenge to the order of the city-state; cf. Castriota 1992: 96–183 for a full discussion in the context of Athenian imperialism. Cartledge 1993 provides an elegant discussion of the homology between the different categories of "other" in Greek thought. On the battle between gods and giants as the mythological model for the rebellion of the birds in the latter part of the play, see 1249–52, and cf. Arrowsmith 1973: 139, and esp. Hofmann 1976: 86 ff. See Vidal-Naquet 1986: 216–18 on the structure of the Aristophanic utopia.

38. Cf. 131–32 and 1137–42 on the reversal of sexual mores; see 793–97 on wings as the perfect equipment for adulterers.

39. See also the reference to the *arkhaioi thesmoi* (ancient sanctions, 331) among the birds, by which human beings were not to be admitted into their realm.

40. The storks' laws are on *kurbeis* (1354), triangular tablets on which some ancient legislation was inscribed at Athens, as opposed to the *stelai* on which modern laws were normally published. Hubbard 1991: 172 treats Pisthetaerus' allusion to the laws of the storks as the ploy of a practiced sophist.

41. The obligation was protected by law; see Harrison 1968: 77.

42. See Finley 1975: 34–59.

43. The word for "delay" is *mellonikian*, a pun on postponing victory (*nikē*) and the dilatory or reluctant policy of Nikias (Nicias) in the Sicilian campaign. Another direct allusion to the Peloponnesian War is the phrase "Melian famine" (186).

44. On the virtue of *sophrosunē* (moderation), see North 1966; Arrowsmith 1973: 124, 140.

45. See Johnston 1980 for a survey of ancient conceptions of the age of Cronus or Saturn; see also Vidal-Naquet 1986: 2–3.

46. There is an analogy here with the development of the individual self,

as it is represented in the psychoanalytical theory of Jacques Lacan. As Gallop 1985: 81 puts it, "The self is constituted through anticipating what it will become, and then this anticipatory model is used for gauging what was before."

47. These are probably not the instruments that Pisthetaerus and Euelpides brought with them (43), which are suitable for a party rather than for defense; see Hamilton 1985. At 62, the hoopoe's servant presumes the two men to be birdcatchers, an inference, perhaps, from their cooking utensils.

48. On tyranny as a commonplace accusation against the ambitions of the well-to-do, cf. *Wasps* 488–507.

49. Henderson 1990: 15, who defends the benevolence of Pisthetaerus' rule, remarks that he "is not doing anything different than the demos had in fact done on the demagogues' advice shortly before"; Henderson sees Pisthetaerus as a representative of the Athenian elite.

50. See Arrowsmith 1973: 131; Alink 1983: 322. For the metaphor of the tyrant city, see Tuplin 1985: 357–58 on Aristophanes (the present passage is not discussed, since it is not an unambiguous reference to imperial tyranny). Tuplin speculates (374) that the ordinary word for king may also have had something of the derogatory significance attaching to the term "tyrant."

51. On the marriage between Pisthetaerus and Basileia, and possible allegorical references to cult and politics, see Hofmann 1976: 140–60; for a more metaphysical interpretation, see Epstein 1981.

52. Contrast Arrowsmith 1973: 139: "The *Birds* . . . is the spectacle of innocent and peaceful *physis* . . . corrupted by superior intelligence whose motive power is man's metaphysical discontent, his lust for divinity—the discontent and *erōs* written into his *physis* and nakedly revealed in this chaotic epiphany of Athenian man and man generally"; see also Carrière 1979: 91–94.

53. Belsey 1980: 94–95; the examples of interrogative texts given by Belsey are Marlowe's *Tamburlaine the Great* and Andrew Marvell's "Horatian Ode" to Cromwell.

54. Cf. Ceccarelli 1982: 30–37.

Chapter 3

1. III.ii.112–28, 137; cited according to Jorgensen 1972.

2. 1162–70; the translation is that of Henderson 1988.

3. Cf. Warner 1987: 331: "Meanings of all kinds flow through the figures of women, and they often do not include who she is herself." Women's bodies may equally serve as a model of utopia or as an image of national identity; cf. Nead 1992; McClintock 1991: 105.

4. Henderson 1988 translation; subsequent translations are my own except where noted.

5. On women's bibulousness, cf. Axionicus frag. 5 (Kassel and Austin 1983–), from a comedy called *Philinna*: "Trust a woman not to drink water!"

6. Cf. Dover 1993: 8 n. 10.

7. Vaio 1973: 369–70.

8. On the parody of civic institutions in *Thesmophoriazusae* (*Women at Festival*), see Haldane 1965; Zeitlin 1981; Bobrick Carter 1987: 106–16.

9. Wilamowitz-Moellendorf 1927: 55; cf. 57.

10. Vaio 1973: 372, 373; cf. 374. Cf. Henderson 1987: xxxii: "The city is assimilated to the individual household" (cf. 129) and Gallant 1991: 170: "The metaphor of the community as merely a household writ large, I believe, lay at the heart of the ancient Greek notion of the *polis*." See also Strauss 1990: 106–7.

11. On the public versus the private role of women in Athens, see Shaw 1975 and the reply by Foley 1982; cf. Saxonhouse 1980, 1983.

12. For a detailed analysis of the political allusions in Lysistrata's image of the carded fleece, see Hugill 1936: 39–102, esp. 40–44; Henderson 1987: 141–42 ad 567–86.

13. On the role of the female body in the legitimization of kingship in the ancient near east, especially in reference to Egypt, see Springborg 1990a: 48: "Although from the beginning there is no doubt that the first monarchies were patriarchal, the processes of empowerment are female." Cf. Springborg 1990b on the corporate aspect of the king's "other body," esp. 679–80 on the female body in this capacity. See also duBois 1988: 28, 42–45 for the association between the female body and the reproductive powers of the earth in early (pre-Platonic) Greek thought, and the significance of this complex for the idea of Athenian autochthony. Vegetti 1983: 41–58 (*Metafora politica e immagine del corpo nella medicina greca*) suggests that in the Hippocratic tradition the body is conceived of as an undifferentiated vessel for humors and the like to enter or exit, whereas Plato and Aristotle developed an "anatomical" image of the body as a kind of polis, in which the internal organs enter into the formation of a coherent structure. According to Vegetti, it is the latter conception that conforms to the ideology of the Athenian city-state. Perhaps the former underwrites Aristophanes' use of the female body to represent Greece as a unified whole. One may contrast Menenius Agrippa's allegory of the revolt of the limbs against the belly (Livy 2.32.9–12; cf. Dionysius Halicarnassus *Antiquities* 6.44 ff.), with which he persuades the rebellious plebs to accept the authority of the aristocracy; here the interdependency of the several parts of the body serves as a justification for the hierarchical ordering of society. No such hierarchical principle is implied in the division of Diallagē's body.

14. For discussion of the utopian elements in their historical context, see Dawson 1992: 37–40.

15. Westlake 1980: 38 argues that there was small likelihood of a negotiated peace at the time *Lysistrata* was produced and concludes: "The *Lysistrata* is a play about peace but not an appeal to the Athenians to try to make peace" (54). Cf. Gomme, Andrewes, and Dover 1981: 190 and Heath 1987: 14: "Peace in *Lysistrata* . . . is a matter of pure fantasy, and can have no direct bearing on the issues of political debate outside the theatre. Contra Hugill 1936: ii–v; Sommerstein 1977: 119.

16. Westlake 1980: 41–42 remarks on the distinct note of gloom in the

play: at the beginning, Lysistrata refuses to utter aloud even the possibility that Athens may be destroyed, whether because it would be a bad omen, or for fear of giving offense to her audience (37–38); later, the commissioner hushes her at the mention of military losses (589–90). López Eire 1994: 71–73, 111–16 emphasizes domestic politics rather than military reversals as the basis of pessimism in the play. For the contrast in tone between *Lysistrata* and the earlier peace plays of Aristophanes, see the excellent discussion in Dillon 1987a.

17. Thucydides 8.1, translation in Crawley 1951.

18. If this oligarchy expected better terms of peace from Sparta (overtures were in fact made toward the Spartans), it was disappointed. Sparta was active on land and sea and was not disposed to negotiate away its advantage.

19. Henderson 1980: 188–89. On the role of class tensions in *Lysistrata*, see especially Newiger 1980: 228–37.

20. Cf. Henderson 1987: 141, 149.

21. Hugill 1936: 13 suggests that the choice of a woman as an advocate for peace exposes the lack of leadership in Athens; as a woman, Lysistrata is above partisanship. On the marginalization of women in Greek society, see Gallo 1984.

22. See Hugill 1936: 50–51 and 55–59 on proposals to widen Athenian citizenship; on the parabasis of *Frogs*, cf. 85–86.

23. Cf. Lamphere 1974. Ardener 1981: 17 noted the ways in which women excluded from public power "operate what may be called a 'muted structure.'" Cf. Wright 1981: 149–51.

24. Verses 81–92, translated in Henderson 1988.

25. Epigram 53 in Green 1991.

26. See Konstan 1993a.

27. Women who behaved sexually in what was perceived to be a masculine way could be characterized as unnatural or monstrous, especially in the Roman period; see Hallett 1988: 1266; Hallett 1989.

28. The possibility of erotic relations among the women might be thought to subvert the premise of their sexual deprivation, but Aristophanes does not represent such activity as a substitute for sex with a husband.

29. Gallop 1989: 16. Cf. Eichenbaum and Orbach 1988: 11: "Connectedness, attachment, affiliation, selflessness have been and still are largely the foundation of women's experience. A woman knows herself and gathers a sense of well-being through her connection and attachment to others." See also Rich 1993: 240; Friedman 1993: 285–87.

30. Modleski 1988: 5–6; she adds: "I want to suggest that woman's bisexual nature, rooted in preoedipality, and her consequent alleged tendency to overidentify with other women and with texts, is less a problem for *women* . . . than it is for patriarchy."

31. While it is common to identify the women of whom Sappho writes as girls, the ancient lexica refer to her circle as composed of friends or coevals (*philai, hetairai*), and there is little evidence in Sappho's own poetry of an age difference between herself and the women she loves. The assumption that Sappho was older may owe something not only to the outdated image of her

as a schoolmistress, but also to the assimilation of sexuality among women to the pederastic model characteristic of males. Love between women was perhaps, unlike male *erōs*, imagined as predicated on likeness rather than on difference; cf. Stigers 1981; Bing and Cohen 1991: 72 n. 3; and Skinner 1993: 133, who observes that Sappho's "model of homoerotic relations is bilateral and egalitarian." Marry 1979: 72–73 and Giacomelli 1980: 140–41, however, ascribe a masculine competitiveness to Sappho's representation of erotic passion. On the idea of "Sapphic romance" involving a younger woman, cf. Vicinus 1993: 438, 441; for an elegant and decisive critique of the schoolmistress hypothesis, see Parker 1993.

32. Cf. Ragland-Sullivan 1989: 43 on the association of naming with masculinity ("father's name over mother's body") in Lacan's psychoanalytic theory.

33. Ardener 1981: 16 observes that women who enter the public arena effectively become "fictive men"; cf. Rodgers 1981: 71.

34. Cf. Henderson 1987: xxxvii–xxxviii; at lines 514–16, Lysistrata seems to refer to an exchange with her husband, though the context (505–20) suggests that she may be speaking on behalf of women generally.

35. Lewis 1955.

36. Henderson 1987: xxviii, xxxv.

Chapter 4

1. Leeuwen 1896: iv–vii.

2. Fraenkel 1962 (ch. 9, "Der Aufbau der Frösche"); Rogers 1902: xvi.

3. Segal 1961; Whitman 1964: 228–58.

4. On the bipartite structure, cf. Müller 1974: 1403; Handley 1985: 386; Harriott 1986: 115: "*Frogs* is intrinsically and unalterably bipartite"; Heath 1987: 44; and Dover 1993: 6. Hooker 1980: 181 argues that "the two principal motifs of the *Frogs*, contest and *katabasis* [descent into the underworld], came into Aristophanes' mind at different times and for different reasons, the former preceding, the latter following the death of Euripides."

5. Strauss 1966; see also Padilla 1992. The author of the ancient prose hypothesis to *Frogs* suggests that Dionysus "sports the lion-skin and club for the purpose of terrifying those he encounters" on his journey to the underworld, but as Dover 1993: 6 n. 2 remarks, this is not supported by what Dionysus says or does in the play.

6. Strauss 1966: 164. Dionysus' quest to bring back a poet is something like Heracles' labor of kidnapping the dog Cerberus, but I would not wish to lay too much emphasis on this analogy.

7. On the divinization of Heracles, see *Odyssey* 11.602, Hesiod frags. 25, 27 Merkelbach-West. Orpheus and Odysseus also descended into the underworld (cf. Lucian, *Nekyom.* 8, cited in Rogers 1902 ad 46), and Theseus as well (*Frogs* 142), but they did not become gods.

8. On the motif of play, see 333, 375, 392, 408, 410, 415, 443, 452.

9. On this sense of "teach," see 687, 1019, 1026 bis, 1035, 1037, 1054, 1055, 1057, 1069.

10. Ancient Greek had a grammatical form for the dual (two objects), as well as for the singular and plural.

11. There is an analogous triadic pattern involving individual power, collective identification, and social reciprocity in Euripides' *Cyclops;* see Konstan 1989.

12. For mutability as a specific characteristic of Dionysus, see Vernant 1985; Frontisi-Ducroux and Vernant 1983; Frontisi-Ducroux and Lissarrague 1983. See also Segal 1961: 221 for the unity of the various aspects of Dionysus.

13. Cf. Segal 1961: 47; Carpenter 1986 (ch. 6, "Dionysos and Herakles"): 99 on the "parallels between Dionysos and Herakles . . . in myth and cult," also 102–3, 122–23, 126 on the political aspects of the cults of Dionysus and Heracles under the reign of Pisistratus; Pascal 1911: 29. It is possible that Aristophanes is alluding to an epic poem on Heracles' descent into the underworld: see Lloyd-Jones 1967; Brown 1991: 49 with n. 34 (bibliography).

14. Whitman 1964: 234. Cf. Lapalus 1934; Tierney 1935; Mylonas 1961: 238 with n. 71; Graf 1974: 40; Brown 1991: 43; Dover 1993: 40. Seaford 1981: 253 supposes that there is "an essential similarity between the Dionysiac mysteries and the Eleusinian"; see also 262 for the theme of rebirth in the Dionysian mysteries, and Lada 1992 for Dionysus as initiand.

15. Bérard 1984: caption to fig. 160a; cf. 144. See also Burkert 1983: 281.

16. Cf. Rogers 1902 ad 830. Hooker 1960 proposed that Dionysus' progression in *Frogs* corresponded to an actual route from the temple of Heracles at Cynosarges to the temple of Dionysus "in the marshes," which he located on banks of the Illisus River outside the city walls of Athens. Slater 1986: 263 would locate the theater in which *Frogs* was performed in the precincts of the Dionysian temple; thus, "Dionysus wends his way into the Dionysion in Limnais, which in turn is the theatre in which he performs." The poetry contest itself may nevertheless have been imagined as occurring inside the walls.

17. Osborne 1985: 178 notes the "lack of fit" between the roles of citizen and initiate, and points to the location of the mysteries "outside the political space."

18. Bérard 1984: 110.

19. Loraux 1984 (ch. 1, "L'autochtonie: une topique athénienne"); on the contrast between the center of the city and the periphery, see also Polignac 1984 (ch. 2, "Le sanctuaire non urbain et la formation de la cité") and 87–88 for Athens as an exceptional case.

20. Czapo 1986: 197 suggests that Dionysus is "a new kind of comic hero," feckless like the youths in New Comedy (and analogous to Menelaus in Euripides' *Helen*), as opposed to the aggressively self-confident kind represented by Philocleon, Pisthetaerus, and the other middle-aged protagonists of the early comedies. As a god, however, Dionysus is exceptional among protagonists in the comedies that survive.

21. Stanford 1963 ad 300, following Radermacher 1954.

22. Turner 1969: 80. For a detailed application of Turner's categories to the interpretation of *Frogs*, see Moorton 1989. Bowie 1987: 112 suggests that mythic structures inform several of Aristophanes' comedies; see also Reckford 1987: 433–39; Goldhill 1991: 176–88.

23. Brown 1991: 42 argues that the encounter with Empusa represents a specific moment in the Eleusinian initiation, namely the experience of terrifying specters (*phasmata*).

24. Donaldson 1970: 5–9.

25. On the festive principle in comedy, see Stallybrass and White 1986: 1–26.

26. Harrison 1962: 15–16.

27. Burkert 1983: 12 and n. 48.

28. See Seaford 1981. Hooker 1980: 179–81 argues that Aristophanes composed the descent part of *Frogs* with Euripides' *Bacchae* in mind, as evidenced by the "choice of Dionysus as protagonist" and a texture of verbal and metrical allusions in the *parodos* (entrance song) of the chorus.

29. Cf. Plepelits 1970: 17; see also Handley 1985: 365–68.

30. For a review of the historical evidence, see Sartori 1974: 420–28.

31. However, Müller 1974: 1404–5 regards Aristophanes as favorable toward the enfranchisement of the slaves.

32. On the exceptional nature of the enfranchisement of the slaves at Athens, see Plutarch *Moralia* 849a and Longinus *On the Sublime* 15, describing the vehement reaction to a similar proposal by the orator Hyperides after the battle of Chaeronea. Ober 1989: 97 observes that "an attempt in 403–02 to limit the franchise to property owners was rejected, as was a proposal to broaden the franchise by granting citizenship to slaves who had helped in the revolution against the thirty. The Athenians thus reasserted both political equality among the citizens and the exclusivity of the citizen body."

33. Arnott 1991 sensibly observes that Aristophanes' advice to restore full civic rights to the conspirators was quite misguided in light of the oligarchic coup by the Thirty Tyrants in the following year, to which the enfranchisement very likely contributed.

34. See Redfield 1962–63: 434–35.

35. Walsh 1984: 91, 87.

36. Walsh 1984: 91. Here one may perhaps detect a serious significance in the association Aristophanes suggests between Euripides and Socrates (1491–92); see Rossetti 1977: 111–20.

37. Walsh 1984: 87. Cf. Euripides' parody of Aeschylus' lyric refrains with the nonsense syllables *tophlattothrattophlattothrat*, 1286 ff.

38. Simonides, as cited by the Byzantine scholar Michael Psellus, *Peri energ. daimonōn* 821 Migne (Edmonds 1924: 258); see also Plutarch *Glor. Ath.* 3 and Harriott 1969: 143.

39. Walsh 1984: 94.

40. Graff 1979: 23 characterizes—and caricatures—a certain type of modernism that opposes to mimetic representation the notion of a creative liter-

ary production; here, "Bad" is associated (according to Graff) with representation and "truth as correspondence," while "Good" is associated with creativity and "truth as invention, fiction."

41. Stanford 1963: xxxix; Walsh 1984: 97. Cf. Dover 1993: 23–24. Heiden 1991: 104 doubts that Aristophanes supported the programs represented by either tragedian and suggests (p. 106) that Aristophanes saw comedy, on which the debate in the *Frogs* is silent, as the genre that might have saved the city.

42. One may note a change in the motivation of Dionysus, who began his journey under the impulse of desire (*pothos*, 52–55, 66–67; *himeros*, 59), but has by the end learned to exercise judgment.

43. Demand 1970. The question whether the chorus of frogs was present on stage, or was invisible behind the back wall, is still debated; for a recent discussion (in favor of invisibility), see Allison 1983; Campbell 1984; contra Dover 1993: 56–57.

44. There is perhaps an allusion to this negative use of language in the proud silence of Aeschylus at the beginning of the poetic contest (832–34); the word *aposemnuneitai* (833) recalls the warning of the chorus to the Athenians (703).

Chapter 5

1. The point is echoed and brought home at 147–48: "For a small bit of silver I was made a slave, because I wasn't so rich."

2. That Plutus is a *daimōn* is evident from 123.

3. The hostility between Zeus and Plutus goes back to the Hesiodic tradition, according to which Zeus is responsible for concealing the earth's bounty from mortals.

4. The logical inference from this exchange, if we accept the inverse relation between justice and wealth, is that nearly all men are rich—at the expense of one or two honest folk like Chremylus. The emphasis, however, falls on the moral theme of unequal distribution and not on the relative numbers; presently, we shall find a conception of general scarcity according to which the populace is basically poor but honest and is exploited by a rather small class of social parasites.

5. But not the only effect. In later scenes, it appears that *all* men have become rich.

6. See Lofberg 1920. To what extent this image of sycophants was truly popular, as opposed to being a product of comic drama and forensic rhetoric, it is difficult to say. The sycophants were not entirely without public importance, any more than the popular political leaders were, and the prejudice against them may well have been partisan. For the sycophants' role in "making life difficult for wealthy men who refused to participate in the democratic working of society," see Osborne 1990: 98; see also Olson 1990: 232, who points to the quietism of the just citizen as a sign of his moderate politics. Cf. Carter 1986; contra Harvey 1990: 113, who observes that sycophancy was a crime and notes the incredulous response of the just citizen.

7. On *polupragmosunē*, see Ehrenberg 1947; Arrowsmith 1973: 126–30.

8. On autarky, see Handley 1965 ad 714; see also Gomme and Sandbach 1973 ad loc.

9. MacDowell 1978: 63 writes: "By the time of his last surviving play, *Wealth*, Aristophanes seems to have mellowed a little, since he allows a sycophant to defend his activities in the following dialogue" (vv. 898–919 are quoted here). But this is perhaps less a case of mellowing than a function of the dramatic structure of the play. The sycophant had been presented a moment before as an unjust figure, who deservedly lost his possessions when Plutus regained his sight. But he is also, as we have seen, hostile to the entire order of Plutus in which wealth creates the possibility of leisure and contentment. He is thus in opposition to Plutus in two respects: he is unjust, and by nature he is unsuited to the god's new golden age.

10. An ironic interpretation of *Wealth* has been developed by a number of German scholars who have attempted to find in the inconsistencies of the plot a "secret hidden meaning" (*geheimer Hintersinn*) that is contrary to the surface sense of the play. See Süss 1954: 289 ff.; Newiger 1957: 173–76; Flashar 1967; Hertel 1969: 13–14, 27–28; Heberlein 1981. For detailed criticism of this view, see Sommerstein 1984: 316–19, 323–30.

11. For a traditional view of economy, see 803 and Finley 1985: 109–10.

12. See, for example, Mossé 1976: 99–100. The idea was perhaps particularly propagated by the aristocracy; cf. Wood 1988: 137–45.

13. Compare the concluding scene of *Assemblywomen*, and see the excellent discussion in Sommerstein 1984: 323; cf. 324–25 on the corresponding scene in *Wealth*. Rothwell 1990: 11 describes *Assemblywomen* as a satire on the "greedy, individualistic attitudes of certain Athenians."

14. See Detienne and Vernant 1978: 41–42 for the significance of this cult title.

15. Many scholars, e.g. Flashar 1967: 167, following the scholia, have interpreted 1189–90 as if Chremylus now identified Plutus with Zeus; see Olson 1990: 237–38 for a spirited defense of this view. Sommerstein 1984: 325 and n. 68 argues cogently that Zeus the Savior is in fact Zeus.

16. See Newiger 1957: 168, 176–77; Vernant 1979: 68–69.

17. In the Oxford Classical Text of Aristophanes (Hall and Geldart 1907), the word *ouranos* (sky, heaven) is not personified, i.e., printed with a capital initial letter; the decision is entirely editorial since ancient Greek did not have minuscules.

18. For bibliography, see Hertel 1969: 19–20; on the later development of the conceit, see Johnston 1980. See also the implicit equation between poverty and virtue in the chorus of *Wasps* (e.g., 462, 1082–90); Menander's *Grouch* 120–31.

19. On the idea that slaves are necessary to perform labor even in an ideal community, see Aristophanes' *Assemblywomen* 651–52; Finley 1975: 187.

20. On the debate between Chremylus and Penia, see Sommerstein 1984: 317–19, esp. 327–30. Sommerstein sees Penia's arguments as failing because they do not take into account the extreme poverty that threatened large num-

bers of Athenians in the years after the Peloponnesian War, and which is represented repeatedly and forcefully in *Wealth* (p. 328); cf. David 1984: 3–14. Poverty, Sommerstein writes, "has extolled the blessings (themselves rather dubious) of moderate poverty and ignored the widespread existence, and the even more widespread fear, of extreme poverty, which Chremylos has vividly brought before the audience" (p. 330); contra David 42, who sees Penia as the spokesman for Aristophanes' own view, and cf. Olson 1990: 235, who argues that Penia "functions as an effective intellectual counterbalance to the constant denunciation of the plight of the laboring classes."

That Aristophanes was sensitive to the condition of poor farmers in his last plays, as Sommerstein suggets (332–33), is plausible (on the attitude toward the rich expressed within the play, cf. David 1984: 15–20; Olson 1990: 225, 233), but I am inclined to doubt that his utopian schemes in *Assemblywomen* and *Wealth* were programmatic. It is not that the plays are ironic, but that the element of fantasy ultimately displaces the social message (cf. Olson 225, 242; Cartledge 1990: 64–65, 68–69). On social conditions in Athens in relation to *Wealth*, see Dillon 1987b, who points to the relative timelessness of the arguments in the play compared to earlier comedies; for the first time, the solution proposed to the evils identified in *Wealth* "has nothing to do with politics" (182); cf. also David 29, 43; Sartori 1972. Heberlein 1980 draws a distinction between the practical and utopian plays of Aristophanes; the former plays look to a possible outcome (specifically, peace, as in *Acharnians*, *Peace*, and *Lysistrata*), while the latter envisage a wholly imaginary or impracticable situation (*Birds*, *Assemblywomen*, and *Wealth*). Heberlein suggests also that in the peace plays the protagonist is a rustic or peasant hero (a *bäuerliche Held*) with whom the audience can identify, and that this is not the case with the utopian hero (e.g., Pisthetaerus in *Birds*). But Heberlein must acknowledge Chremylus as an exception (p. 183), and this to my mind undermines the argument. The complaint of Barkhuizen 1981: 18 that Chremylus is motivated by avarice as opposed to "piety" misses the social issue of the play.

21. Another "bridge" can be seen at 494–97. Chremylus seems to imply (the meaning of 497 is disputed) that Plutus, by avoiding the bad men and rewarding the good, would make *all* men just, since they would change their ways to acquire wealth. Thus would all men eventually become rich. But this idea is never developed, and its usefulness in "unifying" the themes of the play has been much exaggerated.

22. See, e.g., 31, 96, 352, 491, 496, 502; cf. the related use of the vocative as a mild term of abuse at 265, 442, although the former is perhaps a dubious case.

23. Sommerstein 1984: 317 says that this remark, if taken literally, "would be inconsistent with the whole plot of the play." I agree that the utopian finale does not envision unjust riches, since there will be no need for injustice where there is plenty for all; but that dispensation displaces the conception according to which there is not wealth enough for all, and under such circumstances, the desire to be rich will have to be fulfilled at somebody's expense.

24. Olson 1990: 230–31 n. 29 points to Plutus' own beggary (he is in rags,

80–85, 266) as a sign that, at the beginning of the play, sight must be essential to his efficacy in bestowing wealth. I suggest that the appearance of the god leaves the audience confused about his powers, and thus prepares for the shift in plan. There are similar shifts in strategy early in the action of *Birds*, *Lysistrata*, and *Assemblywomen*; cf. also Brock 1986 on *Knights*.

25. See 494–97 and 502–6, and cf. Plutus' prayer of thanksgiving at 774–81, or the sycophant's complaint at 864–67.

26. Euripides' tragedy on the story of Telephus, which Aristophanes never tired of ridiculing, had something of this character, and we may detect analogues also in *Philoctetes* and *Oedipus at Colonus* of Sophocles; but the type is widespread in folktale and mythology. The labors of Heracles, the disguises of Odysseus, and Demeter's search for Persephone in the form of an old woman are all versions of the type. It is possible that some of the tales of this form look back to an Indo-European archetype of the sins of the hero, as Dumézil 1979: 74–76, 96–104 argues; but Plutus should be a third-function deity, which complicates the derivation.

27. See 350–51, and esp. 399–402, where *ta pragmat(a)* in 399 echoes *tōi pragmati* in 348.

28. Neocleides was a well-known speaker at this time, ridiculed for his poor vision also in *Assemblywomen* 254, 398.

29. On the comic utopia, see Carrière 1979: 87–91.

30. On conditions in Athens at the time *Wealth* was produced, see Dillon 1987b; Sommerstein 1984. Rothwell 1990: 2–3 notes that Athens was still relatively prosperous at the beginning of the fourth century, and that class tensions were not so pronounced there as elsewhere in Greece. Cf. Strauss 1986: 44–54, 57, 165: "c. 391–88 Aristophanes was very concerned with the theme of money"; Todd 1987; Olson 1990: 224 with n. 4 (bibliography).

31. Macherey 1976: 18–19.

Chapter 6

1. For luck as a pervasive feature of Menandrean comedy, see Lefèvre 1979: 320–28.

2. On the date of *Grouch*, see Handley 1965: 3, 123–24.

3. Another example is Menander's *Shield (Aspis)*, in which Chaereas confesses that he is in love with his stepfather's niece (288–89). She has, however, been betrothed to him from the beginning; the intended marriage is threatened because a greedy uncle of the girl interferes, in the hope of gaining control of her fortune. Chaereas' passion thus adds pathos to the situation, but is not itself the moving force of the action, as it is in *Grouch*. In Terence's *Girl from Andros (Andria)*, which is based on a comedy of the same name by Menander with elements borrowed from a second Menandrean play called *Perinthia*, a secondary character named Charinus is in love with the daughter of Chremes, a wealthy Athenian; the ancient commentator Donatus specifies, however, that the subordinate plot is not to be found in Menander (ad 301, 977), and it may well be the invention of Terence.

4. There is a problem with the text at 48, and it is not altogether certain that Chaereas accompanied Sostratus on the previous day's outing. Chaereas is identified as a parasite in the dramatis personae, but even if the description is accurate, it does not disqualify the advice he offers.

5. Gomme and Sandbach 1973: 145 ad 50 note that the girl must be free if Sostratus is to marry her (they wonder how he learned her status: "One can only say that the wish had been father to the thought"); the point, however, is that because she is free, Sostratus must have marriage rather than a casual liaison in mind.

6. The beginning of verse 44 is missing. Sandbach, following Bingen, suggests the supplement *erōta* as the object of *ekhein*, in which case Pan specifies that he has induced in Sostratus a passionate desire. The word *entheastikōs* (divinely possessed) emphasizes the role of the god.

7. The participle is used rather than the noun *erastēs* (lover), which would suggest a purely amorous liaison.

8. Zagagi 1990 suggests that the gods in Menander lend an aura of significance to conventional patterns of action.

9. Cf. Konstan 1983b: 24–25.

10. Gomme and Sandbach 1973: 254.

11. On the role of the humor, see also pages 16–17 of this volume, discussing Philocleon's jury mania in Aristophanes' *Wasps.*

12. Cf. Schäfer 1965: 80.

13. Compare the marriage of Glycera in *Shorn Girl.* Patterson 1991: 55 observes that while pledging (*enguē*) a woman in marriage was understood as a transaction between her guardian and her husband to be, the ritual unveiling of the bride in the wedding (*gamos*) perhaps represented a symbolic gesture of assent.

14. For Plautus' *Aulularia,* see Chapter 11 in this volume. Arnott 1988 suggests that the original may have been a comedy by Alexis.

15. On the dramatic coherence of these episodes, see Brown 1992.

16. On the idea that the last act of a Menandrean comedy is a lively and humorous *Nachspiel,* or coda, see Holzberg 1974: 126, 177; Lowe 1987: 133–34; Lloyd-Jones 1987: 314; Brown 1990a: 39–43.

17. Gomme and Sandbach 1973: 268 ad 880–958.

18. Lowe 1987: 130 observes that Cnemo's solitariness "has estranged him not merely from society but from the universal systems of kinship on which society and law are founded."

19. For a more detailed discussion, see Chapter 10 in this volume.

20. The scene perhaps echoes a motif in tragedy, e.g. Euripides' *Electra;* see Goldberg 1980: 18, 77.

21. See Gomme and Sandbach 1973: 174 ad 240.

22. Handley 1965: 258 remarks that with Cnemo's arrangements on behalf of his family, "the complications of the plot are largely solved"; cf. Dedoussi 1988a: 83.

23. Gomme and Sandbach 1973: 205 ad 442–55 note that Cnemo's earlier speech concerning the selfish purpose of sacrifices "prepares for his *apologia.*"

24. On an excessive interest in someone else's business (in Greek, *polupragmosunē*), cf. Ehrenberg 1947; Adkins, 1976.

25. Anderson 1970: 204.

26. Cnemo's view here is undoubtedly extreme in the context of Greek sacrificial practice, but there is perhaps an implicit allusion to the idea that animal sacrifice began after the end of the golden age and was a sign of a decline in natural morality; see Vidal-Naquet 1986: 286–88.

27. Gomme and Sandbach 1973: 205 ad 442–55.

28. On the proposed emendation of 35, see Gomme and Sandbach 1973: 141 ad loc.

29. Ramage 1966: 201.

30. Post 1963: 51. See also Hunter 1985: 111.

31. Anderson 1970: 199.

32. Anderson 1970: 199; cf. Schäfer 1965: 80–82, Holzberg 1974: 21–22. Schäfer 91–95 sees the tension between characterization and plot as a feature of all Menander's comedies.

33. See Handley 1965: 136 ad loc.; on the shift in the prologue from Cnemo to Sostratus, see Holzberg 1974: 19.

34. On the cloak (*khlanis*) as a sign of wealth, cf. Posidippus frag. 33 (Kassel and Austin 1983–): "Everyone, it seems, used to greet my cloak, not me; now no one talks to me." For the characterization of Sostratus as "rich and spoiled," cf. Arnott 1981: 226.

35. See Handley 1965; Gomme and Sandbach 1973 ad loc.

36. Gomme and Sandbach 1973: 182 ad 297.

37. In this earnest protestation there is also a touch of aristocratic bravura, especially in Sostratus' readiness to accept the girl without a dowry (308).

38. Gomme and Sandbach 1973: 190 ad 366ff.

39. Names built on the Greek root *hipp* (horse), like Phidippides, the son of Strepsiades in Aristophanes' *Clouds*, suggested wealth or economic pretensions.

40. For the encounter, see Handley 1965: 271. For the reversal of the comic norm in the young man's sententiousness and Callipides' impatience, see Goldberg 1980: 88: "Sostratos' ability to win his father to the marriage, followed by Gorgias' eventual acceptance of the arrangement, resolves the tension between city and country and between rich and poor that has surfaced at intervals through the play."

41. Cf. Lowe 1987: 129: "The *Dyskolos* seems to be about two things at once: on the one hand Cnemon's self-delusion of autarky . . . , and on the other hand the class tensions between rich and poor in rural Attica." Lowe imaginatively indicates ways in which the stage business may have supported the representation of the themes of the play.

42. See Markle 1976 on the upper-class and self-interested nature of Philip's faction in Athens earlier in the fourth century; also MacKendrick 1969: 66–67 on Menander's aristocratic (but not necessarily plutocratic) connections. Giglioni 1984 argues that Menander's plays are a response to the exclusion from civic rights of a large number of poor Athenians: they give expression to

his compassion for the indigent and project an ideal of social harmony across class lines. See also Whitehorne 1987: 7–8 for some sensible words on the politics of the *Grouch*.

43. Ramage 1966: 211. On *philanthrōpia*, see also Dover 1974: 201–2; Lefèvre 1979: 334–39.

44. See Giglioni 1982: 59–95, esp. the long concluding section on Menander's *Grouch*.

45. For a detailed comparison between Cnemo, Timon, and Alceste as misanthropes, see Konstan 1983a.

Chapter 7

1. My main guide to the play has been Gomme and Sandbach 1973, who review earlier reconstructions of the plot. For a more recent reconstruction, with bibliography, see Blanchard 1983: 349–62. The text is cited according to Sandbach 1990. For Corinth as the scene, see Gomme and Sandbach 1973: 470 ad 125; Körte 1932: 743–44.

2. According to Schwartz 1929: 1–3.

3. One possibility, mentioned simply for the sake of illustration, is Sicyon, the scene of Plautus' *Cistellaria*, and perhaps also that of its Menandrean model, *Synaristosai*. Fredershausen 1912: 205–207 argues that, in comedy, marriage with a noncitizen occurs only in cities other than Athens; cf. Fantham 1975: 58–59 and Konstan 1983b: 105–6.

4. There are two houses on stage in Schwartz 1929: 14 and three houses in Robert 1909: 274 and Körte 1932: 743.

5. That Moschio, who is a foundling, is being raised as a citizen is perhaps a further indication that the setting of the play is not Athens.

6. The old woman was probably of noncitizen status, for it seems unlikely that a citizen woman would be represented in comedy as giving away her daughter on such terms, though it may have been tolerable *exō tou dramatos*, that is, previous to the action of the play. See also Vernant 1980: 46–47, citing a passage in Isaeus (3.39) to show "that a girl could be installed with a man as a concubine, *pallakē*, by the member of her family who had authority over her."

7. Glycera perhaps explained her relationship with Moschio to Myrrhine at the time when she took refuge with her; cf. Blanchard 1983: 355.

8. Contra Gomme and Sandbach 1973: 467–68; but the embrace occurred on the previous evening, and Gomme and Sandbach themselves adopt the hypothesis that the action of the play was confined to a single day.

9. Gomme and Sandbach 1973: 511–13 ad 550; the details have been variously reconstructed.

10. Possibly with a daughter of Myrrhine's husband, according to Robert 1909: 300–301; Schwartz 1929: 14. Gerhard 1910: 34 n. 78 defends the view that Philinus, mentioned at 1026, is not related to Myrrhine.

11. Cf. Fantham 1975: 56–59 for analysis.

12. See Post 1913: 112; Webster 1974: 21–22; Konstan 1983b: 26–29.

13. See Gomme and Sandbach 1973: 514 ad 708 ff. There is perhaps a simi-

lar elegance in Menander's *Hated Man* (*Misoumenos*), where the sword that played a part in the rupture of the relationship may also have been instrumental in the recognition (p. 441).

14. Humphreys 1983: 8 ventures a general proposition that is broadly accurate: "New Comedy provides further evidence for the opposition in Athenian minds between natural affections and legal rules"; *Shorn Girl*, however, must be recognized as at least a partial exception.

15. The suggestion of Blanchard 1983: 359 (cf. 361) that Glycera will not pardon Polemo as long as the problem of Moschio's identity remains unresolved, because she fears new excesses of rage and jealousy on his part, is not, in my view, supported by the text.

16. On *Mother-in-Law*, see Konstan 1983b: 130–141; on *Mother-in-Law* and Menander's *Arbitrants*, which apparently inspired Apollodorus' composition, see Stavenhagen 1910: 580; Fantham 1975: 66–71.

17. Cf. Goldberg 1980: 53: "Polemon is essentially a distraught husband"; true, if we understand "essentially" in the colloquial sense, i.e., "to all appearances." On the distinction between courtesans and concubines in New Comedy, see Brown 1990b: 249–50.

18. Gomme and Sandbach 1973: 477 ad 186. Here also is a discussion of the meaning of *stratiōtēs* as professional soldier, as opposed to a citizen on military campaign for his polis.

19. See Vernant 1980: 47; cf. 45–51 on the relation between marriage and the household ideology in classical Athens; also Fantham 1975: 47–50.

20. In Menander's *Sicyonian* (*Sikuōnios*), the owner of a (putative) slave woman is informally called her *kurios*; see 191 (very badly preserved), 194, 240; at 207 he is called her *despotēs* (master). Gomme and Sandbach 1973: 652–53 ad *Sik.* 193–95 speak of the master as a "de facto" *kurios*. If it was in fact possible to describe the possessor of a noncitizen woman in this way, it is nevertheless the case that such a description is not pertinent to *Shorn Girl*, and it is carefully eschewed.

21. Cf. also *Hated Man* (*Misoumenos*) 307, with Gomme and Sandbach ad loc.

22. Gomme and Sandbach 1973: 498 ad 384–85.

23. Contrast the ironic use of the expression *gametē hetaira* at *Samia* 130. On the behavior of Alcesimarchus in *Cistellaria*, who, in defiance of his father's prohibition promises marriage to Selenium, see Fantham 1975: 58–59. In a new fragment of *Misoumenos* (Turner 1981), Thrasonides, who has given his former slave Crateia her freedom (38–39), announces that he considered her a wife (*gunaika nomisas*, 40). A mutilated line (45) seems to contain the words *oude kuria*, which Turner tentatively translates: "[Even if she were legally her own mistress . . .]." Cf. also Goldberg 1980: 50–51; Barigazzi 1985.

24. Cf. Chariton *Chaereas and Callirhoe* 5.8 for a similar contrast between the self-betrothal of a woman and the role of a father or *kurios* in the marriage transaction; discussion in Konstan 1994b: 73–76.

25. See Vernant 1980: 46 on *kurieia* in marriage, and the contrast with

the *pallakē*, who "installed herself on her own responsibility." Demosthenes 59.46 indicates that a metic woman with no male relatives might be spoken of as *kurios* of herself (cf. Brown 1990a: 56–57 n. 40). The old woman who "gave" (130) Glycera to the soldier was not in a position to contract a binding relationship. Cf. Harrison 1968: 14–15 on the power of a male to give a woman to another male as concubine, and contrast 19, 21, Isaeus 10.10 (cited in Harrison 73 n. 3), and 108–9 on the inability of an Athenian woman to enter into a contract or to "engage her own hand in marriage."

26. Compare the *epiklēros* wife in Menander's *Plokion*, frag. 334 Körte-Thierfelder, in which a husband describes his wife as *kuria* of all their joint possessions. Cf. also Plautus' *Asinaria* 87, where Demaenetus asserts that he sold his *imperium* (= *kurieia*?) for his wife's dowry. On *dotata* (dowered woman) as the Roman translation of *epiklēros*, see Fantham 1975: 73 n. 60.

27. Gomme and Sandbach 1973: 507, 505–6 ad 487.

28. In theory, Moschio might be considered the *kurios* of Glycera, though the possibility is not raised in the text; as an adopted son of Myrrhine, Moschio's relationship with his former family might be felt to be suspended, cf. Humphreys 1983: 65. Humphreys remarks (p. 64): "The concubine, having fewer rights than the wife, might well be, literally, more attached. A similar desire for a more total attachment of the wife to her husband is suggested by Xenophon's advice (*Oeconomicus* vii.4ff.) to marry a young girl and educate her yourself to run the household as you wish it to be run." I cannot agree with Humphreys that this "attachment" represents a desire for "a closer communion"; rather, it indicates the desire for a total domination, and in this respect is at quite the opposite pole from a romantic or sentimental relation with an independent *pallakē*.

29. Cf. Fantham 1975: 51: "In one sense the *hetaera* was the only woman in Greek society who enjoyed a freedom comparable to that of a man," a principle that may be extended here to include a *pallakē* such as Glycera; in general, on the role of *xenai* (foreign women) at Athens, see Fantham 49–51. It should be stressed that there is no question here of frivolousness on Glycera's part. She abandons Polemo, but with cause. Polemo's behavior was, as Pataecus says, *ou kata tropon* (not right) (492).

30. On "free" in the sense of "citizen," see Fantham 1975: 53 n. 26, 57 n. 33; cf. also Menander *Grouch* 290–91, *Samian Woman* 577, 646, and Terence *Eunuch* 558–59 (*civem* = *eleutheran*?). In an earlier age, *eleutheroi* seems more specifically to have distinguished metics or quasi metics (Vernant 1980: 50). More generally on the political history of the term *eleutheros*, see Raaflaub 1983, 1984, 1985.

31. Gomme and Sandbach 1973: 506. On the procedure, they cite (ad *Arbitrants* 641) Harrison 1968: 40–44, 55–56. The passage in *Arbitrants* indicates that witnesses might be summoned as well; see MacDowell 1978: 238 on the need for witnesses in a summons to trial.

32. Gomme and Sandbach 1973: 507. On the rights of a man, under Solonic law, to take action against adultery of a *pallakē* who was taken for the pur-

pose of having "free children" (*ep' eleutherois paisin*), see Vernant 1980: 48; it is to be doubted that this law was in effect in the time of Menander (MacDowell 1978: 89–90).

33. Cf. Goldberg 1980: 48–49 on the force of Polemo's outburst at 506–7.

34. Barigazzi 1979: 43–44 argues that Pataecus' efforts to persuade Glycera were represented in the lacuna after v. 550, although he failed to make an impression on her noble sentiments; this does not strike me as an especially plausible reconstruction. Goldberg 1980: 46 (cf. 49–50) suggests that Moschio assumes "many of the characteristics of the comic soldier," while Polemo "becomes the sympathetic, romantic hero." On the characterization of Polemo, see also Arnott 1979: xxxiii–xxxiv.

35. Marriage is not possible, and Glycera rejects the role of hetaera. Cf. Gomme and Sandbach 1973: 485 ad 305 on Davus' reference to Glycera at her bath as the sign of a hetaera, and ad 340, where Davus distinguishes Glycera from an *aulētris* (flute girl, in the common translation) or *pornidion* (whore). On the contrast between the courtesan and the prostitute, see Calame 1989b: 103–4. Of course, Glycera cannot tell Pataecus the real reason a union with Moschio would be impossible; cf. Blanchard 1983: 359–60.

36. The suggestion of Blanchard 1983: 360 that Glycera's citizen status will justify her having resisted Polemo's violence seems quite alien to the argument of the text.

37. Both quotations from Gomme and Sandbach 1973: 514 ad 708ff.

38. Cf. Gomme and Sandbach 1973: 529 ad 999. Körte 1932: 747 remarks that this scene anticipates Glycera's forgiving Polemo.

39. Webster 1950: 21–25 interprets this sentiment as an indication of Menander's Hellenic humanism.

40. Fortenbaugh 1974: 441 (references to line numbers omitted); cf. Hunter 1985: 174 n. 22. Major contributions to the discussion, all of which, to my mind, overemphasize the technical aspects of the issue, are Tierney 1936: 248; Webster 1950: 7, 204–205 and 1973: 291; Barigazzi 1965: 135–60, 228; Schottlaender 1973: 185–91, whose suggestion that Pataecus effects the reconciliation between Polemo and Glycera seems wide of the mark. Central to the discussion is frag. 359 Körte-Thierfelder, which distinguishes between an *atukhēma* (misfortune) and an *adikēma* (act of injustice), as quoted in Chapter 10 in this volume. Blanchard 1983: 350–51 endorses Fortenbaugh's interpretation.

41. Gomme and Sandbach 1973: 529–30. Most recently, Browne 1974: 48–50 tentatively assigns 1021–22a, 1023 to Glycera, while remarking that the marginal note in the papyrus naming Glycera has been added by a second hand.

42. Gomme and Sandbach 1973: 529–30. On the three-actor rule, see also Sandbach 1975; Frost 1988: 2–3; Brown 1990a: 54; for the addition of a fourth speaking part in Roman adaptations, see Lowe 1991: 39–44.

43. A young woman does speak in Plautus' *Little Carthaginian* (*Poenulus*) after her citizen identity has been discovered, but she is Carthaginian, and the scene may well be an interpolation by Plautus into the Greek original (cf. Lowe

1988). In Plautus' *Persian* (*Persa*) the freeborn daughter of a parasite has a speaking part, but here again the relationship to a Greek model is highly controversial; cf. Lowe 1989 and, for an extreme view of Plautine originality, Stärk 1991.

44. Loraux 1984: 177. Cf. Humphreys 1983: 16: "The rules of modesty for unmarried girls were particularly strict, but even a married woman would never appear at a dinner party or entertain strangers in her husband's absence." See also Henry 1985: 76: "Silence befits a bride; Glykera is no longer *heautēs kyria*. She has undergone several metamorphoses—from citizen by birth, to foundling, concubine, *de facto* wife, imagined hetaira, to citizen once again."

45. Although del Corno 1966: 308 sees *Shorn Girl* as a drama of self-discovery on the principle of "wisdom through suffering," I doubt that moral development, as opposed to the overcoming of ignorance, is thematic in ancient comedy. Cf. Lukács 1975: 108; Bersani 1976: 54–55: "In Molière, the obstacles to the good lovers' marriages are simply pushed aside by happy strokes of fate. The young people's union is not the result of any growth of moral consciousness: *they* have generally been in love from the very start."

46. Fortenbaugh 1974: 443. On the role of the lover-soldier in New Comedy, see Wartenberg 1973; Hofmann and Wartenberg 1973: 35–39 (on *Shorn Girl*); Arnott 1979: xxxiii.

47. Contrast Smedley 1976: 136: "I was proud of Helen. To me her profession seemed as honorable as that of any married woman—she made her living in the same way as they made theirs, except that she made a better living and had more rights over her body and soul. No man dared mistreat her"; al-Saadawi 1983: 91: "All women are prostitutes of one kind or another. Because I was intelligent I preferred to be a free prostitute, rather than an enslaved wife."

48. See Fantham 1975: 57; Anderson 1984: 124–26. Of course, it was permissible for a widow to remarry, as in Menander's *Grouch* and Terence's *Brothers* (based on a Menandrean original). On concealment, see Sissa 1990a: 91, and Chapter 10 n. 23 in this volume.

49. Other comedies of Menander are based on plots more or less similar to that of *Shorn Girl*. Closest of all is *Hated Man*, in which a soldier, Thrasonides, is rejected by a former slave girl, Crateia, to whom he has given her freedom (see Turner 1981; Borgogno 1988: 95–97 on Crateia's status); a recognition scene relatively early in the play reunites Crateia with her father. Thus, the recognition occurs well before the resolution of the tension between soldier and concubine. The cause of the girl's hostility to the soldier is not entirely clear from the fragments (Plutarch, frag. 1, attributes it to the soldier's *alazoneia* [arrogance]); the girl may have suspected the soldier of having killed her brother (cf. Brown 1980; Borgogno 1988: 90). It is impossible to determine what role, if any, the question of a *pallakē*'s independence played in this comedy. See Goldberg 1980: 56 on the difference in effect produced by the placement of the *anagnōrisis*, and 46–47 for a comparison of the two plays.

Sicyonian presents a soldier in possession of a girl who has been kidnapped (as opposed to captured in *Hated Man* and exposed in *Shorn Girl*): her citizenship is revealed, reuniting her with her father; a rival named Moschio is removed when he is revealed as the brother—this time of the soldier, Strato-phanes, whose Athenian citizenship is also demonstrated in the course of the play. From early in the play, the soldier appears eager to restore the girl to her father (238–39). It is not clear whether the girl, Philumene, had a speaking part, and the issue here would seem to be not so much the question of her sta-tus as that of the tension between a citizen's rights to marriage and the senti-mental bond formed through rearing a woman from childhood on (246–57). At the end of the play there is an emphatic reference to the preservation of Philumene's virginity (372); a woman named Malthace, possibly a hetaera, has a speaking part, and stands in contrast to Philumene (frag. 11 Sandbach; but cf. Habrotonum in *Shorn Girl* 482–485).

Webster 1950: 18 suggests that Menander's *Slapped Girl* (*Rhapizomenē*) and *Burnt Girl* (*Empimpramenē*) may have been similar in plot; cf. also 21 on *Arbitrants*, and Goldberg 1980: 51.

50. Webster 1950: 17; on Megadorus, cf. also Konstan 1983b: 41–46.

51. Humphreys 1983: 10–13. On wealth as property within one's control, cf. Aristotle *Rhetoric* 1361a13–23. Such, at all events, was the ideal; in real-ity, figures like Pataecus may well have been motivated by an entrepreneurial spirit not unlike that of early European capitalism; see Thompson 1982: 74–78.

52. Del Corno 1966: 305 n. 23 observes, in connection with Pataecus' loss of his fortune, that *ēkousa* (I heard) in 808 perhaps indicates the news of the shipwreck was false since Pataecus is later in a position to provide a rich dowry for his daughter; alternatively, he adds, one may suppose that Pataecus subse-quently acquired a new fortune.

53. Cf. McKechnie 1989: 16: "It is a commonplace of fourth-century rheto-ric that people who travel, or who live away from home, are disreputable char-acters." McKechnie adds that "the incidence of the 'return motif' in comic plays can be recognized as a symptom of awareness that relatives' absence from home as traders or soldiers, or indeed on state business, created tensions and awkward situations in a world where it was expected that people would nor-mally live their whole lives within the social context of their own city" (p. 190). McKechnie also classifies courtesans as "mobile skilled workers" (pp. 152–54), who move from city to city in pursuit of their trade. We may note that Moschio's position, too, is regularized by the new state of affairs: he will be-come a proper head of household.

Chapter 8

1. Cf., for example, the contrast between Glycerium in Terence's *Andria*, who proves to be an Athenian citizen, and her supposed sister Chrysis, who had become a professional hetaera (69–79), and had multiple lovers (86–88).

2. To be sure, the hetaera can be represented as kind or sincerely affec-tionate, but this does not alter the economic basis of her position. Critics have sought to distinguish the roles of *bona meretrix* and *mala meretrix*, but this formal division has, I think, been rightly rejected in favor of a single type, sim-ply *meretrix*, who may exhibit variations in character or temperament just as

much as any other figure in New Comedy, such as the *senex* or *adulescens*. See Gilula 1980; Brown 1987: 189; Brown 1990b.

3. See Harrison 1971: 19–21, 73 n. 3, 108–9; Vernant 1980: 46 on the role of the *kurios* in marriage. Sealey 1987: 20 states: "In marriage the woman's erstwhile *kyrios* 'entrusted' her to the bridegroom; participially her erstwhile *kyrios* was expressed in the active, the bridegroom in the middle, and the woman in the passive. She was treated not as a person participating in the transaction but as its passive object." For the use of the active verb "marry" (*gēmai*) of men and the passive in the case of women, cf. Pseudo-Ammonius *On the Differences between Similar Words* 120 with Anacreon *Iambi* 7 (West 1980). On conjugal exchange generally, cf. Lévi-Strauss 1969: 60–68.

4. This pertains specifically, of course, to those comedies in which the setting is Athens. On the law of Pericles, see Patterson 1981: 114–15 (a summary of Patterson's views on the motivation behind the law), and 146–47 on the question of whether the law was abrogated at any time previous to its reenactment in 403 B.C. On the representation of citizen brides in New Comedy, see Brown 1990b: 243–44.

5. See Konstan 1983b: 18.

6. It is, of course, possible to see in marriage the mere sale of a woman's body in exchange for sustenance, and thus to collapse the distinction between marriage and prostitution; George Bernard Shaw, for example, exploits the idea programmatically in *Mrs. Warren's Profession*. In New Comedy, an old man may seek to wed a rich heiress, like Smicrines in Menander's *Shield* (*Aspis*); more often, fathers look for profitable connections through the marriages of their children. But marriage and commercial love remain quite distinct in the symbolic code of the genre; contrast Henry 1987: 147, who deconstructs the opposition between wife and courtesan.

7. Cantarella 1985: 75. See also Post 1941: 445: "The distinction between a pallake and a hetaera might not always be clear. . . . The distinction seems to be one of function. The pallake kept house for her consort and was a wife except for her status and that of her children, if there were any. . . . The free hetaera alone can be her own mistress and choose her lover or lovers." On the basis of this last claim, Post assumes that Glycera in *Shorn Girl* must be a hetaera rather than a *pallakē*, but that is precisely to insist on a sharper distinction between the roles than is warranted by the conventions of New Comedy. Certainly, Moschio's silly boast about his attractiveness to hetaerae (303) does not exclude a role as *pallakē* for Glycera.

8. At least, she is tending it by offering it the breast; see Dedoussi 1988b for the view that Chrysis herself had not recently borne a child of her own, and therefore was not (contra Sandbach 1973) in a position actually to offer milk to the child of Moschio and Plango. Dedoussi argues that Chrysis cannot have intended to deceive Demea permanently concerning the status of Moschio and Plango's child, which seems right. This is not, however, inconsistent with the possibility that Chrysis had herself recently lost a baby; how, we cannot tell given the condition of the text, but it is at least conceivable that she would have given it away or had it exposed (56).

9. Moschio, who is perhaps sensitive on the score of origins as a result of his own adopted condition, attempts to reduce the status difference between the *nothos* and a legitimate heir (*gnēsios*) to the purely ethical categories of good and bad (142), a remarkable view which cannot have been taken in earnest by Demea (the text is broken here). It is in fact a view "more striking than any that can be quoted as parallels," according to Gomme and Sandbach 1973: 559–60 ad 141–42, citing Euripides *Andromache* 638 and frag. 141 Nauck², and Sophocles frag. 84 Nauck² = frag. 87 Radt; Euripides frag. 168 Nauck², from his *Antigone*, is perhaps closer: "The bastard is to blame in name only, his nature is equal" (I owe this reference to Ruth Scodel, personal communication).

10. See Chapter 7 n. 35 in this volume on the characterization of Glycera in *Shorn Girl*, and the contrast with the behavior typical of a hetaera. Plutarch *Moralia* 712 C remarks of affairs with hetaerae as they are represented in Menander that (1) they are ruptured if the women are rough in character, or, if they are good, then either (2a) the hetaera turns out to have a citizen father or (2b) the affair continues for some time. Brown 1990a: 59 n. 46 (cf. Brown 1990b) regards the passage as unhelpful, since Plutarch's categories are not exclusive, but if we recognize that type 2a corresponds to the case of the young or novice concubine, while type 1 and type 2b refer to experienced hetaerae (e.g., Bacchis in *Self-Tormentor* and Thais in *Eunuch*, respectively), Plutarch's classification works quite well.

11. Compare the mention of gold (if the reading *chrusi'* is accepted in 382) and servant girls in *Samia*; Sandbach 1990 reads the vocative *Chrysi*.

12. That he abandoned her, rather than the reverse, evidently does not count with him. In his own view, he simply suffered on her behalf while he was gone, disobeying his father and deserting his land for her sake (*propter te*, 256). Was this really the case? Did he run off to Asia with the expressed intention of returning to Antiphila? Had they agreed to such a plan in advance, stipulating the amount of time he would be away? Could he realistically have hoped that the situation at home would somehow be different upon his return? Certainly he has not yet acquired such confidence, since he does not have the courage to confront his father. Was he simply seeking respite, then, from the conflicting demands of love and *pietas*? There is no way to answer these questions, as far as I can see, though these and other anomalies or oversights in the motivations assigned to the characters have been the basis of imaginative reconstructions of the Greek original; see esp. Lefèvre 1973, critically reviewed by Brown 1976; contra: Kroll 1927, who argues that a certain negligence in peripheral aspects of the plot is consistent with ancient Greek dramatic technique, and thus no evidence for interpolation or contamination on the part of the Roman adaptor. It may be simplest to suppose that Clinia merely hoped that Antiphila would remain loyal, undertook to do the same himself, and gave no further thought to what the future might bring, or else that he believed that he would somehow find in himself the will to defy his father, with whatever small hope of success.

13. It is not clear to me whether Syrus has prearranged this meeting of

the women, or whether their simultaneous arrival is coincidental. At all events, Bacchis, with full entourage, intends to spend the night at Clitipho's. Once again, how and why this scheme arose is obscure. Perhaps Terence has altered or omitted something in Menander's original that would have made the situation clearer. Bacchis, at any rate, has already been instructed to play along as Clinia's girlfriend (361).

14. According to, for example, Radice 1976: 118. Forehand 1985: 61 puts the contrast between Bacchis and Antiphila correctly: courtesan vs. "devoted mistress." See also the translation by Bovie 1974: 101: "Once you've chosen to go on living with some man"; and Görler 1982: 172: "Clinia had taken Antiphilia to be the daughter or an unmarried old woman, and so he himself had not seriously considered a marriage."

15. Earlier, Syrus narrated how he suddenly entered Antiphila's house with the news that Clinia has returned and found the young woman at her weaving, dressed in mourning, without ornaments of gold, attended by an old woman and a single slave girl, shabbily attired (285–95). What is more, at the mention of Clinia, she burst into tears (304–6). The scene is an antique male fantasy, most familiar from Tibullus' dream of descending from the skies to find his Delia demurely at the loom (1.3.83–92); cf. Smith 1964[1913] ad loc. for this "genre picture" in Latin literature. Antiphila is virtuous, then, according to literary convention, but she is also her own mistress. Her conduct and her tears reflect her personal commitment. Weaving was, to be sure, one of the household duties of a married woman, but here there is no question of marriage. Antiphila's behavior is a token of her character rather than her social position, which locates her outside the conjugal network.

16. Cf. Terence's *Woman of Andros* (*Andria*) 146, 273 (*pro uxore* = *gametēn nomizei* vel sim.?), 216; also 273–74 (*virum*), of Glycerium, who is thought to be a foreign woman (*peregrina*, 146). The plot of *Andria* differs from that of the plays we have been considering in that Glycerium (a) is known to be a citizen from the beginning of the play, even if Davus, who conveys this information to the audience, does not himself believe it to be true (220), (b) gives birth in the course of the play, and (c) has a mute role, befiting a citizen wife.

17. Brothers argues that it is these additions that Terence had in mind when he claimed, in the prologue, to have made a single plot double (6) in a play otherwise apparently seamless in construction (Brothers 1980: 102 n. 45 allows some venial inconsistencies). Whether the mere fact of having dramatized the roles of Bacchis and Antiphila in two brief episodes is enough to justify the label *duplex argumentum* I cannot say (see Brothers's own doubts on this score, 118–19). Brothers claims that Bacchis' initial speech in the scene under investigation (I omit the second episode as irrelevant to the present discussion) "holds up the action in a quite impossible way" (p. 109), given the expectations of Antiphila's arrival that have been aroused in the audience. Bacchis' didacticism is something of an anticlimax, I agree, but I hesitate to assert that Menander might not have stalled things in this way. In addition, Brothers points out that Clitipho's earlier description of Bacchis' greed and the ostentation of her baggage train are inconsistent with her admiration for

Antiphila's virtue. Finally, there is the evidence of the Bembine scholium, which indicates a possible source (Menander's *Arrhēphoros*) for one of the lines in Bacchis' speech. Brothers concludes that the whole of 381–97 was inserted by Terence to fill in an act division in Menander's play, and that Bacchis' entourage may have served as chorus in the original. Very hesitantly, Brothers proposes that the entire speaking part of Antiphila may have been invented by Terence to dramatize her romantic reunion with Clinia (pp. 117–18). Hunter 1985: 132 sees in the reunion between Clinia and Antiphila a takeoff on the convention of the recognition

18. See Steidle 1974: 257.

19. Forehand 1985: 66 raises the possibility that Chremes' "harshness is a ploy, never a real expression of his feeling" as a way of supporting a favorable view of Chremes' character; cf. Steidle 1974: 247–49, 275.

20. Nardo 1967–68: 137; cf. 150–51. Lefèvre 1973 bases his reconstruction of the Menandrean play on the premise that the original Chremes was in fact a *homo humanus*, whom Terence converts in midcourse into a *homo curiosus*, with drastic results for the structure of the entire plot; Brown 1976: 246 insists that Chremes' curiosity or intrusiveness is the "dramatic core" of Terence's play, and not a casual attribute: "Chremes is comic, and his apparent *humanitas* is exposed to our mockery, from the moment when we realise that this man who devotes his time to setting other people's houses in order is blind to what is going on in his own house." Jocelyn 1973: 23–24 argues the case against Chremes' character most forcefully; after surveying previous interpretations in detail, he concludes: "The scenes following the opening were to reveal in Chremes no sympathetic person but one whom Athenians of Menander's day would have called *polupragmōn* or *periergos* and Romans of Terence's day *curiosus*. He belonged to a type whose discomfiture was welcomed by ordinary men in all the ancient Mediterranean communities." See also Fantham 1971: 979–81; Lefèvre 1986: 40; Goldberg 1986: 137, 143. But Steidle 1974: 247–49 argues convincingly, in my judgment, that Chremes' interest in Menedemus is not mere officiousness, but rather humane concern for a fellow citizen, and entirely in conformity with Athenian expectations of mutual assistance among neighbors; cf. Gallant 1991: 143–69.

One's view of Chremes' behavior at the beginning of the play is likely to determine as well the interpretation of his ruse later in the play to wean his son from Bacchis. Thus Jocelyn 1973: 24–25 imagines the response of a Roman audience: "As they watched Chremes' panic at the threat to his own property and uncontrollable rage at this own son's behaviour (vv. 908–31) they remembered the impertinent concern he had shown about Menedemus' property and the tenor of Clitipho's account (v. 220) of his boasts about his own youthful misdemeanours. . . . It is accordingly unlikely that at the very beginning of the play Terence would have wanted to throw the spectators off the track by giving Chremes a sympathetic presence." Fantham 1971: 981–82, however, sees an amelioration in the character of Chremes toward the end of the play. Steidle 1974: 274–75 sees in Chremes' *simulatio* an echo of the trick devised by Syrus. For a judicious discussion of possible changes in the last act introduced by Terence with a view to enlivening the action, see Maltby 1983.

21. On ancient interpretations of the verse, see Jocelyn 1973: 37–42.

22. Goldberg 1986: 140–142 remarks that Antiphila "*deserves* to be a citizen," and with this I agree. But Goldberg's further claim that when Chremes "threatens to disinherit Clitipho" he "comes dangerously close to repeating Menedemus' error" seems wrong to me. Goldberg emphasizes the similarity of the two affairs: "Clinia and Clitipho make essentially the same progress from illicit love to respectable marriage. Their affairs are so easy to intertwine precisely because they are so similar. . . . The difference comes from the different characters of their lovers. . . . Their significance lies in the challenge they pose to the two fathers and in what the sons reveal about them." I do not place the same emphasis on the contrast between Menedemus and Chremes, but even if it is more central to the play than I have allowed, it is still the case that the nature of the challenge to each is different. Precisely because Antiphila is made to seem deserving, her case is different from that of Bacchis, and rightly evokes a different response from Chremes.

Chapter 9

1. For being a soldier, see Ludwig 1959: 26–27; for not being a soldier, see Knoche 1934–36 and 1938. For a review of the entire problem, see Barsby 1993: 166–74.

2. See Büchner 1974: 231–33; Lowe 1983: 432.

3. Plautus *Merchant* (*Mercator*) 82; cf. Allen 1950a: 262–64.

4. Barsby 1990 argues that Parmeno is characterized in the opening scene as a bungling slave and that his advice is not necessarily consistent or coherent; that he is self-important may be readily conceded, but at least in the verses discussed here his position seems clear, albeit conventional.

5. According to Büchner 1974: 231.

6. Cf. Plautus *Truculentus* 174, 177, 186, 214, 727; Drexler 1938: 78.

7. Lefèvre 1969: 19–21 is in favor of a prologue in Menander's *Eunuch*, contra: Büchner 1974: 243–44; Steidle 1973: 326–29; Lowe 1983: 441–42; Barsby 1993: 161–66. Lowe argues that Terence has curtailed Thais' original monologue, and this might account for the abrupt shift in Terence's version from expressive to expository tenor at 203.

8. See Sandbach 1977: 144–45. Zagagi, 1980: 118–27 has a subtle analysis of the materialization of the courtesan relation by Plautus, and the transformation of the gift-giving practice of the Greeks into a kind of hire. On the whole, I find Zagagi persuasive, although I believe that in Menander, as well as in the Roman comic playwrights, the double-edged character of the "ancient institution of gift-giving" was exposed. See also Büchner 1974: 295, 239; Hunter 1985: 92.

9. Drexler 1938: 98; see also Harsh 1937: 285–87; Lloyd-Jones 1973: 283–84. Gilula 1980: 161–64 emphasizes Thais' deception of Thraso and her mercenary attitude toward Phaedria as evidence that she fits the type of the calculating hetaera.

10. Some of the evidence for the sharing of courtesans in classical Greece is presented in Harsh 1937: 285–87. Ludwig 1959: 37 n. 5 denies the relevance of such analogues to the problem of interpreting *Eunuch*, and emphasizes the dignity of Thais whom he takes to be the central personality in the play. Gilula 1980: 142–65 maintains that courtesans are all of a piece in New Comedy, and that Thais is no exception. (On the good courtesan, cf. Brown 1990b.) Menander, however, seems to have represented courtesans in a particularly sympathetic way, e.g. in *Samia* and *Arbitrants*. For a discussion of Phaedria as a lover, see Croce 1936: 419–20; Parker 1974: 149. Rossi 1979: 57–62 admires the sincerity of passion in New Comedy generally, including its representation in the *Eunuch*.

11. Brown 1990a: 389 n. 43 doubts that the conclusion of the play is consistent with sincerity on the part of Phaedria. But Phaedria's willingness to let Thraso pay the bills is a replay of his earlier concession; instead of a romantic union, Phaedria accepts that Thais both loves him truly and has reason also to cater to the soldier. To put it differently, a rival whose claims must be acknowledged is necessary to the representation of sincere love as an inward fidelity that obtains despite external constraints.

12. The repetition marks closure; for an analysis of such "ring composition" in the opening scene, see Steidle 1973: 334–37.

13. Lefèvre 1969: 25 sees Terence's hand here. My own view is nearest that of Steidle 1973: 333–34, who argues, following Brothers 1969: 315, that everything following the formula *numquid vis aliud* (Want anything else? 191) is the work of Terence. As indicated above, the formula is normally equivalent to a good-bye, and rarely elicits more than a brief reply; contra Lowe 1983: 435 n. 64, who argues rather (pp. 438–40) that the song at 207–24 is Terence's addition, replacing a Menandrean monologue by Parmeno.

14. Less certain as an indication of Terentian composition is the role of Parmeno, who remains on stage with occasional remarks on the conversation between Phaedria and Thais. The ancient commentator Donatus perceived a difficulty here, since Parmeno can presumably surmise that Pamphila is freeborn, yet he later assists Chaerea in the scheme to obtain access to her. Büchner 1974: 235–41, 247, following Nencini 1891: 83–84, inferred that Parmeno's role in the first act must have been Terence's own contribution. But 283–85 seem to indicate clearly that Parmeno, at least in Terence's version, is conscious of Pamphila's possible status even as he advances Chaerea's plan. Perhaps it is best, as Steidle 1973: 337 suggests, to believe Parmeno when he protests that his original suggestion was made in jest; cf. also Lowe 1983: 434, 436–37, on Parmeno's original doubts about the truth of Thais' story, which might incline him to dismiss it later.

15. Cf. Gilula 1980: 164: "The plot of the *Eunuch* is the story of Thais' attempts to secure a patron." This overstates the case, but it is a salutary corrective to a sentimental view of the courtesan's role.

16. For Terentian composition, see Sandbach 1977: 143; Jachman 1921: 76–77; Drexler 1938: 84–90; Bianco 1962: 154. The passage functions as a transition from the comic byplay between Thraso and Gnatho, which is doubtless

patterned on Menander's *Flatterer* (or *Kolax*, the model Terence conflated with *Eunuch*), back to the plot of *Eunuch* proper.

17. According to Drexler 1938: 87–88.

18. Wehrli 1936: 114 notes that Menander likes to vary his recognition scenes and rarely stages them straightforwardly; Jachman 1921: 78–79 saw the incomplete recognition as evidence of Terence's responsibility for the entire scene in which Thraso lays siege to Thais' house.

19. Strictly, Thais is a foreigner (*peregrina* = *xenē*) and would require a *prostatēs* (loosely, a representative), according to Attic procedure, rather than a patron, but the Roman institution of the *clientela* covered connections between Romans and dependent foreigners; see Badian 1958: 154–60; Gelzer 1969: 62–69.

20. The scene is a Terentian interpolation, according to Büchner 1974: 305 and Ludwig 1968: 172–73, both of whom explain the motive for the insertion as comic or farcical effect. Cf. Lowe 1983: 429; Barsby 1993: 174–78. Steidle 1973, who accepts the conclusion as Menandrean, could cite only Harsh 1937 and Webster 1950: 74 as allies. We may add Bianco 1962: 162, who holds that in the Greek *Eunuch* the rival was not a soldier, and hence more acceptable as a partner in the affair with Thais; Lloyd-Jones 1973; Goldberg 1986: 116–22, who stresses the self-interested and submissive nature of all the major characters in *Eunuch*: "Terence has made the stock relationship between soldier and parasite a grotesque paradigm for relationships to which the other characters aspire" and thus the finale is consistent with the moral tone of the comedy as a whole; and Brown 1990a: 49–55, who denies that we can know whether the scene was in Menander's original (though he doubts that Gnatho had a part there), but finds it "an acceptable element in the ending of Terence's play."

21. Holzberg 1974: 159 suggests that Thais ceases to be a hetaera upon acquiring a patron in Phaedria's father, but Brown 1990a: 58–59 is surely right that she remains a courtesan both in Terence's play and in Menander's.

22. Brown 1990a: 57 suggests that Phaedria might have kept Thais as a concubine, but an enduring relationship of concubinage is possible in New Comedy for an older man with a legitimate heir, like Demea in *Samia*, not for a youth like Phaedria.

23. Some critics take Chaerea's passion for Pamphila to be the dominant theme, most recently Goldberg 1986: 114 n. 27, 119–20; but the Chaerea plot is rather thin and wholly contained by the action involving Phaedria and Thais.

24. We might diagram the four terms on a parallelogram:

Here, rape and marriage correspond to the status division between the slave who has no rights (Pamphila before the recognition) and the citizen with connubial rights. The tension between love as a trade and a personal relation is inscribed, in *Eunuch*, within the courtesan role itself. For the semantic parallelogram, see Greimas 1970: 135–55; Greimas and Rastier 1968.

25. The idea goes back at least as far as de Staël 1820: 215–17, cited in Watt 1957: 135.

26. Cf. Szondi 1973: 90 on the function of sentimentality in eighteenth-century bourgeois drama as "the expression of a taboo upon any conflict between members of a family."

27. I believe that Terence found the scene in Menander's *Eunuch*.

28. Romantic sincerity was perhaps more a Roman than a Greek convention and may have drawn its inspiration from Terence's *Eunuch*. Catullus 109 imitates Phaedria's appeal to Thais for truth and sincerity (cf. Catullus 59, echoing *Eun.* 491; Reitzenstein 1940; Büchner 1974: 256–57), and Propertius 2.18 seems to have acknowledged the situation at the beginning of *Eunuch* as a paradigm of the lover's condition (Hubbard 1975: 61); cf. also Horace *Satires* 2.3.259–71, and Lowe 1983: 432. On the characteristic subjectivity of Roman elegy, see Allen 1950b; Luck 1961: 16–17, 37; see Stroh 1971: 1–7 for an overview and history of the idea. See also Griffin 1985: 112–41, and 204–8 on the influence of Roman comedy on love poetry.

29. One may compare in this regard the farcical conclusions to Plautus' *Bacchides* and to Terence's *Brothers*, both based on Menandrean originals, which have troubled critics; for discussion of Menander's endings, see Holzberg 1974: 126, 177; Brown 1990a: 39, 43.

30. Cf. Gilmartin 1975–76: 264–67.

31. See Pepe 1972: 144; Ludwig 1959: 37–38.

Chapter 10

1. I chiefly follow Gomme and Sandbach 1973 for the reconstruction of the lost or fragmentary portions of the play.

2. The text is Sandbach 1990, with addendum on pp. 348–50.

3. Gomme and Sandbach 1973: ad 495–96; cf. 568–71 where Onesimus speculates along just these lines.

4. Cf. Gomme and Sandbach 1973: ad 615–21, 632ff., 637.

5. On the social basis for Smicrines' complaints and Pamphila's loyalty, see Williams 1961, who indicates parallels with the formulas in somewhat later marriage contracts from Hellenistic Egypt.

6. Arnott 1979. Inserts in square brackets are Arnott's; inserts in curly curved brackets are my own. Arnott's text is identical here with that of Sandbach 1990.

7. Fossatoro 1915: 305, cited in Blanchard 1983: 334 n. 59.

8. Stavenhagen 1910: 581, cited in Blanchard 1983: 334 n. 59. Arnott 1981: 221 (cf. 223) judges "Charisios' equation of male and female standards of morality" an isolated exception to the rule that the sentiments expressed by Menander's characters are commonplace and shared by his audience (but cf. *Samian Woman* 142 and Chapter 8 n. 9 in this volume).

9. del Corno 1966: 179.

10. Wilamowitz-Moellendorf 1925: 126.

11. Blanchard 1983: 333–34,

12. Wilamowitz-Moellendorf 1925: 100, commenting on line 918 in Sandbach's numeration.

13. Capps 1910: 111.

14. Sandbach 1990: ad 891, 898, 915. Indeed, Kalbfleisch conjectur *ēdikēka* (I committed a crime) here, comparing frag. adesp. 221 Kock, and this was endorsed by Körte (see Gomme and Sandbach 1973 ad loc.). Sandbach notes: "It gives something which Charisios might have said, if he had not preferred to say *ētukhēka*."

15. Frag. 359 Körte-Thielfelder.

16. Gorgias in his defense of Helen (19) argued notoriously that *erōs* (passion) is godsent and that accordingly "it is not to be blamed as an error [*hamartēma*] but rather to be considered as a misfortune [*atukhēma*]." Aristotle acknowledges such sophistries, for example in the *Magna Moralia* 1.13.1188a 10–33, but states the ordinary view clearly: "Acts committed through sexual desire [*epithumia*] are not involuntary, but voluntary" (*Magna Moralia* 1.12.1188a3–4); for the distinction between crimes and misfortunes, see also Aristotle *Rhetoric* 1.13.1374b4–9.

17. The word "and" (*te*) is epexegetical: fathering the *nothos* specifies the nature of the deed in the previous clause.

18. Contra Wiles 1991: 3, who remarks: "*The Arbitration* turns upon the young man's recognition that he has raped his own future bride, and that he is guilty of sexual double standards;" Lowe 1987: 129 writes that "the *Epitrepontes* highlights the uncomfortable double standard of morality applied to judging the identical sexual offense in men and women," but does not specify the nature of the offense.

19. Cynthia Patterson (personal communication) informs me that the proper term for the illegitimate child of a woman is *parthenios* rather than *nothos*; cf. LSJ s.v. I.2, citing *Iliad* 16.180. I shall continue to refer to the putatively illegitimate child of Pamphila as a *nothos*, however, both for the sake of convenience and in order to bring out the symmetry that Charisius perceives between her situation and his own.

20. The idea that a girl is "soiled" by sexual experience is frequently reported to be the view of men in modern Mediterranean communities; cf. Cohen 1991: 41 n. 19 for bibliography, and Cohen 1992 on the preoccupation with the sexual purity of marriageable women in Renaissance Rome. (The view remains rampant in the United States and elsewhere.) Great caution is required, however, in projecting such attitudes back to the city-state culture of classical Athens.

21. Cf. Euripides *Ion* 26, where Creusa, who has been raped by Apollo and has borne a child, is referred to as *parthenos*; Owen 1939 ad 26 needlessly explains, "*parthenos* = 'like other maidens.'" Sissa 1990a: 73–86 discusses fully the arguments for a purely status-oriented or sociological interpretation of *parthenos* defended by Claude Calame and Angelo Brelich, and gives them a qualified endorsement; Sissa argues that virginity was a sexual matter as well.

See also Dowden 1989: 2: "Although *parthenia* was perceived as adversely affected by premature sexual experience . . . , the real issue was marriageability and the real contrast was between *parthenos* and *gyne*, the married woman. A *parthenos* is a maiden, not a virgin."

22. On the physical signs of virginity, see Sissa 1990a: 105–24; Sissa 1990b: 339–64; Hanson 1990: 324–29; also Hanson 1989, with bibliography.

23. Sissa 1990a: 91 argues that an essential part of the stigma attaching to sexual relations on the part of an unmarried citizen girl was publicity: "Sexuality and virginity were compatible only if sexual activity remained secret." In *Hecyra*, the girl's mother proposes, should news of her daughter's pregnancy get out, to represent the child as Pamphilus', and then expose it (398–400). Clearly, the birth of a child conceived in wedlock with a citizen, though followed by immediate divorce, does not carry the same opprobrium as premarital rape by an unknown male.

24. On the role of lying as part of a strategic manipulation of social norms, see Cohen 1991: 34, 54–69.

25. In a series of myths concerning women who have been raped by gods, and who must face the wrath of their fathers upon the discovery that they have borne a *nothos*, the focus is entirely on the existence of the child rather than on the sexual act per se; see Scafuro 1990 and cf. Seaford 1990: 160–61.

26. In Isaeus 2.7–8, the speaker mentions approvingly that the aging Menecles gave up his young wife and bestowed her on another man in order to spare her the misery of childlessness; it is not imagined that the new husband might entertain any objections to this transaction because he preferred a virgin bride. On the frequency of widowhood in Athens, cf. Gallant 1991: 26–27; Seaford 1990: 170–71.

27. On Greek pederasty, see Halperin 1990: 29–40, with the copious references cited there.

28. Cf. Just 1989: 66: "The notion of 'living in sin,' or the mystical idea that a woman's essentially 'shameful' sexuality can find honourable accommodation only within the confines of legitimate marriage where it is somehow 'sanctified,' appear to have had little place in Athenian views of marriage. . . . The price paid by the woman for such [an informal] union was that she could not claim the veneration of being the producer of legitimate children. . . . [Formal] marriage by *engue* was seen for what it was—a means of ensuring the continuity of the *oikos* by the procreation of legitimate children acceptable to the state."

29. On the Greek ideal of self-mastery in relation to the appetites, see the seminal discussion by Foucault 1984: 111–40. Epicurus *Letter to Menoeceus* 131 illustrates nicely the casual inclusion of sexual desire among the appetites in general: "For what produces the pleasant life is not continuous drinking and parties or pederasty or womanizing or the enjoyment of fish and the other dishes of an expensive talbe, but sober reasoning which tracks down the causes of every choice and avoidance," translation in Long and Sedley 1987: 114; cf. Galen, *Peri tōn idiōn hekastōi pathōn kai hamartēmatōn tēs diagnōseōs* 6.32 (Marquardt 1884): "Whatever one is in love with, he is pleased to make

progress in it; and for this reason you can see drunkards feeling pleasure when they surpass their fellow drinkers, those who are gluttonous taking delight in the quantity of foodstuffs, and those who are gourmets in cakes and pans and dishes and sauces [reading *karukeiais* instead of the misprint *korukeiais*]. I have known some men who have even taken pride in the quantity of their sexual acts" (my translation; the entire treatise has been translated into English in Harkins 1963).

30. Harris 1990 challenges the claim that the Athenians regarded rape as a lesser crime than seduction, and explains away the remark in Lysias 1 as "obviously the slanted interpretation of an advocate" (371; contra Cole 1984: 103; further bibliography in Harris 370 n. 2). Whatever the customary severity of punishment for the two offenses, however, the speaker surely expects that his argument will be received sympathetically by the male jury. Harris does not cite the analogous passage in Xenophon *Hiero* 3.

31. Marchant, in the Loeb edition (vol. 7, 1968: 22–23 n. 2), remarks that "*epei* should be rendered 'though,' not 'since' here, for it introduces a reason why one might suppose that there would be some restriction on the right to kill an adulterer, and *not* the reason why all adulterers may be killed with impunity." But the point is that Hiero is contrasting adultery, which is a capital offense because it alienates the affection of a wife, with rape, which does not.

32. Whether Charisius would have been troubled to learn that Pamphila had been in love with a man before him is irrelevant to Menandrean comedy, which does not ascribe amatory passion to a citizen girl.

33. See Patterson 1990: 55: "The situation usually envisioned in discussions of *nothoi* is that of the child of adultery or premarital union. . . , but the offspring of such unions are not typically called *nothoi*. *Nothoi* were the offspring of *pallakai* or concubines, who generally in Athens were of slave or foreign origin. . . . Likewise in Menander's comedies . . . , premarital children are not called *nothoi*." Patterson argues that the specific meaning of *nothos* is "the paternally recognized offspring of a mismatched or unequal union, which in Athens after 451/50 had both an *oikos* and a polis sense: 'man and concubine' and 'citizen and foreigner'" (p. 56), and that "*nothoi* are a specifically recognized class of 'bastards with fathers,' or 'bastards with families'" (p. 57). On the legal status of the *nothos*, see also Just 1989: 50–60; Sealey 1990: 12–19, 32. On whether the offspring of an unmarried citizen couple was considered a *nothos*, see Cox 1989: 43 with n. 31.

34. On marriage and the *oikos* (household), see Just 1989: 89–95, with references there.

35. One may perhaps understand in this way the thesis of Althusser 1971: 164–65: "All ideology represents in its necessarily imaginary distortion not the existing relations of production (and the other relations that derive from them), but above all the (imaginary) relationship of individuals to the relations of production and the relations that derive from them. What is represented in ideology is therefore not the system of the real relations which govern the existence of individuals, but the imaginary relation of those individuals to the

real relations in which they live." Althusser's analysis represents a partial and not wholly consistent attempt to ground a Marxist conception of ideology in a psychoanalytic (and more particularly, a Lacanian) theory of the construction of the individual subject; see Smith 1984: 128–40. The idea of displacement or distortion distinguishes Althusser's approach from the theory of internalization developed by Talcott Parsons; cf. Habermas 1975: 95.

36. In *Shorn Girl*, however, it is important that Glycera is reconciled to Polemo only after the status barrier is eliminated by means of the recognition, while in *Arbitrants* Charisius decides to accept Pamphila back before he knows that the child is in fact his.

Chapter 11

1. Meier 1980: 9. Cf. Goldmann 1964: 47 n. 1.

2. For a recent attempt to identify a different source (*Lebes* by Alexis), see Arnott 1988.

3. Major differences between the two plays are indicated in editions of *The Miser*. For example, Plautus' Euclio is a poor man wholly mesmerized by his pot of gold, while Harpagon is a bourgeois of some importance, for whom wealth is a sign of status. Cf. Marcou 1920: 26–27; Jouanny 1962: 236: "What difference does it make that the characters do not have a strict coherence in their personalities! What difference, too, that the Miser, at once usurer and hoarder, gathers in himself the legendary—and contradictory—manias of misers of every age. We know that Molière borrowed hastily, without harmonizing them very well, characteristics derived not only from Plautus (*Aulularia*), but also from Ariosto (*I Suppositi*), from Larivey (*Esprits*) and from Boisrobert (*La Belle Plaideuse*)." My concern here, however, is with the systematic transformation of the social code associated with the ancient city-state.

4. The interpretation of *Aulularia* here is based on the analysis in Konstan 1983b: 33–46, to which the reader is referred for full discussion and references.

5. On farcical endings in Menandrean plays, see Brown 1990a: 39–43, and Chapter 6 n. 15 in this volume.

6. See Konstan 1983b: 37–39.

7. Stockert 1983: 43 mentions several other Greek festivals that are also possible candidates; a nocturnal Roman festival for women is unlikely at this period.

8. The idea that Lyconides will have accepted his responsibilities toward the woman he raped because he discovers that she has borne a child perhaps gains some plausibility from the discussion of *Arbitrants* in the preceding Chapter 10, where a man abandons his wife not because she was raped but because she has produced a bastard child (*nothos*). Conversely, when Lyconides perceives that he has a legitimate child, he elects to recognize the woman he violated as his wife.

9. The plays are Plautus' *Casina*, *Merchant*, and *Asinaria*; on the last, see Konstan 1983b: 47–56.

10. In *Shield* (*Aspis*), Menander represents a greedy old man named Smicrines in rivalry with a young man for the hand of his niece, who has come into a fortune; here too, the impropriety of the miser's behavior is underscored by the difference in age between him and the girl he hopes to marry. Menander, however, does not ascribe an erotic motive to Smicrines.

Conclusion

1. Brenkman 1987: 108.

2. Brenkman 1987: 105; cf. Bloch 1971: 16–45, 159–73.

3. Marcuse 1972: 92, cited in Brenkman 1987: 107.

4. Brenkman 1987: 109.

5. Unless perhaps here, too, it is the slaves who are implicitly imagined as performing productive labor; see Longo 1987: 130–31, citing *Assembly-women* 651.

6. Davies 1977–78: 113–14.

7. Arnott 1981: 215.

8. Arnott 1981: 216.

9. On the fetishism or mystification consequent upon the commodity relation, see Geras 1986: 73–80.

10. The exclusivity or parochialism of the modern state is represented, for example, by the principle of *ius sanguinis* enshrined until this year in the German constitution as the criterion for national identity, or in Israel's law of return by which anyone born Jewish may claim Israeli citizenship.

11. Haynes 1992: 12; cf. Williams 1982: 137, 150.

12. Cohen 1985: 84.

References

Adkins, A.W.H. 1976. "*Polupragmosunē* and 'Minding One's Own Business.'" *Classical Philology* 71: 301–27.

Alink, M. J. 1983. *De vogels van Aristophanes: Een structuuranalyse en interpretatie*. Amsterdam: Gieben.

Allen, Archibald W. 1950a. "Elegy and the Classical Attitude toward Love: Propertius I.1." *Yale Classical Studies* 11: 255–77.

Allen, Archibald W. 1950b. "'Sincerity' and the Roman Elegists." *Classical Philology* 45: 145–60.

Allison, Richard H. 1983. "Amphibian Ambiguities: Aristophanes and His Frogs. *Greece and Rome* (2nd ser.) 30: 8–20.

Althusser, Louis. 1971. *Lenin and Philosophy and Other Essays*. Trans. Ben Brewster. New York: Monthly Review Press.

Althusser, Louis and Etienne Balibar. 1970. *Reading Capital*. Trans. Ben Brewster. London: Verso.

Anderson, Michael. 1970. "Knemon's *Hamartia*." *Greece and Rome* (2nd ser.) 17: 199–217.

Anderson, William S. 1984. "Love Plots in Menander and His Roman Adapters." *Ramus* 13: 124–34.

Ardener, Shirley. 1981. "Ground Rules and Social Maps for Women: An Introduction." In Shirley Ardener, ed. *Women and Space: Ground Rules and Social Maps*. London: Croom Helm, 11–34.

Arendt, Hannah. 1958. *The Human Condition*. Chicago: University of Chicago Press.

Arnott, W. Geoffrey, ed. 1979. *Menander*. Vol. 1. Cambridge, MA: Harvard University Press.

Arnott, W. Geoffrey. 1981. "Moral Values in Menander." *Philologus* 125: 215–27.

Arnott, W. Geoffrey. 1988. "The Greek Original of Plautus' *Aulularia.*" *Wiener Studien* 101: 181–91.

Arnott, W. Geoffrey. 1991. "A Lesson from the *Frogs.*" *Greece and Rome* (2nd ser.) 38: 18–23.

Arrowsmith, W. 1973. "Aristophanes' *Birds*: The Fantasy Politics of Eros." *Arion* (n.s.) 1.1: 119–67.

Atkinson, J. E. 1992. "Curbing the Comedians: Cleon versus Aristophanes and Syracosius' Decree." *Classical Quarterly* (n.s.) 42: 56–64.

Austin M. M. and P. Vidal-Naquet. 1977. *Economic and Social History of Ancient Greece.* Trans. M. M. Austin. Berkeley: University of California Press.

Badian, Ernst. 1958. *Foreign Clientelae 264–70 B.C.* Oxford: Clarendon.

Bakhtin, Mikhail M. 1968. *Rabelais and His World.* Trans. Helene Iswolsky. Cambridge, MA: MIT Press.

Bal, Mieke. 1987. *Lethal Love: Feminist Literary Readings of Biblical Love Stories.* Bloomington: University of Indiana Press.

Banks, Thomas R. 1980. "The Ephemeral, the Perennial, and the Structure of Aristophanes' *Wasps.*" *Classical Bulletin* 56: 81–85.

Barigazzi, Adelmo. 1965. *La formazione spirituale di Menandro.* Turin: Bottega d'Erasmo.

Barigazzi, Adelmo. 1979. "Il giuramento di Glicera nella Periciromene di Menandro e la preparazione del riconoscimento." *Prometheus* 5: 21–44.

Barigazzi, Adelmo. 1985. "Menandro: L'inizio del *Misumenos.*" *Prometheus* 11: 97–125.

Barkhuizen, J. J. 1981. "The *Plutus* of Aristophanes." *Acta Classica* 24: 17–22.

Barsby, John A. 1990. "The Characterisation of Parmeno in the Opening Scene of Terence's *Eunuch.*" *Prudentia* 22: 4–12.

Barsby, John A. 1993. "Problems of Adaptation in the *Eunuchus* of Terence." *Drama* 2: 160–79.

Belsey, Catherine. 1980. *Critical Practice.* London and New York: Methuen.

Bennington, Geoffrey. 1990. "Postal Politics and the Institution of the Nation." In Homi K. Bhabha, ed., *Nation and Narration.* London and New York: Routledge, 121–37.

Bérard, C. 1984. *La cité des images: Religion et société en grèce antique.* Lausanne: Fernand Nathan.

Bersani, Leo. 1976. *A Future for Astyanax: Character and Desire in Literature.* Boston: Little, Brown.

Bianco, Orazio. 1962. *Terenzio: problemi e aspetti dell'originalità.* Rome: Edizioni dell'Ateneo.

Bing, Peter and Rip Cohen. 1991. *Games of Venus: An Anthology of Greek and Roman Erotic Verse from Sappho to Ovid.* New York: Routledge.

Blanchard, Alain. 1983. *Essai sur la composition des comédies de Ménandre.* Paris: Belles Lettres.

Blaydes, Fredericus H. M. 1882. *Aristophanis Aves.* Halis Saxonum.

Bloch, Ernst. 1971. *On Karl Marx.* Trans. John Cumming. New York: Herder and Herder.

Blumenberg, H. 1979. "The Concept of Reality and the Possibility of the Novel." In R. E. Amacher and V. Lange, eds., *New Perspectives in German Literary Criticism*. Princeton: Princeton University Press, 29–48.

Bobrick Carter, Elizabeth. 1987. "Actor, Author and Audience in Aristophanes' *Thesmophoriazusae*." Ph.D. dissertation. Baltimore: Johns Hopkins University.

Borgogno, Alberto. 1988. "Sul nuovissimo *Misumenos* di Menandro." *Quaderni Urbinati di Cultura Classica* 59: 87–97.

Borthwick, E. K. 1968. "The Dances of Philocleon and the Sons of Carcinus in Aristophanes' *Wasps*." *Classical Quarterly* (n.s.) 18: 44–51.

Bovie, Palmer, trans. 1974. *Self-Tormentor*. In Douglass Parker, ed., *The Complete Comedies of Terence*. New Brunswick, NJ: Rutgers University Press, 71–143.

Bowie, A. M. 1987. "Ritual Stereotype and Comic Reversal: Aristophanes' *Wasps*." *Bulletin of the Institute of Classical Studies* 34: 112–25.

Bremer, J. M. 1993. "Aristophanes on His Own Poetry." In J. M. Bremer and E. W. Handley, eds., *Aristophane*. Entretiens Hardt 38. Geneva: Reverdin and Grange, 125–72.

Brenkman, John. 1987. *Culture and Domination*. Ithaca, NY: Cornell University Press.

Brock, R. W. 1986. "The Double Plots in Aristophanes' *Knights*." *Greek, Roman, and Byzantine Studies* 27: 15–27.

Brothers, A. J. 1969. "Terence, *Eunuchus* 189–206." *Classical Quarterly* (n.s.) 19: 314–19.

Brothers, A. J. 1980. "The Construction of Terence's *Heautontimorumenos*." *Classical Quarterly* (n.s.) 74: 94–119.

Brown, Christopher G. 1991. "Empousa, Dionysus and the Mysteries: Aristophanes, *Frogs* 285 ff." *Classical Quarterly* (n.s.) 41: 41–50.

Brown, P. 1985. "'This Thing of Darkness I Acknowledge Mine': *The Tempest* and the Discourse of Colonialism." In Jonathan Dollimore and Alan Sinfield, eds., *Political Shakespeare: New Essays in Cultural Materialism*. Ithaca, NY: Cornell University Press, 48–71.

Brown, P.G.McC. 1976. "Review of Lefèvre 1973." *Gnomon* 48: 244–49.

Brown, P.G.McC. 1980. "Review of Turner, E. G., *The Lost Beginning of Menander, Misoumenos*." *Classical Review* (n.s.) 30: 3–6.

Brown, P.G.McC. 1987. "Masks, Names and Characters in New Comedy." *Hermes* 115: 181–202.

Brown, P.G.McC. 1990a. "The Bodmer Codex of Menander and the Endings of Terence's *Eunuchus* and other Roman Comedies." In E. W. Handley and Andre Hurst, eds., *Relire Menandre. Recherches et Rencontres* 2: 37–61.

Brown, P.G.McC. 1990b. "Plots and Prostitutes in Greek New Comedy." *Papers of the Leeds International Latin Seminar* 6: 241–66.

Brown, P.G.McC. 1992. "The Construction of Menander's *Dyskolos*, Acts I–IV." *Zeitschrift für Papyrologie und Epigraphik* 94: 8–20.

Browne, G. M. 1974. "The End of Menander's *Perikeiromene*." *Bulletin of the Institute of Classical Studies* 21: 43–54.

Büchner, Karl. 1974. *Das Theater des Terenz*. Heidelberg: C. Winter.

Burkert, Walter. 1983. *Homo Necans: The Anthropology of Ancient Greek Ritual and Myth*. Trans. Peter Bing. Berkeley: University of California Press.

Calame, Claude. 1989a. "Démasquer par le masque: effets énonciatifs dans la comédie ancienne." *Revue de l'Histoire des Religions* 206: 357–76.

Calame, Claude. 1989b. "Entre rapports de parenté et relations civiques: Aphrodite l'hetaire au banquet politique des *hetairoi*." In *Aux sources de la puissance: sociabilité et parenté*. Actes du Colloque de Rouen 12–13 novembre 1987. Publications de l'Université de Rouen 148. Rouen: L'Université de Rouen, 101–11.

Calame, Claude. 1991. "Eros initiatique et la cosmogonie orphique." *Recherches et Rencontres* 3: 227–47.

Campbell, David A. 1984. "The Frogs in the *Frogs*." *Journal of Hellenic Studies* 104: 163–65.

Cantarella, Eva. 1985. *L'Ambiguo malanno: Condizione e immagine della donna nell'antichità greca e romana*. 2nd ed. Rome: Riuniti.

Carpenter, T. H. 1986. *Dionysian Imagery in Archaic Greek Art: Its Development in Black-Figure Vase Painting*. Oxford: Clarendon.

Carrière, Jean Claude. 1979. *Le carnival et la politique: une introduction à la comédie grecque*. Annales littéraires de l'université de Besançon 212. Paris: L'Université de Besançon.

Carter, L. B. 1986. *The Quiet Athenian*. Oxford: Clarendon.

Cartledge, Paul. 1990. *Aristophanes and His Theatre of the Absurd*. Bristol: Bristol Classical Press.

Cartledge, Paul. 1993. *The Greeks: A Portrait of Self and Others*. Oxford: Oxford University Press.

Castriota, David. 1992. *Myth, Ethos, and Actuality: Official Art in Fifth-Century B.C. Athens*. Madison: University of Wisconsin Press.

Ceccarelli, Paola. 1992. "Le monde sauvage et la cité dans la comédie ancienne." *Etudes de lettres. Revue de la Faculté des Lettres, Université de Lausanne*: 23–37.

Cohen, David. 1991. *Law, Sexuality and Society: The Enforcement of Morals in Classical Athens*. Cambridge: Cambridge University Press.

Cohen, Thomas V. 1992. "Agostino Bonamore and the Secret Pigeon." In Marlene Kadar, ed., *Exploring and (Re)Defining Life Writing*. Toronto: University of Toronto Press, 94–112.

Cohen, Walter. 1985. *Drama of a Nation: Public Theater in Renaissance England and Spain*. Ithaca, NY: Cornell University Press.

Cole, Susan G. 1984. "Greek Sanctions against Sexual Assault." *Classical Philology* 79: 97–183.

Connor, W. R. 1971. *The New Politicians of Fifth-Century Athens*. Princeton: Princeton University Press.

Cox, Cheryl Anne. 1989. "Incest, Inheritance and the Political Forum in Fifth-Century Athens." *Classical Journal* 85: 34–46.

Craik, Elizabeth M. 1987. "'One for the Pot': Aristophanes' *Birds* and the Anthesteria." *Eranos* 85: 25–34.

Crawley, Richard, trans. 1934. *The Complete Writings of Thucydides*. New York: Modern Library.

Croce, Benedetto. 1936. "Intorno alle commedie di Terenzio." *La critica* 34: 401–23. English transl. by C. Sprigge in B. Croce, *Philosophy, Poetry, History* (London: Oxford University Press, 1966): 776–801.

Culler, Jonathan. 1979. "Jacques Derrida." In John Sturrock, ed., *Structuralism and Since: From Lévi-Strauss to Derrida*. Oxford: Oxford University Press, 154–80.

Culler, Jonathan. 1982. *On Deconstruction: Theory and Criticism after Structuralism*. Ithaca, NY: Cornell University Press.

Czapo, Eric G. 1986. "Stock Scenes in Greek Comedy." Ph.D. dissertation. Toronto: University of Toronto.

David, E. 1984. *Aristophanes and Athenian Society of the Early Fourth Century B.C. Mnemosyne* supplement 81.

Davies, John K. 1977–78. "Athenian Citizenship." *Classical Journal* 73: 105–21.

Dawson, Doyne. 1992. *Cities of the Gods: Communist Utopias in Greek Thought*. New York: Oxford University Press.

de Certeau, Michel. 1980. *L'Invention du quotidien*. Vol. 1. Paris: Union Générale d'Editions.

del Corno, Dario, ed. 1966. *Menandro: Le commedie*. Vol. 1. Milan: Istituto Editoriale Italiano.

Dedoussi, Christina. 1988a. "The Borrowing Play in *Dyskolos* 891–930." *Bulletin of the Institute of Classical Studies* 35: 79–83.

Dedoussi, Christina. 1988b. "The Future of Plangon's Child in Menander's *Samia*." *Liverpool Classical Monthly* 13.3: 39–42.

Demand, Nancy. 1970. "The Identity of the Frogs." *Classical Philology* 65: 83–87.

Detienne, Marcel and Jean-Pierre Vernant. 1978. *Cunning Intelligence in Greek Culture and Society*. trans. Janet Lloyd. Hassocks: Harvester Press.

Dillon, Matthew. 1987a. "The *Lysistrata* as a Post-Dekeleian Peace Play." *Transactions of the American Philological Association* 117: 97–104.

Dillon, Matthew. 1987b. "Topicality in Aristophanes' *Ploutos*." *Classical Antiquity* 6: 155–83.

Dobrov, Gregory. 1990a. "The Dramatic Sources of *Nephelokokkugia*." In Gregory Dobrov, ed., *Aristophanes' Birds and Nephelokokkugia: Charting the Comic Polis*. Papers of the APA Seminar. Syracuse, NY: Trugedy Press, 17–25.

Dobrov, Gregory. 1990b. Introduction to Gregory Dobrov, ed., *Aristophanes' Birds and Nephelokokkugia: Charting the Comic Polis*. Papers of the APA Seminar. Syracuse, NY: Trugedy Press, 3–4..

Dobrov, Gregory. 1993. "The Tragic and the Comic Tereus." *American Journal of Philology* 114: 189–234.

Donaldson, Ian. 1970. *The World Upside-Down: Comedy from Jonson to Field-ing.* Oxford: Clarendon.

Dorfman, A. 1983. *The Empire's Old Clothes.* New York: Pantheon.

Dover, K. J. 1972. *Aristophanic Comedy.* Berkeley: University of California Press.

Dover, K. J. 1974. *Greek Popular Morality in the Time of Plato and Aristotle.* Berkeley: University of California Press.

Dover, K. J. 1993. *Aristophanes: Frogs.* Oxford: Clarendon.

Dowden, Ken. 1989. *Death and the Maiden: Girls' Initiation Rites in Greek Mythology.* London: Routledge.

Drexler, Hans. 1938. "Terentiana." *Hermes* 73: 39–98.

duBois, Page. 1988. *Sowing the Body: Psychoanalysis and Ancient Represen-tations of Women.* Chicago: University of Chicago Press.

Dumézil, Georges. 1979. *The Destiny of the Warrior.* Trans. Alf Hiltebeitel. Chicago: University of Chicago Press.

Eagleton, Terry. 1983. *Literary Theory: An Introduction.* Minneapolis: Uni-versity of Minnesota Press.

Eco, U. 1984. "Science Fiction and the Art of Conjecture." *Times Literary Supplement* 4257 (2 November): 1257.

Edmonds, J. J., ed. 1924. *Lyra Graeca.* Vol. 2. New York and London: Loeb Library.

Edmunds, Lowell. 1980. "Aristophanes' 'Acharnians'." *Yale Classical Stud-ies* 26: 1–42.

Edmunds, Lowell. 1987. *Cleon, Knights, and Aristophanes' Politics.* Lanham, MD: University Press of America.

Edwards, Anthony T. 1990. "Commentary." In Gregory Dobrov, ed., *Aristo-phanes' Birds and Nephelokokkugia: Charting the Comic Polis.* Papers of the APA Seminar. Syracuse, NY: Trugedy Press, 53–62.

Edwards, Anthony T. 1991. "Aristophanes' Comic Poetics: Τρύξ, Scatology, Σκῶμμα." *Transactions of the American Philological Association* 121: 157–79.

Ehrenberg, Victor. 1947. "Polypragmosyne: A Study in Greek Politics." *Jour-nal of Hellenic Studies* 67: 44–67.

Ehrenberg, Victor. 1961. *The People of Aristophanes: A Sociology of Old Attic Comedy.* 2nd ed. New York: Schocken.

Eichenbaum, Luise and Susie Orbach. 1988. *Between Women: Love, Envy, and Competition in Women's Friendships.* New York: Viking.

Epstein, P. D. 1981. "The Marriage of Peisthetairos to *Basileia* in the *Birds* of Aristophanes." *Dionysius* 5: 5–28.

Fantham, Elaine. 1971. "*Heautontimorumenos* and *Adelphoe*: A Study of Fatherhood in Terence and Menander." *Latomus* 30: 970–98.

Fantham, Elaine. 1975. "Sex, Status, and Survival in Hellenistic Athens: A Study of Women in New Comedy." *Phoenix* 29: 44–74.

Ferguson, William Scott. 1911. *Hellenistic Athens: An Historical Essay.* Lon-don: Macmillan.

Finley, M. I. 1975. *The Use and Abuse of History.* New York: Viking.

Finley, M. I. 1985. *The Ancient Economy.* 2nd ed. Berkeley: University of California Press.

Fisher, N.R.E. 1993. "Multiple Personalities and Dionysiac Festivals: Dicaeopolis in Aristophanes' *Acharnians.*" *Greece and Rome* (2nd ser.) 40: 31–47.

Flashar, Helmut. 1967. "Zur Eigenart des aristophanischen Spätwerks." *Poetica* 1: 154–75. Repr. in H. J. Newiger, ed., *Aristophanes und die alte Komödie* (Darmstadt: Wissenschaftliche Buchgesellschaft, 1975): 405–34.

Foley, Helene P. 1982. "The 'Female Intruder' Reconsidered: Women in Aristophanes' *Lysistrata* and *Ecclesiazusae.*" *Classical Philology* 77: 1–21.

Forehand, Walter E. 1985. *Terence.* Boston: Twayne.

Fortenbaugh, W. W. 1974. "Menander's *Perikeiromene*: Misfortune, Vehemence, and Polemon." *Phoenix* 28: 430–43.

Fossatoro, P. 1915. "Gli 'Epitrepontes' di Menandro e l''Hecyra' terenziana." *Athenaeum* 3: 305–18.

Foucault, Michel. 1984. *Histoire de la sexualité.* Vol. 2. *L'Usage des plaisirs.* Paris: Gallimard.

Fraenkel, Eduard. 1962. *Beobachtungen zu Aristophanes.* Rome: Edizioni di Storia e Letteratura.

Fredershausen, O. 1912. "Weitere Studien über das Recht bei Plautus und Terenz." *Hermes* 47: 199–249.

Friedman, Marilyn. 1993. "Feminism and Modern Friendship: Dislocating the Community." In Neera Kapur Badhwar, ed., *Friendship: A Philosophical Reader.* Ithaca, NY: Cornell University Press, 285–302.

Frontisi-Ducroux, Françoise and François Lissarrague. 1983. "De l'ambiguïté à l'ambivalence: un parcours dionysiaque." *Annali del seminario di studi del mondo classico del istituto universitario orientale di Napoli* (Archeologia e storia antica) 5: 11–32.

Frontisi-Ducroux, Françoise and Jean-Pierre Vernant. 1983. "Figures du masque en Grèce ancienne." *Journal de psychologie* 1/2: 53–69. Repr. in Jean-Pierre Vernant and Pierre Vidal-Naquet, *Mythe et tragédie en Grèce ancienne,* Vol. 2 (Paris: Editions La Découverte, 1986): 25–43.

Frost, K. B. 1988. *Exits and Entrances in Menander.* Oxford: Clarendon.

Frow, John. 1986. *Marxism and Literary History.* Cambridge, MA: Harvard University Press.

Gallant, Thomas W. 1991. *Risk Survival in Ancient Greece: Reconstructing the Rural Domestic Economy.* Cambridge: Polity Press.

Gallo, Luigi. 1984. "La donna greca e la marginalità." *Quaderni Urbinati di Cultura Classica* (n.s.) 18: 7–51.

Gallop, Jane. 1985. *Reading Lacan.* Ithaca, NY: Cornell University Press.

Gallop, Jane. 1989. "The Monster in the Mirror: The Feminist Critic's Psychoanalysis." In Richard Feldstein and Judith Roof, eds., *Feminism and Psychoanalysis.* Ithaca, NY: Cornell University Press, 13–24.

Gelley, Alexander. 1987. *Narrative Crossings: Theory and Pragmatics of Prose Fiction.* Baltimore: Johns Hopkins University Press.

Gelzer, Matthias. 1969. *The Roman Nobility*. Trans. Robin Seager. New York: Barnes and Noble.

Gelzer, Thomas. 1976. "Some Aspects of Aristophanes' Dramatic Art in the *Birds*." *Bulletin of the Institute of Classical Studies* 23: 1-14.

Geras, Norman. 1986. *Literature of Revolution: Essays on Marxism*. London: Verso.

Gerhard, G. A. 1910. "Zu Menanders Perikeiromene." *Philologus* 69: 10-34.

Giacomelli, Anne. 1980. "The Justice of Aphrodite in Sappho Fr. 1." *Transactions of the American Philological Association* 110:135-42.

Giglioni, Gabriella B. 1982. "Communità e solitudine: Tensioni sociali nei rapporti fra città e campagna nell'Atene del quinto e del quarto secolo A.C." *Studi classici e orientali* 32: 59-95.

Giglioni, Gabriella B. 1984. *Menandro e la politica della convivenza: La storia attraverso i testi letterari*. Como: Edizioni New Press.

Gill, Christopher. 1985. "Ancient Psychotherapy." *Journal of the History of Ideas* 46: 307-25.

Gilmartin, Kristine. 1975-76. "The Thraso-Gnatho Subplot in Terence's *Eunuchus*." *Classical World* 69: 264-67.

Gilula, Dwora. 1980. "The Concept of the *Bona Meretrix*: A Study of Terence's Courtesans." *Rivista di Filologia e di Istruzione Classica* 108: 142-65.

Goldberg, Sander M. 1980. *The Making of Menander's Comedy*. Berkeley: University of California Press.

Goldberg, Sander M. 1986. *Understanding Terence*. Princeton: Princeton University Press.

Goldberg, Sander M. 1990. "Act to Action in Plautus' *Bacchides*." *Classical Philology* 85: 191-201.

Goldhill, Simon. 1991. *The Poet's Voice: Essays on Poetics and Greek Literature*. Cambridge: Cambridge University Press.

Goldmann, Lucien. 1964. *The Hidden God: A Study of the Tragic Vision in the Pensées of Pascal and the Tragedies of Racine*. Trans. Philip Thody. London: Routledge.

Gomme, A. W. 1938. "Aristophanes and Politics." *Classical Review* 52: 97-109.

Gomme A. W. and F. H. Sandbach, eds. 1973. *Menander: A Commentary*. Oxford: Oxford University Press.

Gomme, A. W., A. Andrewes and K. J. Dover. 1981. *A Historical Commentary on Thucydides*. Oxford: Clarendon.

González de Tobia, Ana M. 1994. "Composición de espacios para una utopía en *Aves* de Aristófanes." *Synthesis* 1: 93-113.

Görler, Woldemar. 1972. "Doppelhandlung, Intrige und Anagnorismos bei Terenz." *Poetica* 5: 164-82.

Graf, F. 1974. *Eleusis und die orphische Dichtung: Athens in vorhellenistischer Zeit*. Religionsgeschichtliche Vorsache und Vorarbeiten 33. Berlin: De Gruyter.

Graff, Gerald. 1979. *Literature against Itself: Literary Ideas in Modern Society*. Chicago: University of Chicago Press.

Green, R.P.H. 1991. *The Works of Ausonius*. Oxford: Clarendon.

Green, W. C., ed. 1868. *Aristophanes: The Wasps*. London: Rivingtons.

Green, W. C., ed. 1879. *The Birds of Aristophanes*. Cambridge: Cambridge University Press.

Greimas, A.-J. 1970. *Du sens*. Paris: Editions du Seuil.

Greimas, A.-J. and F. Rastier. 1968. "The Interaction of Semiotic Constraints." *Yale French Studies* 41: 86–105.

Griffin, Jasper. 1985. *Latin Poets and Roman Life*. Chapel Hill: University of North Carolina Press.

Gruen, Erich S. 1990. *Studies in Greek Culture and Roman Policy*. Cincinnati Classical Studies (n.s.) 7. Leiden: E. J. Brill.

Habermas, Jürgen. 1975. *Legitimation Crisis*. Trans. Thomas McCarthy. Boston: Beacon.

Haldane, J. A. 1965. "A Scene in the *Thesmophoriazusae* (295–371)." *Philologus* 109: 39–46.

Hall, Edith. 1989. *Inventing the Barbarian: Greek Self-Definition through Tragedy*. Oxford: Clarendon.

Hall, F. W. and W. M. Geldart, eds. 1907. *Aristophanis Comoediae*. 2nd ed. Oxford: Clarendon.

Hallett, Judith P. 1988. "Roman Attitudes toward Sex." In Michael Grant and Rachel Kitzinger, eds., *Civilization of the Ancient Mediterranean: Greece and Rome*. Vol. 2. New York: Scribners, 1265–78.

Hallett, Judith P. 1989. "Female Homoeroticism and the Denial of Roman Reality in Latin Literature." *Yale Journal of Criticism* 3: 209–27.

Halliwell, Stephen. 1984. "Aristophanic Satire." In Rawson, C., ed., *English Satire and the Satiric Tradition*. Oxford: Oxford University Press, 6–20.

Halperin, David M. 1990. *One Hundred Years of Homosexuality and Other Essays on Greek Love*. New York: Routledge.

Hamilton, Richard. 1985. "The Well-Equipped Traveller: *Birds* 42." *Greek, Roman, and Byzantine Studies* 26: 235–39.

Händel, Paul. 1963. *Formen und Darstellungsweisen in der aristophanischen Komödie*. Heidelberg: C. Winter.

Handley, E. W., ed. 1965. *The Dyskolos of Menander*. London: Methuen.

Handley, E. W. 1985. "Comedy." In P. E. Easterling and B.M.W. Knox, eds., *The Cambridge History of Classical Literature*. Vol. 1. Cambridge: Cambridge University Press, 355–425.

Hanson, Ann Ellis. 1989. "Greco-Roman Gynecology." *Newsletter of the Society for Ancient Medicine and Pharmacy* 17: 83–92.

Hanson, Ann Ellis. 1990. "The Medical Writers' Woman." In David M. Halperin, John J. Winkler, and Froma T. Zeitlin, eds., *Before Sexuality: The Construction of Erotic Experience in the Ancient Greek World*. Princeton: Princeton University Press, 309–39.

Harkins, P. W. 1963. *Galen on the Passions and Errors of the Soul*. With Introduction and Interpretation by W. Riese. Columbus: Ohio State University Press.

Harman, E. G. 1920. *The Birds of Aristophanes Considered in Relation to Athenian Politics.* London: E. Arnold.

Harriott, Rosemary M. 1969. *Poetry and Criticism before Plato.* London: Methuen.

Harriott, Rosemary M. 1986. *Aristophanes: Poet and Dramatist.* Baltimore: Johns Hopkins University Press.

Harris, Edward M. 1990. "Did the Athenians Regard Seduction as a Worse Crime than Rape?" *Classical Quarterly* (n.s.) 40: 370–77.

Harrison, A.R.W. 1968 and 1971. *The Law of Athens.* 2 vols. Oxford: Clarendon.

Harrison, Jane Ellen. 1962. *Themis: A Study of the Social Origins of Greek Religion.* 2nd ed. Cleveland and New York: New York University Books.

Harsh, Philip W. 1937. "Certain Features of Technique Found in both Greek and Roman Drama." *American Journal of Philology* 58: 282–93.

Harvey, David. 1990. "The Sykophant and Sykophancy: Vexatious Redefinition?" In Paul Cartledge, Paul Millett, and Stephen Todd, eds., *Nomos: Essays in Athenian Law, Politics and Society.* Cambridge: Cambridge University Press, 103–21.

Haynes, Jonathan. 1992. *The Social Relations of Jonson's Theater.* Cambridge: Cambridge University Press.

Heath, Malcolm. 1987. *Political Comedy in Aristophanes.* Hypomnemata 87.

Heberlein, Friedrich. 1980. *Pluthygieia: Zur Gegenwelt bei Aristophanes.* Frankfurt am Main: Haag und Herchen.

Heberlein, Friedrich. 1981. "Zur Ironie im 'Plutus' des Aristophanes." *Würzburger Jahrbücher für die Altertumswissenschaft* 7: 27–49.

Heiden, Bruce. 1991. "Tragedy and Comedy in the *Frogs* of Aristophanes." *Ramus* 20: 95–111.

Henderson, Jeffrey. 1975. *The Maculate Muse: Obscene Language in Attic Comedy.* New Haven, CT: Yale University Press.

Henderson, Jeffrey. 1980. "'Lysistrate': The Play and Its Themes." *Yale Classical Studies* 26: 153–218.

Henderson, Jeffrey. 1987. *Aristophanes: Lysistrata.* Oxford: Clarendon.

Henderson, Jeffrey. 1988. *Aristóphanes' Lysistrata.* Cambridge, MA: Focus Information Group.

Henderson, Jeffrey. 1989. "The Demos and the Comic Competition." In John J. Winkler and Froma Zeitlin, eds., *Nothing to Do with Dionysus? Athenian Drama in its Social Context.* Princeton: Princeton University Press, 271–313.

Henderson, Jeffrey. 1990. "Peisetairos and the Athenian Elite." In Gregory Dobrov, ed., *Aristophanes' Birds and Nephelokokkugia: Charting the Comic Polis.* Papers of the APA Seminar. Syracuse, NY: Trugedy Press, 8–16.

Henry, Madeleine M. 1985. *Menander's Courtesans and the Greek Comic Tradition.* Frankfurt am Main: P. Lang.

Henry, Madeleine M. 1987. "*Ethos, Mythos, Praxis*: Women in Menander's Comedy." *Helios* 13: 141–50.

Hertel, Gerhard. 1969. *Die Allegorie von Reichtum und Armut*. Nuremberg: Hans Carl.

Hofmann, Heinz. 1976. *Mythos und Komödie: Untersuchungen zu den Vögeln des Aristophanes*. Spudasmata 33.

Hofmann, W. and G. Wartenberg. 1973. *Der Bramarbas in der antiken Komödie*. Berlin: Akademie-Verlag.

Holzberg, Niklas. 1974. *Menander: Untersuchungen zur dramatischen Technik*. Nuremberg: Hans Carl.

Hooker, G.T.W. 1960. "The Topography of the *Frogs.*" *Journal of Hellenic Studies* 80: 112–17.

Hooker, J. T. 1980. "The Composition of the Frogs." *Hermes* 108: 169–82.

Hubbard, Margaret. 1975. *Propertius*. London: Duckworth.

Hubbard, Thomas. 1991. *The Mask of Comedy: Aristophanes and the Intertextual Parabasis*. Ithaca, NY: Cornell University Press.

Hugill, William Meredith. 1936. *Panhellenism in Aristophanes*. Chicago: University of Chicago Press.

Humphreys, Sally. 1983. *The Family, Women and Death: Comparative Studies*. London: Routledge.

Hunter, R. L. 1985. *The New Comedy of Greece and Rome*. Cambridge: Cambridge University Press.

Jachman, Günther. 1921. "Der *Eunuchus* des Terenz." *Nachrichten von der Gesellschaft der Wissenschaft zu Göttingen*: 69–88.

Jacob, Christian. 1980. "The Greek Traveler's Areas of Knowledge: Myths and Other Discourses in Pausanias' *Description of Greece.*" *Yale French Studies* 59: 65–84.

Jameson, Fredric. 1981. *The Political Unconscious: Narrative as a Socially Symbolic Act*. Ithaca, NY: Cornell University Press.

Jameson, Michael, ed. 1966. *Ben Jonson: Three Comedies*. Harmondsworth: Penguin.

Jebb, Richard. 1928. *Sophocles: The Plays and Fragments*. Vol. 3: *The Antigone*. 3rd ed. Cambridge: Cambridge University Press.

Jocelyn, H. D. 1973. "Homo sum: humani nihil a me alienum puto (Terence, *Heauton Timorumenos* 77)." *Antichthon* 7: 14–42.

Johnston, Patricia. 1980. *Vergil and the Golden Age: A Study of the Georgics*. *Mnemosyne* supplement 60.

Jones, A.H.M. 1953. "The Athenian Democracy and Its Critics." *Cambridge Historical Journal* 9: 1–26. Repr. in A.H.M. Jones, *Athenian Democracy* (Oxford: Oxford University Press, 1975): 41–72.

Jorgensen, Paul A., ed. 1972. *William Shakespeare: The Comedy of Errors*. Rev. ed. New York: Penguin.

Jouanny, Robert, ed. 1962. *Molière: Oeuvres complètes*. Vol. 2. Paris: Garnier.

Just, Roger. 1989. *Women in Athenian Law and Life*. London: Routledge.

Kassel, R. and C. Austin, eds. 1983–. *Poetae Comici Graeci*. Berlin: De Gruyter.

Katz, B. 1976. "The *Birds* of Aristophanes and Politics." *Athenaeum* 54: 353–81.

Kavanagh, James H. 1981. "'Marks of Weakness': Ideology, Science, and Textual Criticism." *Praxis* 5: 23–38.

Kells, J. H. 1963. "Problems of Interpretation in the *Antigone.*" *Bulletin of the Institute of Classical Studies* 10: 47–64.

Knoche, U. 1934–36 and 1938. "Über einige Szenen des *Eunuchus.*" *Nachrichten von der Gesellschaft der Wissenschaft zu Göttingen* (n.s.) 1: 145–84 and 3: 31–87.

Koch, Klaus-Dietrich. 1965. *Kritische Idee und Komisches Thema: Untersuchungen zur Dramaturgie und zum Ethos der Aristophanischen Komödie. Jahrbuch der Wittheit zu Bremen* 9.

Köchly, H.A.T. 1857. "Über die Vögel des Aristophanes." In *Gratulationsschrift . . . August Boeckh.* Zurich: Zürcher und Furrer.

Konstan, David. 1983a. "A Dramatic History of Misanthropes." *Comparative Drama* 17: 97–123.

Konstan, David. 1983b. *Roman Comedy.* Ithaca, NY: Cornell University Press.

Konstan, David. 1985. "The Politics of Aristophanes' *Wasps.*" *Transactions of the American Philological Association* 115: 27–46.

Konstan, David. 1986. "Love in Terence's *Eunuch*: The Origins of Erotic Subjectivity." *American Journal of Philology* 107: 369–93.

Konstan, David. 1987a. "Between Courtesan and Wife: A Study of Menander's *Perikeiromene.*" *Phoenix* 41: 121–39.

Konstan, David 1987b. "Politique, poétique, et rituel dans les *Grenouilles* d'Aristofane." *Mētis* 1: 291–308.

Konstan, David. 1989. "An Anthropology of Euripides' *Kyklōps.*" In John J. Winkler and Froma Zeitlin, eds., *Nothing to Do with Dionysus? Athenian Drama in Its Social Context.* Princeton: Princeton University Press, 207–27.

Konstan, David. 1990a. "Aristophanes' *Birds* and the City in the Air." *Arethusa* 23: 183–207.

Konstan, David. 1990b. "The Dramatic Fortunes of a Miser: Ideology and Form in Plautus and Molière." In Andrew Milner and Chris Worth, eds., *Discourse and Difference: Post-Structuralism, Feminism and the Moment of History.* Melbourne: Centre for General and Comparative Literature of Monash University, 177–89.

Konstan, David. 1993a. "Friends and Lovers in Ancient Greece." *Syllecta Classica* 4: 1–12.

Konstan, David. 1993b. "Women and the Body Politic: The Representation of Women in Aristophanes' *Lysistrata.*" In S. Halliwell, J. Henderson, A. H. Sommerstein, and B. Zimmerman, eds., *Tragedy, Comedy and the Polis.* Bari: Levante Editori, 431–44.

Konstan, David. 1993c. "The Young Concubine in Menandrean Comedy." In Ruth Scodel, ed., *Theatre and Society in the Classical World.* Ann Arbor: University of Michigan Press, 139–60.

Konstan, David. 1994a. "Premarital Sex, Illegitimacy, and Male Anxiety in Menander and Athens." In Alan Boegehold and Adele Scafuro, eds.,

Athenian Identity and Civic Ideology. Baltimore: Johns Hopkins University Press, 217–35.

Konstan, David. 1994b. *Sexual Symmetry: Love in the Ancient Novel and Related Genres.* Princeton: Princeton University Press.

Konstan, David and Matthew Dillon. 1981. "The Ideology of Aristophanes' *Wealth*." *American Journal of Philology* 102: 371–94.

Körte, Alfred. 1932. "Menandros (9)." In A. Pauly, G. Wissowa, and W. Kroll, eds., *Real-Encyclopädie der classischen Altertumswissenschaft.* Vol. 15. Stuttgart: Metzler, 707–61.

Körte, Alfred and Andreas Thierfelder, eds. 1957 and 1959. *Menandri quae supersunt.* 2 vols. 3rd ed. Leipzig: Teubner.

Kroll, Wilhelm. 1927. "Die Handlung des Hautontimorumenos." *Jahresbericht der schlesischen Gesellschaft für vaterländische Kultur* 100: 122–32.

Kunst, Karl. 1919. *Studien zur griechisch-römischen Komödie mit besonderer Berüchsichtigung der Schlußz-Szenen und ihrer Motive.* Vienna and Leipzig: C. Gerold's.

Lacey, W. K. 1968. *The Family in Classical Greece.* Ithaca, NY: Cornell University Press.

Laclau, Ernesto. 1977. *Politics and Ideology in Marxist Theory.* London: Verso.

Lada, Ismene. 1992. "Dionysus in Aristophanes' *Frogs*." Ph.D. dissertation. Cambridge: Trinity College.

Lamphere, Louise. 1974. "Strategies, Cooperation, and Conflict among Women in Domestic Groups." In Michelle Zimbalist Rosaldo and Louise Lamphere, eds., *Women, Culture, and Society.* Stanford: Stanford University Press, 97–112.

Landfester, Manfred. 1977. *Handlungsverlauf und Komik in den frühen Komödien des Aristophanes.* Berlin: De Gruyter.

Lapalus, Etienne. 1934. "Le Dionysos et l'Héraclès des *Grenouilles*." *Revue des Etudes Grecques* 47: 1–20.

Lateiner, Donald. 1981. "An Analysis of Lysias' Political Defense Speeches." *Rivista Storica dell'Antichità* 11: 147–60.

Lateiner, Donald. 1982. "'The Man Who Does Not Meddle in Politics': A *Topos* in Lysias. *Classical World* 76: 1–12.

Lawler, Lillian B. 1974. *The Dance of the Ancient Greek Theater.* Iowa City: University of Iowa Press.

Leeuwen, J. van., ed. 1896. *Aristophanis Ranae.* Leyden: Sijthoff.

Lefèvre, Eckard. 1969. *Die Expositionstechnik in der Komödien des Terenz.* Darmstadt: Wissenschaftliche Buchgesellschaft.

Lefèvre, Eckard. 1973. "Der 'Heautontimorumenos' des Terenz." In E. Lefèvre, ed., *Die römische Komödie: Plautus und Terenz.* Wege der Forschung 236. Darmstadt: Wissenschaftliche Buchgesellschaft, 443–62.

Lefèvre, Eckard. 1978. *Der Phormio des Terenz und der Epidikazomenos des Apollodor von Karystos.* Munich: C. H. Beck.

Lefèvre, Eckard. 1979. "Menander." In Adolf Gustav Seeck, ed., *Das griechische Drama.* Darmstadt: Wissenschaftliche. Buchgesellschaft, 307–53.

Lefèvre, Eckard. 1986. "Ich bin ein Mensch, nichts Menschliches ist mir fremd." In *Wegweisende Antike: Zur Aktualität humanistischer Bildung. Humanistische Bildung* Beiheft 1: 39–49.

Lenz, Lutz. 1980. "Komik und Kritik in Aristophanes' 'Wespen.'" *Hermes* 108: 15–44.

Lévi-Strauss, Claude. 1969. *The Elementary Structures of Kinship.* Trans. James Harle Bell, John Richard von Sturmer, and Rodney Needham. Boston: Beacon Press.

Lewis, D. M. 1955. "Notes on Attic Inscriptions, II." *Annual of the British School at Athens* 50: 1–36.

Lissarague, François. 1990. *The Aesthetics of the Greek Banquet: Images of Wine and Ritual.* Trans. Andrew Szegedy-Maszak. Princeton: Princeton University Press.

Lloyd-Jones, Hugh. 1967. "Heracles at Eleusis: P. Oxy. 2622 and P.S.I. 1391." *Maia* 19: 206–29.

Lloyd-Jones, Hugh. 1973. "Terentian Technique in the *Adelphi* and the *Eunuchus.*" *Classical Quarterly* (n.s.) 23: 279–84.

Lloyd-Jones, Hugh. 1987. "The Structure of Menander's Comedies." *Dioniso* 57: 313–21.

Lofberg, J. O. 1920. "The Sycophant-Parasite." *Classical Philology* 15: 61–72.

Long, A. A. and D. N. Sedley, eds. *The Hellenistic Philosophers.* Vol. 1. Cambridge: Cambridge University Press.

Longo, Oddone. 1987. "Società, economia e politica in Aristofane." *Dioniso* 57: 111–34.

López Eire, Antonio. 1994. *Aristofanes: Lisístrata.* Salamanca: Hesperides.

Loraux, Nicole. 1980–81. "L'Acropole comique." *Ancient Society* 11–12: 119–50. Rev. version in Nicole Loraux, *Les enfants d'Athéna: Idées athéniennes sur la citoyenneté et la division des sexes.* 2nd. ed. (Paris: F. Maspero, 1984): 157–96.

Loraux, Nicole. 1984. *Les enfants d'Athéna: Idées athéniennes sur la citoyenneté et la division des sexes.* 2nd ed. Paris: F. Maspero.

Lowe, J.C.B. 1983. "The *Eunuchus*: Terence and Menander." *Classical Quarterly* (n.s.) 33: 428–44.

Lowe, J.C.B. 1988. "Plautus *Poenulus* I 2." *Bulletin of the Institute of Classical Studies* 35: 101–10.

Lowe, J.C.B. 1989. "The *Virgo Callida* of Plautus, *Persa.*" *Classical Quarterly* (n.s.) 39: 390–99.

Lowe, J.C.B. 1991. "Prisoners, Guards, and Chains in Plautus, *Captivi.*" *American Journal of Philology* 112: 29–44.

Lowe, N. J. 1987. "Tragic Space and Comic Timing in Menander's *Dyskolos.*" *Bulletin of the Institute of Classical Studies* 34: 126–38.

Luck, Georg. 1961. *Die römische Liebeselegie.* Heidelberg: C. Winter.

Ludwig, Walther. 1959. "Von Terenz zu Menander." *Philologus* 103: 1–38. Repr. in Eckard Lefèvre, ed., *Die Römische Komödie: Plautus und Terenz* (Darmstadt: Wissenschaftliche Buchgesellschaft, 1973): 354–408.

Ludwig, Walther. 1968. "The Originality of Terence and His Greek Models. *Greek, Roman, and Byzantine Studies* 9: 169–92.

Lukács, Georg. 1975. *The Theory of the Novel.* Trans. Anna Bostock. Cambridge, MA: MIT Press.

MacDowell, Douglas M., ed. 1971. *Aristophanes' Wasps.* Oxford: Oxford University Press.

MacDowell, Douglas M. 1978. *The Law in Classical Athens.* Ithaca, NY: Cornell University Press.

Macherey, Pierre. 1976. "The Problem of Reflection." Trans. S. S. Lanser. *Sub-Stance* 15: 6–20.

Macherey, Pierre. 1978. *A Theory of Literary Production.* Trans. Geoffrey Wall. London. Routledge.

Macherey, Pierre and Etienne Balibar. 1978. "Literature as an Ideological Form: Some Marxist Propositions." Trans. Ian McLeod, John Whitehead, and Ann Wordsworth, *Oxford Literary Review* 3.1.4–12. Repr. in Robert Young, ed., *Untying the Text: A Post-Structuralist Reader* (London: Routledge, 1981): 79–99.

MacKendrick, Paul. 1969. *The Athenian Aristocracy 399–31 B.C.* Martin Classical Lectures 23. Cambridge, MA: Harvard University Press.

Maltby, Robert. 1983. "The Last Act of Terence's *Heautontimorumenos.*" *Papers of the Liverpool Latin Seminar* 4: 27–41.

Marchant, E. C., ed. and trans. 1968. *Xenophon.* Vol. 7. Cambridge, MA: Harvard University Press.

Marcou, M., ed. 1920. *Molière: L'Avare.* Paris: Garnier.

Marcuse, Herbert. 1972. *Counterrevolution and Revolt.* Boston: Beacon.

Marianetti, Marie C. 1992. *Religion and Politics in Aristophanes' Clouds.* Altertumswissenschaftliche Texte und Studien 24. Hildesheim: Olms Weidmann.

Markle, M. M. III. 1976. "Support of Athenian Intellectuals for Philip: A Study of Isocrates' *Philippus* and Speusippus' *Letter to Philip.*" *Journal of Hellenic Studies* 96: 80–99.

Markle, M. M. 1985. "Jury Pay and Assembly Pay at Athens." In Paul A. Cartledge and F. D. Harvey, eds., *Crux: Essays Presented to de Ste. Croix on his 75th Birthday. History of Political Thought* 6: 265–97.

Marquardt, I., ed. 1884. *Galeni scripta minora.* Vol. 1. Leipzig: Teubner.

Marry, John. 1979. "Sappho and the Heroic Ideal." *Arethusa* 12: 71–92.

McClintock, Anne. 1991. "'No Longer in a Future Heaven': Women and Nationalism in South Africa." *Transition* 51: 104–23.

McKechnie, Paul. 1989. *Outsiders in the Greek Cities in the Fourth Century B.C.* London: Routledge.

Meier, Christian. 1980. *Die Entstehung des Politischen bei den Griechen.* Frankfurt am Main: Suhrkamp.

Miller, Norma, trans. 1987. *Menander: Plays and Fragments.* Harmondsworth: Penguin.

Modleski, Tania. 1988. *The Women Who Knew Too Much: Hitchcock and Feminist Theory.* New York and London: Methuen.

Moorton, Richard F., Jr. 1989. "Rites of Passage in Aristophanes' *Frogs*." *Classical Journal* 84: 308–24.

More, Thomas. 1910. *Utopia*. Ed. John Warrington. New York: Dutton.

Mossé, Claude. 1976. "Les salariés à Athènes du IVième siècle." *Dialogues d'histoire ancienne* 21: 97–101.

Müller, Isolde. 1974. "Der Wandel der Stoffwahl und der komischen Mittel in den Komödien des Aristophanes durch die Krise der attischen Polis." In E. C. Welskopf, ed., *Hellenische Poleis: Krise-Wandlung-Wirkung*. Vol. 3. Berlin: Akademie-Verlag, 1389–1412.

Murray, Oswyn. 1983. "The Greek Symposion in History." In E. Gabba, ed., *Tria Corda: Scritti in onore di Arnaldo Momigliano*. Como: Edizioni New Press, 257–72.

Mylonas, George E. 1961. *Eleusis and the Eleusinian Mysteries*. Princeton: Princeton University Press.

Nardo, Dante. 1967–68. "Terenzio e l'ironizzazione del sapiens." *Atti del Istituto Veneto di scienze, lettere, ed arti* 126: 131–74.

Nauck, August, ed. 1964. *Tragicorum Graecorum Fragmenta*. 2nd ed. Hildesheim: G. Olms.

Nead, Lynda. 1992. "Framing and Freeing: Utopias of the Female Body." *Radical Philosophy* 60: 12–15.

Neil, Robert Alexander, ed. 1901. *The Knights of Aristophanes*. Cambridge: Cambridge University Press.

Nencini, F. 1891. *De Terentio eiusque fontibus*. Livorno: Giusti.

Nesselrath, Heinz-Günther. 1990. *Die attische Mittler Komödie: Ihre Stellung in der antiken Literaturkritik und Literaturgeschichte*. Berlin: De Gruyter.

Newiger, Hans-Joachim. 1957. *Metapher und Allegorie: Studien zu Aristophanes*. Zetemata 16.

Newiger, Hans-Joachim. 1980. "War and Peace in the Comedy of Aristophanes." *Yale Classical Studies* 26: 219–37.

North, H. 1966. *Sophrosyne: Self-Knowledge and Self-Restraint in Greek Literature*. Ithaca, NY: Cornell University Press.

Ober, Josiah. 1989. *Mass and Elite in Democratic Athens: Rhetoric, Ideology, and the Power of the People*. Princeton: Princeton University Press.

Olson, S. Douglas. 1990. "Economics and Ideology in Aristophanes' *Wealth*." *Harvard Studies in Classical Philology* 93: 223–42.

Osborne, Robin. 1985. *Demos: The Discovery of Classical Attika*. Cambridge: Cambridge University Press.

Osborne, Robin. 1990. "Vexatious Litigation in Classical Athens: Sykophancy and the Sykophant." In Paul Cartledge, Paul Millett, and Stephen Todd, eds., *Nomos: Essays in Athenian Law, Politics and Society*. Cambridge: Cambridge University Press, 83–102.

Ostwald, M. 1969. *Nomos and the Beginnings of Athenian Democracy*. Oxford: Clarendon.

Owen, A. S. 1939. *Euripides: Ion*. Oxford: Clarendon.

Padilla, Mark. 1992. "The Heraclean Dionysus: Theatrical and Social Renewal in Aristophanes' *Frogs.*" *Arethusa* 25: 359–84.

Parker, Douglass. 1974. Introduction to *The Eunuch.* In Douglass Parker, ed., *The Complete Comedies of Terence.* Brunswick, NJ: Rutgers University Press, 147–52.

Parker, Holt N. 1993. "Sappho Schoolmistress." *Transactions of the American Philological Association* 123: 309–51.

Pascal, Carlo. 1911. *Dioniso: Saggio sulla religione e la parodia religiosa in Aristofane.* Catania: Battiato.

Patterson, Cynthia B. 1981. *Pericles' Citizenship Law of 451–50 B.C.* Salem, NH: Ayer.

Patterson, Cynthia B. 1990. "Those Athenian Bastards." *Classical Antiquity* 9: 40–72.

Patterson, Cynthia B. 1991. "Marriage and the Married Woman in Athenian Law." In Sarah B. Pomeroy, ed., *Women's History and Ancient History.* Chapel Hill: University of North Carolina Press, 48–72.

Pellizer, Ezio. 1983. "Della zuffa simpotica." In Massimo Vetta, ed., *Poesia e simposio nella Grecia antica.* Rome and Bari: Laterza, 31–41.

Pepe, George M. 1972. "The Last Scene of Terence's *Eunuchus.*" *Classical World* 65: 141–45.

Platnauer, Maurice, ed. 1964. *Aristophanes: Peace.* Oxford: Clarendon.

Plebe, Armando. 1952. *La teoria del comica da Aristotele a Plutarco.* Turin: Università.

Plepelits, Karl. 1970. *Die Fragmente der Demen des Eupolis.* Vienna: Verlag Notring.

Polignac, François de. 1984. *La naissance de la cité grecque.* Paris: Editions La Découverte.

Post, C. R. 1913. "The Dramatic Art of Menander." *Harvard Studies in Classical Philology* 24: 111–45.

Post, L. A. 1941. "Woman's Place in Menander's Athens." *Transactions of the American Philological Association* 71: 420–59.

Post, L. A. 1963. "Some Subtleties in Menander's *Dyscolus.*" *American Journal of Philology* 84: 36–51.

Quirini, Bruno Zannini. 1987. *Nephelokokkygia: La prospettiva mitica degli Uccelli di Aristofane.* Rome: "L'Erma" di Bretschneider.

Raaflaub, Kurt. 1983. "Democracy, Oligarchy, and the Concept of the 'Free Citizen' in Late Fifth-Century Athens." *Political Theory* 11: 517–44.

Raaflaub, Kurt. 1984. "Freiheit in Athen und Rom: Ein Beispiel politischer Begriffsentwicklung in der Antike." *Historische Zeitschrift* 238: 529–67.

Raaflaub, Kurt. 1985. *Die Entdeckung der Freiheit: Zur historischen Semantik und Gesellschaftgeschichte eines politischen Grundbegriffes der Griechen.* Munich: Beck.

Radermacher, L., ed. 1954. *Frösche.* 2nd ed. Revised by W. Kraus. *Sitzungsberichte der österreichischen akademie der Wissenschaften in Wien* 198.4.

Radice, Betty. 1976. *Terence: The Comedies*. Harmondsworth: Penguin.

Radt, Stefan, ed. 1977. *Tragicorum Graecorum Fragmenta*. Vol. 4: *Sophocles*. Göttingen: Vandenhoeck & Ruprecht.

Ragland-Sullivan, Ellie. 1989. "Seeking the Third Term: Desire, the Phallus, and the Materiality of Language." In Richard Feldstein and Judith Roof, eds., *Feminism and Psychoanalysis*. Ithaca, NY: Cornell University Press, 40–64.

Rahe, Paul. 1984. "The Primacy of Politics in Classical Greece." *American Historical Review* 89: 265–93.

Ramage, Edwin S. 1966. "City and Country in Menander's 'Dyskolos'." *Philologus* 110: 194–211.

Rau, Peter. 1967. *Paratragodia: Untersuchung einer komischen Form des Aristophanes*. Zetemata 45.

Reckford, Kenneth J. 1977. "Catharsis and Dream-Interpretation in Aristophanes' *Wasps*." *Transactons of the American Philological Association* 107: 283–312.

Reckford, Kenneth J. 1987. *Aristophanes' Old-and-New Comedy*. Vol. 1: *Six Essays in Perspective*. Chapel Hill: University of North Carolina Press.

Redfield, James. 1962–63. "Die 'Frösche' des Aristophanes: Komödie und Tragödie als Spiegel der Politik." *Antaios* 4: 422–39.

Reinhardt, Karl. 1938. "Aristophanes und Athen." *Europäische Revue* 14: 754–67. Repr. in Karl Reinhardt, *Tradition und Geist: Gesammelte Essays zur Dichtung* (Göttingen: Vandenhoeck & Ruprecht, 1960): 257–73.

Reitzenstein, E. 1940. *Terenz als Dichter. Albae Vigiliae* 4.

Rich, Adrienne. 1993. "Compulsory Heterosexuality and Lesbian Existence." In Henry Abelove, Michèle Aina Barale, and David M. Halperin, eds., *The Lesbian and Gay Studies Reader*. New York: Routledge, 227–54.

Richter, Friedrich. 1933. "Die Frösche und der Typ der aristophanischen Komödie." Ph.D. dissertation. Frankfurt am Main: Erlangen Universität.

Richter, Iulius, ed. 1858. *Aristophanis Vespae*. Berlin: Schneider.

Robert, C. 1909. "Bemerkungen zur Perikeiromene des Menander." *Hermes* 44: 260–303.

Rodgers, Silvia. 1981. "Women's Space in a Men's House: The British House of Commons." In Shirley Ardener, ed., *Women and Space: Ground Rules and Social Maps*. London: Croom Helm, 50–71.

Rogers, Benjamin Bickley, ed. 1902. *The Frogs of Aristophanes*. London: G. Bell.

Rogers, Benjamin Bickley, ed. 1911. *The Lysistrata of Aristophanes*. London: G. Bell.

Romer, Frank. 1990. "Good Intentions and the *hodos hē es korakas*." In Gregory Dobrov, ed., *Aristophanes' Birds and Nephelokokkugia: Charting the Comic Polis*. Papers of the APA Seminar. Syracuse, NY: Trugedy Press, 27–41.

Rose, Peter W. 1992. *Sons of the Gods, Children of Earth: Ideology and Literary Form in Ancient Greece*. Ithaca, NY: Cornell University Press.

Rossetti, Livio. 1977. *Aspetti della letteratura socratica antica*. Messina: Editoriale Studium.

Rossi, Amato. 1979. *Donne, prostituzione e immoralità nel mondo greco e romano*. Rome: L. Lucarini.

Rothwell, Kenneth S., Jr. 1990. *Politics and Persuasion in Aristophanes' Ecclesiazusae. Mnemosyne* supplement 111.

Rusten, Jeffrey, et al., trans. Forthcoming. *The Birth of Comedy: Fragments of Greek Drama 520–250 B.C.* Baltimore: Johns Hopkins University Press.

al-Saadawi, Nawal. 1983. *Woman at Point Zero*. Trans. Sherif Hetata. London: Zed Books.

Ste. Croix, G.E.M. de. 1972. *The Origins of the Peloponnesian War*. Ithaca, NY: Cornell University Press.

Ste. Croix, G.E.M. de. 1981. *The Class Struggle in the Ancient Greek World*. Ithaca, NY: Cornell University Press.

Sandbach, F. H. 1975. "Menander and the Three-Actor Rule." In Jean Bingen, Guy Cambier, and Georges Nachtergael, eds., *Le monde grec: pensée, littérature, histoire, documents: hommages à Claire Préaux*. Brussels: Editions de l'université de Bruxelles, 197–204.

Sandbach, F. H. 1977. *The Comic Theatre of Greece and Rome*. London: Chatto and Windus.

Sandbach, F. H., ed. 1990. *Menandri reliquiae selectae*. Rev. ed. Oxford: Oxford University Press.

Sartori, Franco. 1972. "Elementi storici del tardo teatro aristofanico e documentazione contemporanea." *Akten des VI. Internationalen Kongresses für griechische und lateinische Epigraphik*, 327–43.

Sartori, Franco. 1974. "Riflessi di vita politica ateniese nelle 'Rane' di Aristofane." In Luigi Barbesi, ed., *Scritti in onore di Caterina Vassalini*. Verona: Fiorini, 413–41.

Saxonhouse, Arlene W. 1980. "Men, Women, War and Politics: Family and Polis in Aristophanes and Euripides." *Political Theory* 8.1: 65–81.

Saxonhouse, Arlene W. 1983. "Classical Greek Conceptions of Public and Private." In S. I. Benn and G. F. Gaus, eds., *Public and Private in Social Life*. London: Croom Helm, 363–84.

Scafuro, Adele C. 1990. "Discourses of Sexual Violation in Mythic Accounts and Dramatic Versions of 'The Girl's Tragedy'." *Differences* 2.1: 126–59.

Scafuro, Adele C. 1995. *The Forensic Stage: Settling Disputes in Graeco-Roman New Comedy*. Cambridge: Cambridge University Press.

Schäfer, Armin. 1965. *Menanders Dyskolos: Untersuchungen zur dramatischen Technik*. Beiträge zur klassischen Philologie 14. Meisenheim am Glan: Anton Hain.

Schareika, H. 1978. *Der Realismus der aristophanischen Komödie: Exemplarische Analysen zur Funktion des Komischen in den Werken des Aristophanes*. Frankfurt am Main: Lang.

Schottlaender, Rudolf. 1973. "Menander's Bedeutung für seine und unsere Zeit." In W. Hofmann and H. Kuch, eds., *Die gesellechaftliche Bedeutung des antiken Dramas für seine und für unsere Zeit*. Berlin: Akademie-Verlag, 185–95.

Schwartz, E. 1929. "Zu Menanders Perikeiromene." *Hermes* 64: 1–16. Repr. in E. Schwartz, *Gesammelte Schriften*, Vol. 2 (Berlin: Walter de Gruyter, 1956): 190–206.

Schwinge, Ernst-Richard. 1975. "Kritik und Komik: Gedanken zu Aristophanes' Wespen." In Justus Cobet, Rüdiger Leimbach, and Ada B. Neschke-Hentschke, eds., *Dialogos: Für Harald Patzer zum 65. Geburtstag.* Wiesbaden: Steiner, 35–47.

Seaford, Richard. 1981. "Dionysiac Drama and Dionysiac Mysteries." *Classical Quarterly* (n.s.) 31: 252–75.

Seaford, Richard. 1990. "The Structural Problems of Marriage in Euripides." In Anton Powell, ed., *Euripides, Women, and Sexuality.* London: Routledge, 151–76.

Sealey, Raphael. 1987. *The Athenian Republic: Democracy or the Rule of Law?* University Park: Pennsylvania State University Press.

Sealey, Raphael. 1990. *Women and Law in Classical Greece.* Chapel Hill: University of North Carolina Press.

Segal, Charles Paul. 1961. "The Character and Cults of Dionysus and the Unity of the *Frogs.*" *Harvard Studies in Classical Philology* 65: 207–42.

Shaw, Michael. 1975. "The Female Intruder: Women in Fifth-Century Drama." *Classical Philology* 70: 255–66.

Sifakis, G. M. 1992. "The Structure of Aristophanic Comedy." *Journal of Hellenic Studies* 112: 123–39.

Silk, Michael S. 1987. "Pathos in Aristophanes." *Bulletin of the Institute of Classical Studies* 34: 78–111.

Sinclair, Robert K. 1988. "Lysias' Speeches and the Debate about Participation in Athenian Public Life." *Antichthon* 22: 54–66.

Sissa, Giulia. 1990a. *Greek Virginity.* Trans. Arthur Goldhammer. Cambridge, MA: Harvard University Press.

Sissa, Giulia. 1990b. "Maidenhood without Maidenhead: The Female Body in Ancient Greece." In David M. Halperin, John J. Winkler, and Froma I. Zeitlin, eds., *Before Sexuality: The Construction of Erotic Experience in the Ancient Greek World.* Princeton: Princeton University Press, 339–64.

Skinner, Marilyn B. 1993. "Woman and Language in Archaic Greece, or, Why Is Sappho a Woman?" In Nancy Sorkin Rabinowitz and Amy Richlin, eds. *Feminist Theory and the Classics.* New York: Routledge, 125–44.

Slater, Niall. 1986. "The Lenaean Theatre." *Zeitschrift für Papyrologie und Epigraphik* 66: 255–64.

Slater, Niall. 1990. "Performing the City in the *Birds.*" In Gregory Dobrov, ed., *Aristophanes' Birds and Nephelokokkugia: Charting the Comic Polis.* Papers of the APA Seminar. Syracuse, NY: Trugedy Press, 42–52.

Smedley, Agnes. 1976. *Daughter of Earth.* Old Westbury, NY: Feminist Press.

Smith, Kirby Flower. 1964[1913]. *The Elegies of Albius Tibullus.* Darmstadt: Wissenschaftliche Buchgesellschaft.

Smith, Steven B. 1984. *Reading Althusser: An Essay on Structural Marxism.* Ithaca, NY: Cornell University Press.

Sommerstein, A. H. 1977. "Aristophanes and the Events of 411." *Journal of Hellenic Studies* 97: 112–26.

Sommerstein, A. H. 1984. "Aristophanes and the Demon Poverty." *Classical Quarterly* (n.s.) 34: 314–33.

Sommerstein, A. H., ed. 1987. *The Comedies of Aristophanes*. Vol. 6: *Birds*. Warminster: Aris and Phillips.

Spatz, Lois. 1978. *Aristophanes*. Boston: Twayne.

Springborg, Patricia. 1989. "Arendt, Republicanism and Patriarchalism." *History of Political Thought* 10: 499–523.

Springborg, Patricia. 1990a. "The Feminine Principle in 'The Birth of the State'." *Political Theory Newsletter* 2.1: 45–63.

Springborg, Patricia. 1990b. "'His Majesty Is a Baby?': A Critical Response to Peter Hammond Schwartz." *Political Theory* 18: 673–89.

Stallybrass, Peter and Allon White. 1986. *The Politics and Poetics of Transgression*. Ithaca, NY: Cornell University Press.

Stanford, W. B., ed. 1963. *Aristophanes: The Frogs*. 2nd ed. London: Macmillan.

Stärk, Ekkehard. 1991. "*Persa* oder *Ex oriente fraus*." In Eckard Lefèvre, Ekkehard Stärk, and Gregor Vogt-Spira, eds. *Plautus barbarus: Sechs Kapitel zur Originalität des Plautus*. Tübingen: Gunter Narr Verlag, 141–162.

Starkie, W.J.M., ed. 1897. *The Wasps of Aristophanes*. London: Macmillan.

Stavenhagen, K. 1910. "Menanders Epitrepontes und Apollodors Hekyra." *Hermes* 45: 564–82.

Steidle, Wolf. 1973 and 1974. "Menander bei Terenz." *Rheinisches Museum für Philologie* 116: 303–47 and 117: 247–76.

Stigers [Stehle], Eva. 1981. "Sappho's Private World." In Helene P. Foley, ed., *Reflections of Women in Antiquity*. New York: Gordon and Breach, 219–45.

Stockert, Walter, ed. 1983. *Plautus: Aulularia*. Stuttgart: Teubner.

Strauss, Barry S. 1986. *Athens after the Peloponnesian War: Class, Faction and Policy 403–386 B.C.* Ithaca, NY: Cornell University Press.

Strauss, Barry S. 1990. "*Oikos* and *Polis*." In J. Rufus Fears, ed., *Aspects of Athenian Democracy*. Copenhagen: Museum Tusculanum Press, 101–127.

Strauss, Leo. 1966. *Socrates and Aristophanes*. New York: Basic Books.

Stroh, W. 1971. *Die römische Liebeselegie als werbende Dichtung*. Amsterdam: Adolf M. Hakkert.

Suevern, J. W. 1827. "Über Aristophanes Vögel." *Abhandlungen der Akademie der Wissenschaften, Berlin, historisch-philologische Kl.* 1–109. English version, trans. by W. R. Hamilton, *Essay on "The Birds" of Aristophanes* (London, 1835).

Süss, Wilhelm. 1954. "Scheinbare und wirkliche Inkongruenzen in den Dramen des Aristophanes." *Rheinisches Museum für Philologie* 97: 289–316.

Sutton, Dana Ferrin. 1980. *Self and Society in Aristophanes*. Lanham, MD: University Press of America.

Szondi, Peter. 1973. *Die Theorie des bürgerlichen Trauerspiele im 18. Jahrhundert: Der Kaufmann, der Hausvater und der Hofmeister*. Ed. G. Mattenklott. Frankfurt am Main: Suhrkamp.

Taillardat, Jean. 1965. *Les images d'Aristophane: Etudes de langue et de style.* Rev. ed. Paris: Belles Lettres.

Thompson, John B. 1984. *Studies in the Theory of Ideology.* Cambridge: Polity Press.

Thompson, Wesley G. 1982. "The Athenian Entrepreneur." *L'Antiquité Classique* 51: 51–85.

Tierney, M. 1935. "The Parodos in Aristophanes' *Frogs.*" *Proceedings of the Royal Irish Academy* 42, section C: 199–202.

Tierney, M. 1936. "Aristotle and Menander." *Proceedings of the Royal Irish Academy* 43: 241–54.

Todd, C. 1987. "Factions in Early-Fourth-Century Athens." *Polis* 7: 32–49.

Toynbee, A. 1981. *The Greeks and Their Heritages.* Oxford: Oxford University Press.

Tuplin, Christopher. 1985. "Imperial Tyranny: Some Reflections on a Classical Greek Political Metaphor." In Paul A. Cartledge and F. D. Harvey, eds., *Crux: Essays Presented to G.E.M. de Ste. Croix on his 75th Birthday. History of Political Thought* 6: 348–75.

Turner, E. G., ed. 1981. "P. Oxy. 3371 A." *Oxyrinchus Papyri* 48: 1–21.

Turner, Victor. 1969. *The Ritual Process.* Chicago: Aldine.

Vaio, John. 1971. "Aristophanes' *Wasps*: The Relevance of the Final Scenes." *Greek, Roman, and Byzantine Studies* 12: 335–51.

Vaio, John. 1973. "The Manipulation of Theme and Action in Aristophanes' *Lysistrata.*" *Greek, Roman, and Byzantine Studies* 14: 369–80.

Vegetti, Mario. 1983. *Tra Edipo e Euclide: Forme del sapere antico.* Milan: Il Saggiatore.

Vernant, Jean-Pierre. 1979. "A la table des hommes." In Marcel Detienne and Jean-Pierre Vernant, *La cuisine du sacrifice en pays grec.* Paris: Gallimard, 37–132.

Vernant, Jean-Pierre. 1980. *Myth and Society in Ancient Greece.* Trans. Janet Lloyd. Sussex: Harvester Press.

Vernant, Jean-Pierre. 1985. "Le Dionysos masqué des *Bacchantes* d'Euripide." *L'Homme* 93 25.1: 31–58. Repr. in Jean-Pierre Vernant and Pierre Vidal-Naquet, *Mythe et tragédie en Grèce ancienne,* Vol. 2 (Paris: Editions La Découverte): 237–70.

Vicinus, Martha. 1993. "'They Wonder to Which Sex I Belong': The Historical Roots of the Modern Lesbian Identity." In Henry Abelove, Michèle Aina Barale, and David M. Halperin, eds., *The Lesbian and Gay Studies Reader.* New York: Routledge, 432–52.

Vidal-Naquet, Pierre. 1986. *The Black Hunter: Forms of Thought and Forms of Society in the Greek World.* Trans. Andrew Szegedy-Maszak. Baltimore: Johns Hopkins University Press.

Volosinov, V. N. (= M. Bakhtin). 1973. *Marxism and the Philosophy of Language.* Trans. L. Matejka and I. R. Titunik. New York: Seminar Press.

Walsh, George. 1984. *The Varieties of Enchantment: Early Greek Views of the Nature and Function of Poetry.* Chapel Hill: University of North Carolina Press.

Warner, Marina. 1987. *Monuments and Maidens: The Allegory of the Female Form*. London: Pan.

Wartenberg, Günther. 1973. "Der miles gloriosus in der griechisch-hellenistischen Komödie." In W. Hofmann and H. Kuch, eds., *Die gesellschaftliche Bedeutung des antiken Dramas für seine und für unsere Zeit*. Berlin: Akademie-Verlag, 197–205.

Watt, Ian. 1957. *The Rise of the Novel: Studies in Defoe, Richardson and Fielding*. London: Chatto and Windus.

Webster, T.B.L. 1950. *Studies in Menander*. Manchester: Manchester University Press.

Webster, T.B.L. 1973. "*Woman Hates Soldier*: A Structural Approach to New Comedy." *Greek, Roman, and Byzantine Studies* 14: 287–99.

Webster, T.B.L. 1974. *An Introduction to Menander*. Manchester: Manchester University Press.

Wehrli, Fritz. 1936. *Motivstudien zur griechischen Komödie*. Zurich: Niehans.

West, Martin L. 1980. *Delectus ex iambis et elegis graecis*. Oxford: Clarendon.

Westlake, H. D. 1980. "The *Lysistrata* and the War." *Phoenix* 34: 38–54.

Whitehorne, John, trans. 1987. *Menander: The Dyskolos*. Ancient Society Resources for Teachers 17.2. Sydney: Macquarie University.

Whitman, Cedric H. 1964. *Aristophanes and the Comic Hero*. Martin Lectures 19. Cambridge, MA: Harvard University Press.

Wilamowitz-Moellendorf, Ulrich von. 1911. "Über die Wespen des Aristophanes." *Sitzenberichte der Königlichen preussischen Akademie der Wisenschaften*: 484–85. Repr. in *Kleine Schriften*, Vol. 1 (Berlin: Wiedmann, 1935): 312–13.

Wilamowitz-Moellendorff, Ulrich von, ed. 1925. *Das Schiedsgericht*. Berlin: Wiedmann.

Wilamowitz-Moellendorff, Ulrich von. 1927. *Aristophanes Lysistrate*. Berlin: Wiedmann.

Wiles, David. 1991. *The Masks of Menander: Sign and Meaning in Greek and Roman Performance*. Cambridge: Cambridge University Press.

Williams, Raymond. 1982. *The Sociology of Culture*. New York: Schocken.

Williams, Thomas. 1961. "Menanders Epitrepontes im Spiegel der griechischen Eheverträge aus Agypten." *Wiener Studien* 74: 43–58.

Wolf, Eric. 1982. *Europe and the People without History*. Berkeley: University of California Press.

Wood, Ellen Meiksins. 1988. *Peasant-Citizen and Slave: The Foundations of Athenian Democracy*. London: Verso.

Wright, Susan. 1981. "Place and Face: Of Women in Doshman Ziari, Iran." In Shirley Ardener, ed., *Women and Space: Ground Rules and Social Maps*. London: Croom Helm, 136–57.

Zagagi, Netta. 1980. *Tradition and Originality in Plautus: Studies of the Amatory Motifs in Plautine Comedy*. Hypomnemata 62.

Zagagi, Netta. 1990. "Divine Interventions and Human Agents in Menander." In E. W. Handley and Andre Hurst, eds., *Relire Menandre. Recherches et Recontres* 2: 63–91.

Zeitlin, Froma I. 1981. "Travesties of Gender and Genre in Aristophanes' *Thesmophoriazusae.*" In Helene P. Foley, ed., *Reflections of Women in Antiquity.* New York: Gordon and Breach, 169–217.

Zimmerman, Bernhard. 1983. "Utopisches und Utopie in den Komödien des Aristophanes." *Würzburger Jahrbücher für die Altertumswissenschaft* 9: 57–77.

Zimmerman, Bernhard. 1987. "L'Organizzazione interna delle commedie de Aristofane." *Dioniso* 57: 49–64.

Index

acropolis: 50, 54, 65
adikēma (act of injustice): 146, 194n.40
adulterer: 111
adultery, male reaction to: 150
Aeschylus, Prometheus Bound: 82,
    178n.36
Aesop, fables: 37
agōn (contest; formal section in Old
    Comedy): 56, 74, 171n.10; in Frogs,
    63–64
agora (marketplace): 65, 68
agrarian society: 167
agroikos (rustic): 100
Alcibiades: 31–32, 43
Alexander the Great: 3
Alexis, Lebes: 208n.2
Alink, M. J.: 33, 176n.19
allegory: 31–32
Althusser, Louis: 207n.35
amicus (friend): 136
Ammonius (pseudo-): 197n.3
Anacreon, Iambi: 197n.3
anagnōrisis (recognition): 108, 122, 152,
    195n.49
anapeithō (persuade, suborn): 173n.42
Anderson, Michael: 99–101
anēr (acc. andra, husband, man): 110
anger: 18–19
animus (mind, heart): 134
anomy (anomia): 33–39, 43
antagonist: 17
antinomy (antinomia): 34, 39–40
anxiety: over bastard child, 148; over
    women's sexuality, 148–49

Aphrodite: 59
Apollo: 76, 79, 86
Apollodorus of Carystus: 109, 149
archon basileus: 112
Arginusae, battle of: 70
Ariosto, I suppositi: 156–57, 208n.3
aristocracy, withdrawal from politics of:
    24–25
aristokrateisthai (rule as an aristocrat):
    42
Aristophanes: life, 3; as political
    conservative, 26–27; Acharnians, 4,
    15, 19, 54, 57, 105–6, 175n.1, 187n.20;
    Assemblywomen, 15, 23, 38, 53–54,
    175n.3, 186nn.13 and 19, 187n.20,
    188n.24, 209n.5; Birds, 3, 7–8, 15–16,
    29–44, 54–55, 66, 74, 81, 187n.20,
    188n.24; Clouds, 17, 21, 190n.39;
    Frogs, 7–8, 17, 54, 56, 61–74, 166,
    177n.28, 182n.5; Knights, 17, 177n.27,
    188n.24; Lysistrata, 4, 7–8, 15, 45–60,
    73, 166, 172n.20, 175n.3, 187n.20,
    188n.24; Peace, 3, 15, 19, 54, 172n.20,
    175n.1, 187n.20; Wasps, 7–8, 15–28,
    43, 73–74, 105, 166, 179n.48, 186n.18,
    188n.28, 189n.11; Wealth, 7–8, 15, 23,
    54, 75, 90, 105, 175n.3; Women at
    Festival, 48, 50, 180n.8
Aristotle: 114, 116; and the body politic,
    180n.13; on boorishness, 100; Magna
    Moralia, 205n.16; Politics, 84;
    Rhetoric, 196n.51, 205n.16
Arnott, Geoffrey: 144, 167, 204n.8
Arrowsmith, William: 32, 179n.52

art: 165
artisans: 77
Asclepius: 79, 86, 88–89
assault: 26–27, 113
astos (fem. *astē*, citizen): 151
Athena: 75, 82
Athens, as scene of comedy: 107–8
atimos (without honor or rights): 34, 39, 69
atukhēma (misfortune): 145–47, 194n.40, 205n.16
audience, of Menandrean comedy: 167
aulētis (flute girl): 194n.35
Ausonius, *Epigrams*: 58
autarky: 27, 79, 81, 99, 102, 105–6, 156
autochthony of Athenians: 66
Axionicus, *Philinna* fragment 5: 179n.5

bachelors: 117–18
Bal, Mieke: 5
Balibar, Etienne: 176n.14
Banks, Thomas: 26
barbarism: 175n.2
bastard: 146–8; concealment of, 149–50; as reason for divorce, 148–51. *See also* illegitimate child; *nothos*
Belsey, Catherine: 43
beneficium (favor): 136
Bennington, Geoffrey: 169n.7
Bérard, C.: 64–65
Bersani, Leo: 195n.45
betrothal: 111, 189n.13
bisexuality, of women: 58–59
Blanchard, Alain: 145
Blaydes, Fredericus H. M.: 175n.3
blight (agricultural metaphor): 133
blindness, of Wealth: 86–89
Bloch, Ernst: 165
blocking figure: 95–96, 103, 157
blood, and loss of virginity: 149
Blumenberg, H.: 176n.21
body, female: as city, 180n.13; of courtesan, 139–40; dissected, 59–69; and kingship, 180n.13; as map, 45–46, 49, 53, 58–59
Boisrobert, *La belle plaidoise*: 158, 208n.3
bonding, among women: 58–59
boundary: 35, 37
Brenkman, John: 165
Brothers, A. J.: 125
Brown, P.G.McC.: 200n.20, 203n.20
Burkert, Walter: 69

Cantarella, Eva: 121
capitalism: 161, 163–64, 167–68
Capps, Edward: 146
carnival: 171n.4
Catullus: 205n.28
Cecrops: 66
ceramicus: 65–66
Ceres, festival of: 155
character: 5, 22, 27, 43, 173n.29; of courtesan, 140; Greek, 114; of Lysistrata, 59; of misanthrope, 99–100, 105–6; as role, 118
Chariton, *Chaereas and Callirhoe*: 58, 192n.24
Chodorow, Nancy: 58
chronos (time): 33
citizenship: 27; and concubine, 117; exclusiveness of, 70–71, 130, 151–52, 159, 163, 184n.32; and marriage, 97, 99, 110, 116, 120, 126–27, 131, 151, 163; at Rome, 155
city: 35–36; in Hades, 65; as household, 51, 105–6; and laws, 111; and marriage, 97–99; parochialism of, 162–63; as *polis*, 36, 41, 43; of women, 51
civic space: 65, 155
class and class conflict: 21–24, 27–28, 47, 56, 71; in Hellenistic period, 104; mediated by marriage, 102–4; and Peloponnesian war, 165–66; and plot, 105; rich vs. poor, 76, 90
Cleon: 19–20, 25–26
clientela (clientship): 203n.19
cloak, as sign of wealth: 190n.34
Cohen, Walter: 168
coincidence: 4
commerce: and courtesan's trade, 132–33, 137–38; and marriage, 120–21, 138; right of, at Rome, 155
commodities: 161, 167
commune: 53
communalism. *See* solidarity
complaint at law: 113
concubinage: 9, 107, 110, 121–22, 191n.6; and marriage, 110–11, 117; permanent, 203n.22
consilium (rationality): 133
constitution of Athens: 40
contest: 63–65, 74. *See also agōn*
contradiction: 5–6, 8, 37–38, 43–44, 48–49, 90, 110, 163–64, 176n.16
cook, in New Comedy: 97
Corinth: 107, 124

courtesan: 73, 94, 120–21; contradictions in representation, 140; good vs. bad type of, 135, 202n.10; in Greece vs. Rome, 135, 140; vs. lover, 135, 139–40; overdetermined, 132–35; sharing of, 135, 202n.10; sympathetically represented by Menander, 202n.10; and travel, 196n.53
courts, in Athens: 16–27
cowardice: 20–21
crimes: 205n.16
Cronus: 41, 83
cultures, comparison of: 153
curiosus (meddlesome): 200n.20

daimōn (deity): 76
daimonion (power, deity): 144
Davies, John K.: 166–67
deification: 62
del Corno, Dario: 145
Demand, Nancy: 74
Demeter: 69; search for Persephone, 188n.26
Demetrius, of Phalerum: 3
Demetrius, son of Antigonus: 3
democracy: 22–24, 32
dēmos (the people): 23, 32, 50
Demosthenes: 193n.25
derision: 68
desire: 38, 40, 185n.42; and capitalism, 161–62; and New Comedy, 93–94; in the Renaissance, 156; of women, 129, 141
despotēs (master): 192n.20
Diallagē (Reconciliation): 46, 180n.13
dicasts. *See* jurors
didaskō (teach, train a chorus): 63
differentiation: 35–38, 67–68
Dillon, Matthew: 187n.20
Dionysius of Halicarnassus: 180n.13
Dionysus: 7, 64–67
disenfranchisement: 34, 39, 69–70
disguise: 62, 67, 69
distribution of wealth: 83, 85, 89
Dobrov, Gregory: 32
domestic economy (and public economy): 51–54
domesticity: 47–48; and New Comedy, 93
Donaldson, Ian: 68
Donatus: 188n.3, 202n.14
Dorfman, Ariel: 37–38
dotata (dowered woman): 193n.26
double standard, between the sexes: 145–48
Dover, Kenneth: 19, 27

Dowden, Ken: 206n.21
dowry: 104, 154, 156, 161–62; foregoing of, 160; women with, 193n.26
dual (grammatical): 64
dunamis (power, capacity): 87
Duskolos: 93. *See also* Menander: *Grouch*
duskolos (grouchy): 101

Eco, Umberto: 33
economics: 22–23
economy, of Athens: 118
Edwards, Anthony T.: 176n.15
Eichenbaum, Luise: 181n.29
ekklēsia (assembly): 50
elegiac poetry: 204n.28
Eleusinian mysteries: 62, 64–65
eleutheros (free, well-bred): 94, 100–101; as citizen, 193n.30; and guardian, 112
Empusa: 66, 68
enfranchisement, of slaves: 70, 73, 184n.32
enguē (betrothal): 111, 189n.13, 206n.28
enkalēma (complaint at law): 113
ephēbeia (transition to adulthood): 171n.12
Epicurus, *Letter to Menoeceus*: 206n.29
epiklēros (heiress): 193n.26
equality: 8
erastēs (lover): 189n.7
Erichthonius: 66
erōs (erotic love): 16, 32, 58–59, 178n.36, 179n.52, 182n.31; godsent, 205n.16; and leisure, 101; and marriage, 94-95, 99; in New Comedy, 93-94, 141; as transgressive, 130; and wealth, 161–62
Eros (god of love): 59
erotic love: 4. *See also erōs*; love
error (opposed to misfortune): 146
escapism: 167
eunomy (*eunomia*): 34, 40
euphemism: 146
Eupolis, *Dēmoi*: 69
Euripides: death of, 61; *Andromache*, 198n.9; *Andromeda*, 61; *Antigone*, 198n.9; *Bacchae*, 69, 184n.28; *Cyclops*, 183n.11; *Electra*, 189n.20; *Helen*, 183n.20; *Heracles*, 65; *Ion*, 205n.21; *Telephus*, 188n.26; fragment 141 Nauck, 198n.9
eutopia: 34
exchange: 156, 160, 162–63
exclusiveness. *See* citizenship: exclusiveness of

exempflicatory scenes, in Aristophanes: 79–80
exposure, of infants: 108, 118, 142, 149–50

faith. *See* good faith
fantastic: 33
farmers: 77–78; character of, 100–104
father: authority of, 126; beating of, 39–40; and daughter, 117; in love, 157, 159; and military service, 47; as rival, 160–61; and son, 128, 159; support for, 39–40
feminism, in Menander: 145, 148
festivals: and comedy, 68; dramatic, 74; and rape, 143; women's, 52
festive comedy: 140, 174n.4
fetishism: 158, 161–62, 209n.9
fides (good faith): 155
Fides (goddess): 154–55
foreigners: 71. *See also* courtesan; mercenary soldier
form, in art: 168
Fortenbaugh, William: 114–16
Fossatoro, P.: 145, 148
foundling: 107
Fraenkel, Eduard: 61
free status: of citizen, 193n.30; and guardian, 112; of women, 94, 103. *See also* independence
friends: 58; women, 181n.31
frogs: 74
Frow, John: 5, 176n.16

Galen, *On the Individual Passions and the Diagnosis of Errors*: 206n.29
Gallant, Thomas W.: 180n.10
Gallop, Jane: 58, 179n.46
gametē (lawfully wedded): 111, 192n.23; of a courtesan: 122
gamos (wedding): 189n.13
Gelley, Alexander: 176n.21
gēmai (marry): 197n.3
generations: conflict of, 18–22; solidarity among, 47
generosity: 104
Gennep, Arnold Van: 67, 73
gifts: 131–32, 134–35, 137
Gilula, Dwora: 202n.15
gnēsios (legitimate heir): 151, 198n.9
gods, traditional and new: 72
Goldberg, Sander: 190n.40, 192n.17, 201n.22, 203n.20
golden age: 8, 37, 40–42, 75, 80–81, 83, 89; and leisure, 79

Goldhill, Simon: 6, 170n.16
Gomme, A. W.: 95, 97–98, 100, 102, 110–15, 143, 189n.5
gonimos (productive): 72
good faith: 154-55
Gorgias, *Helen*: 205n.16
Görler, Woldemar: 199n.14
Graff, Gerald: 184n.40
greed: 84–85; of courtesans: 120, 132–33, 157–59
Green, W. C.: 31–32
guardian of a woman: 111
guardianship of oneself: 112, 116
gunē (woman, wife): 111, 149, 206n.21

hamartanein (commit an error): 146
hamartēma (error): 205n.16
harmony, among rich and poor: 104–5
harpagō (grasp): 162
Harrison, Jane: 68–69
Haynes, Jonathan: 168
head of household: 18, 97–98
Heath, Malcolm: 5–6, 170n.16, 180n.15
Heberlein, Friedrich: 187n.20
hēdonē (pleasure): 173n.27
heir: 122, 124, 138, 143, 198n.9
Henderson, Jeffrey: 26, 31, 56, 59, 179n.49, 180n.10
Henry, Madeleine M.: 195n.44
Heracles: and Dionysus, 62, 64; as initiate, 64–65; labors of, 188n.26; and underworld, 183n.13
Hermes: 80–81, 88
hero, comic: 15–16, 170n.1, 183n.20, 187n.20; figure of, 188n.26
heroism: 63
Herodotus, *Histories*: 33, 34, 37
Hesiod: and farmers's life, 82; and Zeus, 185n.3; *Theogony*, 178n.36; *Works and Days*, 166; fragments 25 and 27, 182n.7
hetaira (courtesan): 94, 120, 192n.23, 193n.29, 194n.35, 198n.10; in Athens versus Rome, 135
hipp (horse), as element in names: 190n.39
Hippocratic tradition, and the body: 180n.13
hoarding: 158, 160, 163
Homer: *Iliad*, 205n.19; *Odyssey*, 34, 69, 177n.31, 182n.7
homosexuality. *See* pederasty; sex: between women
honesty, among citizens: 77–78

honor: 35
Hooker, J. T.: 182n.4
Horace, *Satires:* 204n.28
household: 18, 47–49; ambivalence of, 60; as city, 51–53, 105–6; and economy, 118; and marriage, 97
Hubbard, Thomas: 175n.4
hubris (assault): 113, 175n.56
humanity: 128
humor (obsessional character): 16–17, 95, 103, 106, 154; wit, 6, 170n.18
Humphreys, Sally: 118, 192n.4, 193n.28, 195n.44
hunting: 101
husband: as guardian of wife, 117, 151; Greek word for, 110, 124
hymen: 149
Hyperides: 184n.32
hypothesis (ancient preface) to *Frogs*: 69, 182n.5

Iacchus: 64, 69
identity: 67, 69, 167; national, 209n.10
ideology: 4–7, 163–65; Althusser's definition of, 207n.35; and Aristophanes, 22, 27, 30, 43, 79, 90; and Menander, 110, 119, 122, 132, 141; and resolution of comedy, 152
illegitimate child: 122, 146–48; and adultery, 150; and Pericles' law, 151; and rape, 150
imitation: 67–69
imperialism: 30–31, 40–43, 60
imperium (authority): 193n.26
independence, of women: 112, 114–16, 124, 129
individualism: 64, 163
infatuation: 161–62
inheritance. *See* heir
inimicus (enemy): 136
initiates: 62, 64–65, 68
injustice: act of, 146, 194n.40; and wealth, 76, 80, 85
interest: 157
interpolations by Terence: 125, 129, 131, 133, 136–40, 198nn.12–13, 200n.20, 202nn.13–14 and 16, 203n.20
inversion: 68
investment: 157
irony: 79
Isaeus: 191n.6, 193n.25, 206n.26
ius conubii et commercii (right of marriage and commerce): 155–56, 162
ius sanguinis (right of blood): 209n.10

Jameson, Fredric: 5
Jocelyn, H. D.: 200n.20
Jonson, Ben: 168; *Epicene,* 95; *Everyman in His Humour,* 171n.9
Jouanny, Robert: 208n.3
jurors, in Athens: 16–27
Just, Roger: 206n.28
justice: and citizens, 78–79, 85; and poverty, 76

kaloi kagathoi (well-born citizens, gentlemen): 71
khlamis (rich cloak): 190n.34
kinship, and political unity: 46–47, 56
Köchly, H.A.T.: 31–32
kurbeis (tablets): 178n.40
kurieia (authority): 116–17, 172n.15, 192n.25
kurios (head of household): 18, 97–98; and citizenship, 112; as guardian, 111; and marriage, 117, 124, 197n.3; as master of one's body, 76; as master of oneself, of women, 112, 116, 192nn. 20 and 23–24

Lacan, Jacques: 179n.46, 182n.32, 208n.35
Laches: 20, 25
Laclau, Ernesto: 170n.12
land, and Athenian economy: 118
language, as creative: 72–73
Larivey, *Esprits:* 208n.3
Lateiner, Donald: 24
law: 32–33, 39–40; and the household, 151; and reclaiming of a wife, 111; and women, 112
lawful wife: 111
legitimacy. *See* illegitimate child; *nothos*
leisure: 79; and love, 101–2
leveling: 68
limen (threshold): 67–68
liminality: 67–70, 72
litigiousness: 29–30
Livy: 180n.13
Longinus, *On the Sublime*: 184n.32
Loraux, Nicole: 65–66, 115, 170n.18
love: and business, 137–39; between courtesan and citizen, 123–26, 132; expression of, 134–35; between husband and wife, 150–51; as madness, 132–33; in Molière, 168; mutual, 139; and rape, 139; and riches, 101; and sincerity, 139–40. *See also eros*

Lowe, N. J.: 189n.18, 190n.41, 205n.18
Lysias: 24, 150, 207n.30
Lysimache (priestess of Athena): 59

MacDowell, Douglas: 186n.9
Macedonian policy, toward Athens: 104
Macherey, Pierre: 5, 90, 176n.14
madness: 16
male anxiety: 148–49
Marcuse, Herbert: 165
Markle, M. M.: 173n.33
Marlowe, Christopher, *Tamburlaine the Great*: 179n.53
marriage: 9, 48; at Athens, 117, 120; ceremonies, absence of, 110; and citizenship, 116, 131; and the city, 97, 99, 105; and concubinage, 110–11; at Corinth, 107; in Menander, 93–95; between rich and poor, 103–5; right of at Rome, 155; and virginity, 116, 120; and women's independence, 115
Marvell, Andrew, "Horatian Ode": 179n.53
master: 192n.20. *See also despotēs*; head of household; *kurios*
McKechnie, Paul: 196n.53
meddlesomeness: 77, 79, 99, 127–28, 200n.20
megalonomy (*megalonomia*): 34, 40–41, 43
Meier, Christian: 153
men, and public space: 49, 51
Menander: and escapism, 167; life, 3; *Arbitrants*, 8, 10, 141–52, 192n.16, 193n.31, 196n.49, 202n.10, 208n.8; *Arrhēphoros* (*Maiden in Procession*), 200n.17; *Burnt Girl* (*Empimpramenē*), 196n.49; *Double Deceiver* (*Dis exapatōn*), 170n.21; *Eunuch*, 131–32, 203n.20; *Flatterer* (*Kolax*), 203n.16; *Grouch*, 8–10, 93–106, 115, 118, 140, 150, 153–57, 166, 186n.18, 193n.30, 195n.48; *Hated Man* (*Misoumenos*), 192n.20, 195n.49; *Perinthian Woman*, 188n.3; *Plokion* (*Lock*), 192nn.13, 21, and 23, 193n.26, 195n.49; *Samian Woman* (*Samia*), 121–22, 124, 192n.23, 193n.30, 198n.11, 202n.10, 204n.8; *Self-Tormentor* (*Heautontimoroumenos*), 125; *Shield* (*Aspis*), 88n.3, 197n.6, 209n.10; *Shorn Girl*, 8–9, 107–19, 122, 129, 152, 189n.13, 198n.10, 208n.36; *Sicyonian*, 192n.20, 195n.49; *Slapped Girl* (*Rhapizomenē*), 196n.49; *Synaristosai* (*Women Breakfasting Together*), 191n.3; fragment 359, 146

Menenius Agrippa: 180n.13
mercenary soldier: 110, 117; as career, 122, 132
merchants: 77, 118
meretrix (courtesan): 135, 196n.2. *See also* courtesan
Meton: 37
Michael Psellus: 184n.38
Middle Comedy: 169n.2
misanthrope: 95–96, 99–101, 106
Misanthrope: 93. *See also* Menander: *Grouch*; Molière
miser: 96, 153–64
misfortune: 145–47, 194n.30, 205n.16
misthos (wages): 172n.15
Modleski, Tania: 58
moikhos (adulterer): 111
Molière: 195n.45; *Dom Juan*, 161; *The Misanthrope*, 106; *The Miser*, 8, 10–11, 153–64
money: 35, 76; and circulation, 158; and commodities, 161; desire for, 84; and universality, 163; and wealth, 83
moral development, in comedy: 195n.45
More, Thomas: 33–34
mystai (initiates): 62–63, 66–66
mysteries (Eleusinian): 62
myth of origins: 38

names: 67–69, 105
Nardo, Dante: 128
nation (in Renaissance comedy): 159, 163, 167–68
nature: 32, 35
Neocleides: 89
Nephelokokkugia (Cloudcuckooland): 34
networking, among women: 57
New Comedy: 3–4, 10, 93–96; and class divisions, 104; and concubine's role, 128–30; final scene, 97, 140, 154; and marriage, 110, 120–24; and modern comedy, 151; plot form, 99, 108–9; and rape, 149–50; resolution of, 152; and sexual code, 116
Nicias: 25, 31, 178n.43
nomadism: 35
nomos (law, custom): 32–34, 39–40, 43
nostalgia: 20–21, 89
nothos (illegitimate child): 122, 146–48, 198n.9; definition of: 207n.33; as reason for divorce, 148–52, 208n.8
nowhere (and utopia): 35
Nymphs: 94, 100

Ober, Josiah: 184n.32
obsessional character: 16–17, 158–59
Odysseus: 82, 188n.26
office: 35
oikeiotēs (relative): 98
oikos (household): 1, 118, 152; and
 children: 206n.28
Old Comedy: 3–4, 93
oligarchy at Athens (411 B.C.): 55–56,
 69–71
Olson, S. Douglas: 187n.20
Olympian deities: 81, 88
Orbach, Suzie: 181n.29
orgē (anger, temper): 19
Orphic cosmogony: 178n.36
Ouranos: 82
ousia (substance, property): 118
overdetermination: 6–8, 10, 21, 23, 60,
 72, 90, 102; of character vs. plot, 105,
 118; of courtesan's role, 121; of social
 role, 129–30

pallakē (concubine): 107, 110–13, 121,
 191n.6, 193nn.25, 28–29, and 32,
 195n.49, 207n.33
Pan: 94–95, 100
pan-Hellenism: 56–57, 60, 166
parabasis: 4, 39, 56, 69–70
partheneia (maidenhood): 206n.121
parthenios (illegitimate child of a
 woman): 205n.19
parthenon: 178n.37
parthenos (maiden): 149
passion, in New Comedy: 93–94; as
 unstable: 133. *See also* desire; *erōs*
passivity, sexual: 58
patronage, at Rome: 138
Patterson, Cynthia: 205n.19, 207n.33
pederasty: 58–59, 150, 182n.31
Peloponnesian War: 30–31, 46–47, 56,
 70, 178n.43; as class conflict, 165–66;
 possibility of truce in, 55
Penia. *See* Poverty
peregrina (foreign woman): 203n.19
Pericles: 31; citizenship law of, 97, 120,
 151
Persian War: 18–19, 172n.18
personal satire: 169n.6
persuasion: 27, 40
philanthrōpia (generosity): 104
philēliastēs (lover of courts): 16
philia (love): 150
philos (friend; fem. *philē*): 58, 181n.31
Phrynichus (comic poet): 74

Phrynichus (tragic poet): 18
phusis (nature): 32, 179n.52
piety: 63; filial, 157
Plato: and the body politic, 180n.13;
 Gorgias, 177n.25; *Republic*, 34
Plautus: *Asinaria*, 193n.26, 208n.9;
 Bacchides, 170n.21, 204n.29; *Braggart
 Soldier (Miles gloriosus)*, 95; *Casina*,
 208n.9; *Cistellaria (Play of the Chest)*,
 108, 124, 157, 191n.3, 192n.23; *Little
 Carthaginian (Poenulus)*, 194n.43;
 Merchant: 132, 208n.9; *Persian*,
 195n.43; *Play of the Pot (Aulularia)*,
 10, 96, 118, 153–64; *Pseudolus*, 95;
 Pugnacious (Truculentus), 149, 201n.6
playfulness: 63
plēthos (people, majority): 22
plot: 2–6; of Aristophanic comedy,
 15–16, 29–30, 54, 75, 177n.32; and
 class, 105; discontinuity in, 47–48,
 50–51, 53, 175n.3, 188n.24; double in
 Wealth, 87–88; of Menandrean
 comedy, 93–95, 107–9, 147; in
 Molière, 157; of Terentian comedy,
 131, 199n.17; tripartite in *Frogs*,
 61–62; utopian form, 15–16, 54,
 187n.20
Plutarch: 93; *On the Glory of the
 Athenians*, 184n.38; *Life of Alcibiades*,
 32; *Life of Lucullus*, 171n.4; *Moralia*,
 184n.32, 198n.10
Plutus (god of wealth): 75–90
poetry: 63, 71–73
poetry contest: 61, 63–64, 71–74
poets, as teachers: 63
polis (city-state): 36; used for acropolis:
 54, 111
political discourse: 74
politicians: 77
politics, and literature: 4–6
pollution, sexual: 14, 150–51, 205n.20
polos (pole, sky): 36
polupragmosunē (meddlesomeness):
 190n.24, 200n.20
polupragmonein (be meddlesome): 77, 79
ponēros (wretched, bad): 85
ponos (toil): 85
pornē (whore): 135
pornidion (whore): 194n.35
Poseidon: 41
Posidippus, fragment 33: 190n.34
Post, L. A.: 100, 197n.7
poststructuralism: 164
potestas (authority): 155

poverty: 21, 75; in Athens, 186n.20; of farmers, 101–3; as goad to virtue, 83–84
Poverty (personified): 79, 83
power, will to: 40–42
primitivism: 37
private sphere: 49, 51–52
proboulos (special commissioner): 55
profit: 158
prologue: in Menander, 94–95, 108, 133; in Plautus, 154; in Terence, 136, 142
Prometheus: 82
Propertius: 204n.28
property: 37, 43, 53, 55, 151
prostatēs (representative): 203n.19
prostitute: 193n.35, 195n.47
protagonist, in Aristophanic comedy: 175n.1
prudentia (good sense): 133
public sphere: 49, 51–52
purity, sexual: 205n.20

Quirini, Bruno Zannini: 177n.35

Ramage, Edwin S.: 100, 104
rape: 109, 120–21, 131; and childbirth, 149; and citizenship, 155; concealment of, 149–50; and divorce, 109, 142; by gods, 206n.25; and love, 139; male reaction to, 150–51; and marriageability, 137–38, 141–48, 154
ratio (reason): 133
reaggregation (in ritual process): 67–68, 73
reason: 133
reciprocity, and civic life: 64, 154–56, 158, 163
recognition: 108–9, 113–14, 122, 159; placement of, 152, 195n.49; postponed, 137–38, 142; and status, 104–5
Reconciliation (personified): 46, 54, 59–60
redistribution of wealth: 75, 77
rejuvenation: 17
remarriage: 150
representation (poetic): 72
resident alien: 27, 120
resolution, of New Comedy: 152, 155
ressurection: 62
revenge: 113
ring composition: 202n.12
ritual process: 67–69, 73
Rogers, Benjamin Bickley: 71

Rose, Peter: 8
rustic character: 100, 103

al-Saadawi, Nawal: 195n.47
sacrifice: 100, 190n.26
Ste. Croix, G.E.M. de: 26–27
Samos: 122
Sandbach, F. H.: 95, 97–98, 100, 102, 110–15, 143, 146, 189n.5, 205n.14
Sappho: 181n.31
satirical comedy: 17, 171n.10
scarcity: 75, 83, 85–86
Schäfer, Armin: 101
Schareika, H.: 32
scientia (knowledge, good sense): 133
scortum (whore): 135
Sealey, Raphael: 197n.3
secrecy: 206nn.23–24
seduction: 150
Segal, Charles: 62
self-control: 116
selfishness: 100
self-sufficiency: 27, 79, 81, 96–97, 99, 105–6
Seneca, *Moral Epistles*: 128
separation, of husband and wife: 141–43
sex: 150; and citizenship, 139; in *Dom Juan*, 161–62; double standard in, 145–47; as drive, 47–49; and male anxiety, 148–49; premarital, 141, 148; and women's behavior, 120–23; between women, 57–59
sex strike: 47, 49–51
Shakespeare, William: *Comedy of Errors*, 45–46; *Romeo and Juliet*, 96; *Tempest*, 177n.35; *Timon of Athens*, 106
Shaw, George Bernard, *Mrs. Warren's Profession*: 197n.6
Sicilian expedition: 30–31, 55
signified and signifier: 72–73
Silvanus: 154
Simonides: 72
sincerity: 134–36, 138–40, 202nn.11 and 28
Sissa, Giulia: 206n.23
skōptein (mock): 68
Slater, Niall: 183n.16
slavery: 27; absence of in *Birds*, 35, 39, 43; and production, 83, 209n.5; and torture, 67; and wages, 81
slaves: enfranchisement of, 70; as lovers, 40; and money, 76
Smedley, Agnes: 195n.47

Socrates: 21, 184n.36
soldier (professional or mercenary): 110, 192n.18; as lover, 132, 195nn.46 and 49; and travel, 196n.53
solidarity: 37, 41–42, 44, 47–53, 166; of initiates, 64, 74, 89; and New Comedy, 105, 118; sexualized, 58
soliloquy: 116
Sommerstein, A. H.: 175n.4, 186n.20, 187n.23
sophism: 43
Sophocles: 61; *Antigone*, 177n.28; *Oedipus at Colonus*, 177n.25, 188n.26; *Philoctetes*, 69, 188n.26; *Tereus*, 175n.2; fragment 87 Radt, 198n.9
Sovereignty (personified): 30, 42, 54
space, civic: 65
Spartans: 26
Springborg, Patricia: 180n.13
Stallybrass, Peter: 171n.4
Stanford, W. B.: 66, 73
stasis (civil strife): 37, 42
state, at Athens: 20–21; and women: 51–53, 90
status: 70, 166; and illegitimacy, 151; and marriage, 108–9, 120–21, 126–28, 159
Stavenhagen, K.: 145, 148
stratiōtēs (professional soldier): 192n.18
Strauss, Leo: 62
Suevern, J. W.: 31
sycophant (public informer): 76–81
symposium: 26, 174n.47

teacher, poet as: 63
tekmar (boundary): 35
Terence: 4, 8–9; and double plot, 131, 199n.17; interpolations in Menandrean models, 125, 129, 131, 133, 136–38, 140, 198nn.12–13, 200n.20, 202nn.13–14 and 16; *Brothers*, 118, 131, 195n.48, 204n.29; *Eunuch*, 9–10, 131–40, 151, 193n.30, 198n.30; *Mother-in-Law*, 109, 149, 206n.23; *Self-Tormentor*, 9, 120–31, 152, 157; *Woman of Andros* (*Andria*), 108, 131, 188n.3, 196n.1, 199n.16
Tereus: 29
theater, where *Frogs* performed: 183n.16
theft: 19–20, 154; analogy to rape, 154–55
Theophrastus: 100
Thesmophoria: 155

Thompson, John: 170n.12
three-actor rule: 115
Thucydides: 31, 55
Tibullus: 199n.15
timē (honor, office): 35
timōria (revenge, punishment): 113
toil: 82
topos (place): 33, 36
torture: 67
trade: 77, 118, 196n.53
travel: 196n.53
tribes, Athenian: 66
trux (dregs): 171n.4
turannos (tyrant): 42
Turner, Victor: 67
tyranny: 22, 42–43, 179n.48; of Zeus, 82
tyrant city: 42–43

unity: 5–6, 27, 30, 85, 90, 101, 110, 165, 168, 170n.12, 187n.21
universalism: and Menander, 167; and Molière, 162–63
upside-down world: 34, 39, 68
urbanity: 101, 104
use-value: 84
usury: 158, 160, 162–63, 168
utopianism: 8–10, 33–34, 54, 56, 167; and everyday life, 165; and pan-Hellenism, 130; and plot form, 15–17, 187n.20

Vaio, John: 26, 48, 51
Vegetti, Mario: 180n.13
verbum (word, phrase): 134
Vernant, Jean-Pierre: 191n.6
violence, and rape: 150
vir (man, husband): 124
Virgil, *Georgics*: 82
virginity: 149; and male anxiety, 150–51; and marriage, 116, 120, 147–51; tests for, 14
virtue, women's: 124–26

wages: 22–23, 42, 172n.15, 173n.33; and slavery, 81
walls: 42, 54, 154–55
Walsh, George: 71–73
war: and widowhood, 150; and women, 52
Warner, Marina: 179n.3
wealth: 75–90; desire for, 80, 161–62; as god (*see* Plutus); as mightier than Zeus, 79; versus money, 83, 196n.51; unequal distribution of, 75. *See also* miser; usury

244 Index

Webster, T.B.L.: 117
Westlake, H. D.: 180nn.15–16
White, Allon: 171n.4
Whitman, Cedric: 32, 62, 64–65,
174n.45
widows, and remarriage: 150
wife, lawful: 111; and citizen status,
124; legal claim on, 112
Wilamowitz-Moellendorf, Ulrich: 50,
145–46
Wiles, David: 205n.18
Williams, Raymond: 168
withdrawal from politics: 24–25
women: and bisexuality, 58–59; body of,
45–46; and chaperones, 98; desire of,
in Renaissance comedy, 156–57; and
the double standard, 145–48;
independence of, 110–12, 124; and the

law, 112; as libidinous, 47–48; and
love, 124, 156; and male anxiety,
148–49; and marriage, 96, 139,
193n.25; and networking, 57; as
outsiders, 54, 56; and remarriage, 150;
seclusion of, 195n.44; sex among,
57–59; sexual behavior of, 122–26;
silence of, 96, 98; and the state, 52–54
writing: 23

Xenophon: *Hiero*, 150–51, 207nn.30–31;
Oeconomicus, 174n.45, 193n.28; *Ways
and Means* (*Poroi*), 23
xenos (foreigner): 193n.29, 203n.19
xungenēs (kinsman): 46

Zeus: 41, 71, 76, 79, 81–83, 87; the
Savior, 186n.15